MW00805024

CROSSING CULTURES

A SICILIAN AND AMERICAN FAMILY IN WESTERN NEW YORK

Thomas MacPherson

Milne Library

© 2016 Thomas MacPherson

ISBN: 978-1-942341-33-8 (print)
978-1-942341-34-5 (ebook)

This work is licensed under a Creative Commons Attribution-NonCommercial-ShareAlike 3.0 Unported License, with the exception of original paintings by the author, which are licensed under a Creative Commons Attribution-NonCommercial-NoDerivatives 4.0 International License:

You are free to:
Share—copy and redistribute the material in any medium or format
Adapt—remix, transform, and build upon the material
The licensor cannot revoke these freedoms as long as you follow the license terms.
Under the following terms:
Attribution—You must give appropriate credit, provide a link to the license, and indicate if changes were made. You may do so in any reasonable manner, but not in any way that suggests the licensor endorses you or your use.
NonCommercial—You may not use the material for commercial purposes.
ShareAlike—If you remix, transform, or build upon the material, you must distribute your contributions under the same license as the original.

Photos courtesy of the author.

Published by Milne Library
State University of New York at Geneseo,
Geneseo, NY 14454

ACKNOWLEDGMENTS

My debts are great. My sense of gratitude, especially to those who have to live with me, is very deep. I want to thank my Aunt Dorothy O'Geen who was very honest with her opinion of this project. Her memories of times long past helped me correct misconceptions I had. Her insights were most welcome and have made this book a more accurate record of what life was like for the first and second generation Sicilians in Western New York. I also want to thank my sister, Mary, who has a better memory about the details than I do.

I also am indebted to the many relatives who supplied me with photographs, invaluable information about my parents, their parents, their recollections of events, and of family history. My cousin Pauline Seekins was the most important source for information on the MacPhersons and told me many stories about my father, Great-Aunt Kitty, my grandparents, and my great-grandparents. David Frost was an invaluable source for the history of the MacPhersons when they first emigrated from Scotland and their life throughout the nineteenth century. David also found me an amazing letter that my great-grandfather sent to his grandfather while he was serving as a corporal in the Civil War. Chuck Barone, Marie Argana, Michael, Rita, and Louie Cinquino all shared with me priceless stories about the first generation of our Sicilian family that would have been lost to the ages. Nancy Hough, Bob Schrader, Jim MacPherson, Don MacPherson, and Bill MacPherson were all generous with their time and supplied me with a treasure trove of biographical information about their family life, especially intimate insights into the lives of their parents. I am eternally indebted to Aunt Beverly MacPherson for looking though her family artifacts and finding long forgotten newspaper articles on my father, Great-Aunt Kitty and of course her husband, my Uncle Bill, and her photographic albums where she found two incredible nineteenth century photos of my great-grandparents, Don and Sarah MacPherson. Charlie "Ace" O'Geen graciously related to me stories of his experiences in World War II, and Rusty O'Geen generously shared with me family documents from Sicily and his boxes of photographs that I found fascinating. And last but not least, Joe Burkart allowed me the opportunity to pour through literally hundreds of photographs, some over one hundred years old, to find some real gems that I turned into egg tempera portrait paintings and others that made many of the chapters come alive.

This project would have never gotten off the ground if it wasn't for my dear friend and colleague, Dr. Lynette Bosch, who encouraged me to expand the biographies that accompanied the egg tempera paintings of family members that I began way back in 2006. At Lynette's insistence, I traveled to New York City in the fall of 2005 to learn the Renaissance painting technique egg tempera in order to paint my relatives in a way that said "Italian" and by encouraging me to undertake a literary endeavor that I didn't know I had in me. Both Lynette and her British husband and my friend Dr. Charles Burroughs opened new avenues for me that paved the way for me to travel to Italy and to Scotland to experience the culture of my ancestors.

Special thanks has to go to my dear friend Helen Thomas, for her discerning reading of the manuscript, who spent several years reading my gibberish and helping me transform my ideas and stories into English.

A special debt of gratitude goes to Lynne Belluscio, Director of the LeRoy Historical Society, and her amazing memory of all things LeRoy. Without her help searching the historical society's archives for newspaper articles on my father and Great-Aunt Kitty (plus her World War I military record), pertinent historical photographs, and sharing with me the oral history of LeRoy, writing the book would have been much harder and much less interesting to read.

Finally to Allison Brown, Digital Publishing Services Manager at Milne Library, SUNY Geneseo, for her faith in the project and to Ben Burdett for his perceptive and insightful perspectives while editing the book.

And my wife and best friend, Linda, who listened patiently to these stories for over forty-five years, helped edit the manuscript, and gave me her opinion when I lost my way. Her support and belief in me gave me the strength to do new things that were out of my comfort zone.

Please accept my deep and humble gratitude.

CROSSING CULTURES

Table of Contents

The Immigration of Great-Grandpa Calogero Barone and Great-Grandma Maria Orazia Guzzetta

Life in Sicily in the late nineteenth century was chaotic, where exploitation by northern Italians, rule by foreign powers, and a feudal system that governed the economy prevented poor Italians from improving their lives.[1] It was against this backdrop that my great-grandfather, Calogero Barone, gathered his young family and emigrated Italy to settle in the United States. It was in 1896 that they left Sicily and made their way to Naples, where they booked passage on a ship, the Elysia, bound for America. After crossing the ocean and passing through Ellis Island, they settled in Avon, New York among other relatives and families they knew from Sicily, and eventually moved to LeRoy, New York in 1903, only a few miles to the West. One day I asked my grandmother if she ever wanted to go visit Sicily. She replied, "Why would I want to do that? If it was so great, why did we leave?" Thus, while nostalgia for the old country is a recurring theme for some immigrant narratives, it was not part of my family's tradition. My family considered that in Italy they already lived as foreigners and that their new country was where their real home would be found.

Because my family represents a narrative that unfolded in a rural setting, their story is a less familiar one in the culture of immigration to the United States, which is more often told in the context of large cities. Although my Sicilian family settled in a Sicilian neighborhood in LeRoy, there weren't enough Sicilians in the area to comprise an enclave. Assimilation was difficult for new and different immigrants, such as my mother's Sicilian family, in a place where the close proximity of different northern European ethnic groups accentuated division and prejudice. However, the small town setting also encouraged mixing, exemplified by my parents' multicultural marriage as well as that of other relatives who married into northern European families. The resulting mixtures of religious and ethnic differences eventually produced a generation of Americans whose diverse, European backgrounds were replaced by more mainstream attitudes generated by the new country.

The Sicilian Barones can be traced in church records to about 1790. But for me, the Barone family history begins at the time of their immigration to America in 1896, because it was their arrival in America that began their lives as Italian-Americans. Their participation in this hybrid culture shaped my life and now provides me with a significant part of the subject for my egg tempera paintings, which record my experience of being born into a Scottish and Sicilian family.

For my Sicilian family, the narrative of upward mobility displaced the narrative of nostalgia and they never looked back. Eventually, my Sicilian great-grandparents were able to realize the American dream and buy their own home, and in the process improve themselves

---

1 Nicola Colella, "Southern Italian Immigration," *ItalianAmerica.org*, 2007, http://www.italiamerica.org/id49.htm.

in a way that they would have never been able to do in Sicily. The discrimination and obstacles they met in LeRoy, New York, were familiar because they were similar to those they had known in the old country. But in America, they could surmount the discrimination they could not fight in Italy. Nonetheless, Sicilians in LeRoy were met with hostility and were treated as second-class citizens. To illustrate their plight, one can look at the obstacles encountered when the Italians in LeRoy decided to begin a parish of their own.

The purchasing of property for a new church was not an easy task for the parishioners, as they met opposition from non-Italians. The Very Reverend Dean L. Vanderpool, pastor of St. Peter's Roman Catholic Church, a predominantly Irish parish at the time, recorded in his journal that the LeRoy News publicly stated that the Italians were not welcome by LeRoyans. It was thought that if the Italians were given a chance to purchase property to build a church, they would establish permanent roots in LeRoy. To get around the discrimination, Sicilians had to purchase the property through a third party—in this instance, a Mr. T. P. Sullivan. During the negotiation of the sale, the seller stipulated that if the property were to be sold to the Italians, the agreement would be null and void. Mr. Sullivan refused to have this clause included. Rev. Vanderpool stated in his journal, "the Italians had the last laugh": on June 9, 1907, a house was purchased on Lake Street. Church services were held on the ground floor of the newly purchased house and the second floor became a residence for the church's priest, Father Gambino. I remember hearing stories about Father Gambino from Grandma, and in her eyes he was a remarkable priest. For two years, the priest and parishioners struggled against great odds, the greatest of these being financial difficulties, to start the building of the new church. Finally, in June of 1909, Bishop Colton of Buffalo blessed and dedicated the cornerstone for the new church and on September 5, 1909, the church was ready for public service.[2]

SICILIAN CULTURE CLASHES WITH AMERICAN SOCIETY

What was the basis for all of this hostility, especially from American Catholics? According to writer George Pozzetta, "Italian mass migration coincided with the growth of a nativism that identified southern and eastern Europeans as undesirable elements. Inspired by the pseudo-scientific findings of eugenics and social Darwinism, turn-of-the-century nativists often branded southern Italians as especially inferior."[3] Catholicism as it existed in southern Italy was totally different and unique to the way it was practiced in America, and when the *contadini* (peasants) arrived in the New World they brought it with them to the horror of Catholics and Protestants in the towns where they settled.[4] As Rudolph J. Vercoli writes in his article on Italian-American religious practices, "Pagan! Heathen! Idolater! These were among the epithets hurled at the Italian immigrants around the turn of the century."[5] In addition to being called mafiosi, Italians had the further burden of being regarded as believ-

---

2   For a complete history, see St. Joseph's Church Anniversary Bulletin, 2007.

3   George Pozzetta, "Italian Americans," *Everyculture*, May 2008, http://www.everyculture.com/multi/Ha-La/Italian-Americans.html.

4   R.J. Vecoli, "Cult and Occult in Italian-American Culture: The Persistence of a Cultural Heritage," in *Immigrants and Religion in Urban America*, ed. T.D. Marzik and R.M. Miller (Philadelphia: Temple University Press, 1977), 33.

5   Vecoli, "Cult and Occult," 1.

ers of anti-Christian beliefs and practices.[6] As R.J. Vecoli wrote, "Their folk religion was a syncretic melding of ancient pagan beliefs, magical practices, and Christian liturgy. Cult and occult had fused into a magical-religious worldview that was deeply rooted in the psyche of this people."[7]

In Sicily, remnants of the Roman past were still in evidence as late as the early twentieth century. Louise Caico lived for an extended period of time in an isolated Sicilian mountain town called Montedoro (just south of Valledolmo) and in 1910 wrote an account of her experiences (*Sicilian Ways and Days*) on the manners and customs she observed in this region that had not yet been affected by the outer world. She observed the Rogation outdoor service on the Sunday before Ascension Day when a parish priest went out to bless the cornfields:

In the fresh, early dawn, before the summer glare has begun to pour the torrents of fire on the hills and plains, the Vicar, in surplice, followed by most of the villagers, walks to the top of a hill, from where, in a sweeping glance, he can see far and near, and look on all the fields of ripe golden corn the one hope and fortune of these poor people and there raising his right arm, whilst an acolyte shakes an incense burner, he blesses the whole country round, and ask for God's help and protection during the now impending season.[8]

For Caico, "This reminds us, as it should, of an old Roman custom. In a spot half an hour from Rome, on the Via Campana, there was a wood sacred to the goddess Dia (Nature, also called Maia, whence the month of May). The *frati Aravali camperstres sacerdotes* lived there and offered sacrifices for the welfare of agriculture, especially during the three days of May..."[9]

At harvest time she observes the peasants extolling the virtues of "his favourite saints, his incantations to them before, during, and after work. The quaint and beautiful 'Praises of the Lord,' sung on the threshing floor, must have been a very ancient origin; many have traced in them the worship of Demeter and Persphone, and the same pagan origin can be given to the habit of dividing the corn by beginning to count with the words 'In the name of God.' Does not this remind us of the pagan *ab Jove principio* [let's begin with Jupiter]?"[10]

The problematic religion my family brought to LeRoy was formed in the social customs of Sicily, where family life and religion revolved around the village, or *paese*. "This spirit of *campilismo* (excessive village loyalty and parochialism) was expressed in the veneration of local sanctities: each *paese* had its churches and shrines dedicated to its patron saints and Madonnas. In religious as in other matters, the *contadini* subscribed to the system of *clien-*

---

6 Pozzetta, "Italian Americans," 9.

7 Vecoli, "Cult and Occult," 2.

8 Louise Caico, *Sicilian Ways and Days* (New York: D. Appleton and Company, 1910), 115. *Sicilian Ways and Days* is an ebook that has been made available by the University of California and can be downloaded as a pdf at http://archive.org/details/sicilianwaysdays00caicrich.

9 Caico, *Sicilian Ways and Days*, xiii.

10 Caico, *Sicilian Ways and Days*, xiv. I am thankful to classics scholar Dr. Charles Burroughs for his translation and opinion on the phrase *ab Jove principio*. "I thought it seems a bit odd—the quotation should be *ab Jove principium* so: everything begins with Jupiter, or: lets begin with Jupiter comes from a poem by Vergil (Eclogues 3. 60)—a poet/shepherd says to the other 'the muse begins with Jupiter.' Then they argue about which deity is more responsible for poetic inspiration. In antiquity Sicily was famous as the home of pastoral poetry, and Vergil set some of his eclogues (pastoral poems) on the island."

telismo,[11] or a special devotion to a saint who might be petitioned for protection or to give one favors. The thinking was that God was a distant figure and far too busy to listen to a peasant and his mundane affairs, but a local saint, as a friend of God, could intercede on one's behalf. The cult of the saint would serve as the focus for their devotional rituals in a way that was significantly different from the standard Catholic idea as saints as intercessors.[12] The relationship between the person/family and the saint was one of close and personal ties based on special favors garnered through ritual behavior.

In Italy and Sicily, the culmination of this devotion reached its climax with the feast of the patron saint. The *feste* was more than a religious affair where the statue of the saint was carried through the streets in a grand procession; it was also a county fair. They "were great occasions for celebration including music, dancing, eating and fireworks displays."[13] During my youth, St. Joseph's Church, the Church to which the local Irish Catholics consigned the Sicilians, had a lawn fete that resembled the *feste* to create income for the Church to defray operating costs of the parish. The lawn fete had carnival rides, bingo, games of chance, Italian music played by my cousin, Roxy Cacamise, fireworks and, of course, Italian food tents. It was the old traditional Sicilian *feste*, only Americanized and made into more of an American pageant – fireworks and all.

Such behavior was a far cry from the tasteful recitations of the rosary, the novenas, and the individual candles lit before altars that was customary among Irish-American Catholics, as well as among other Italian-American groups. Sicilian Americans believed in lavish display of lit candles and in obvious displays of belief in the power of the saints. In 1924, Monsignor Amleto G. Cicognani commented that thanks to Italian immigrants, the practice of lighting candles had become widespread throughout America.[14] In the Italian churches, the sale of candles was a major source of income for parishes: "almost every church, no matter how small collects from four to ten thousand dollars a year, and even more."[15] I can attest that in my family, lighting candles was a normal religious activity and the power of the patron saint or the Madonna was real and tangible. While visiting the Sta. Maria in Trastevere off the Piazza Trastevere in Rome, Italy, I noticed that the cult of the saint is still alive and well. A statue of St. Anthony, the patron saint of lost articles, was covered with little pieces of paper enlisting the saint for his help in finding lost articles. All around the statue of the saint was ablaze with candles. The Mass as it is celebrated in Italy still retains its ancient religious origins and Mediterranean identity, and is full of mysticism and passion unlike the "sanitized" Mass found in the United States. It was quite a spectacle.

Along with the cult of the saint, the immigrants brought with them their occult beliefs and practices.[16] In Italian there are two words used for the word "witch." *Strega* literally means "female witch" and *stregone* means "male witch." The old Italian word for "witchcraft"

---

11   Vecoli, "Cult and Occult," 3.

12   Vecoli, "Cult and Occult," 3.

13   Pozzetta, "Italian Americans," 14.

14   Vecoli, "Cult and Occult," 6.

15   Vecoli, "Cult and Occult," 6.

16   Two very good books on *stregheria* are Raven Grimassi's book *Italian Witchcraft: The Old Religion of Southern Italy* and Thomas Hauschild's social anthropological study, *Power and Magic in Italy,* based his years of research and interviews with *strege.*

is *stregheria*.[17] In Sicily and Italy, the church tolerated village witches even during the Italian Inquisition (1575–1647). As Raven Grimassi has recorded in Italian Witchcraft, the church, although obliged to persecute the "*stregas*" and "*stregheria*," nonetheless let the village witches off with either a brief flogging or a short jail term, and so the Sicilian covens flourished despite pro-forma persecution.[18] Because the witches, on the whole, did not reject Catholicism, the "old ways" were blended with Catholicism in a syncretic process that enabled a substitution of saints in place of the "old spirits and deities." As succeeding generations of Christianized/Catholic witches passed on their knowledge, Sicilian Catholicism became a blend of the pagan and the holy that to Sicilians seemed to be wholly Catholic.[19] Thus, when my grandmother lit candles to the Blessed Mother, or prayed for the intercession of the saints, the manner in which she prayed or asked for intercession was not free of the pagan practices. They were still present in the extravagance of her gestures, the manner in which she recited the prayers, and the way in which she handled the candles and their placement in front of the images to which she prayed. My grandmother was enacting old rituals couched in the language of the Catholic Church, and she and her family and neighbors were not aware of the origins of their practices. Generation after generation remembered and honored their predecessors by passing on the ancient traditions until the origins were forgotten. Sicilian prayers are often thinly disguised spells, such as "the Spell of St. Anthony," which a *strega* can cast when a girl wishes to reclaim a lover.[20] The spell belongs to the old ways, but becomes Catholic because it is addressed to St. Anthony, who was endowed by his Sicilian devotees with the power of *La Vecchia Religione* (The Old Religion). Transferred to this country, Sicilian Catholicism was destined not to play well in an Irish Catholic town to Irish-Americans who would be scandalized by our Sicilian ways. And let me say that my father's Protestant family was not happy either at suddenly finding themselves related to a group of *strege*. This diversity of religious practices meant that my Sicilian family would be subjected to religious as well as social discrimination, even though they considered themselves to be strict and devout Catholics.

Alongside the syncretic practices, couched within the Catholic cult of the saints, the overt occult beliefs and practices based on the *Stregheria* of *La Vecchia Religione* only made the Sicilians further outcasts in LeRoy. My family's response to negative events and tragic circumstances that affected their lives that were beyond the power of police, priest or doctor required the help of a *strega* (female magician) or *stregone* (male magician) to remove the evil eye or *mal'occhio*. To Protestants and other Catholic Americans this appeared to be a ridiculous response to the events of life, but to the Sicilians this was the only way they knew how to cope with unexplainable events, and I once had the opportunity to experience this personally (see Chapter 7). Each crisis was faced with the support and love of family and *paesani*, and increased the sense of community by affirming my family's Sicilian identity.[21]

---

17   Raven Grimassi, *Italian Witchcraft: The Old Religion of Southern Europe* (St. Paul, Minnesota: Llewellyn Publications, 2000), xv.
18   Grimassi, *Italian Witchcraft*, 58.
19   Grimassi, *Italian Witchcraft*, 58.
20   Grimassi, *Italian Witchcraft*, 201.
21   Vecoli, "Cult and Occult," 7.

When the Sicilians of LeRoy started attending Mass at St. Peter's Church at the turn of the twentieth century, their encounter with "the dominant Catholic model" must have been a shock to both them and the American Catholics.[22] Their brand of Catholicism was considered too scandalous for the more conservative American Catholics. American (Irish) Catholicism was based on respect and obedience to the clergy, faithfulness in attendance at Mass, and in partaking of the sacraments and generous in supporting the Church. The Italians fell far short of these ideals and were judged to be not Catholic at all. Men rarely came to church unless it was Easter or the feast day of the patron saint, and they had no great reverence for priests.[23] To the American priests, Catholicism as the Italians practiced it was all emotionalism and external display. The *feste* particularly scandalized Irish Catholics.[24] The clash of cultural traditions between the Catholics in LeRoy inevitably fueled the idea for Sicilians to leave St. Peter's Church, a predominantly Irish parish, and start their own church just a half a block away. As George Pozzetta wrote, "The Irish hierarchy agonized over the 'Italian problem,' and suspicion and mistrust initially characterized relations between the groups, leading to defections among the immigrant generation and demands for separate parishes."[25]

The exteriors of the two churches were as different as the people who worshipped inside them. The exterior of St. Peter's Church was a large cathedral-like structure made out of cut stone. From an architectural point of view it had very interesting elements that featured a tall belfry, multiple entrances and prominent stained glass windows. As interesting as it was to look at, it also was a cold and intimidating structure.

By contrast, the exterior of St. Joseph's Church a half a block away resembled a large house. The church had a very simple floor plan and was constructed of white clap-

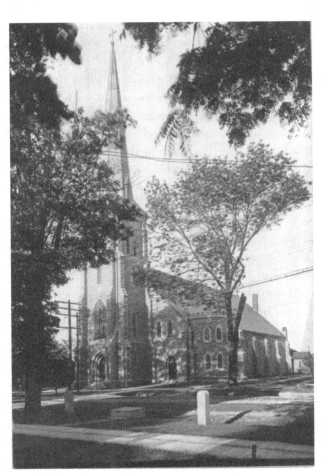

St. Peter's Church, circa 1920. LeRoy Historical Society.

22   Vecoli, "Cult and Occult," 9.

23   Italian men were not as religious as their Sicilian counterparts.

24   Vecoli, "Cult and Occult," 8.

25   Pozzetta, *Italian Americans*, 13.

boards with a peaked roof. It was an inviting building and welcomed worshippers to come inside. This church was also a symbolic representation of the congregation of immigrants who had limited sources of income, so the structure was very modest in comparison to the more impressive Catholic church of well-to-do Irish parishioners down the street.

The interiors also provided an interesting contrast between the two churches. While St. Joseph's Church was smaller and more intimate on a human scale, St. Peter's Church was much larger and more cavernous, and was neither welcoming nor forbidding. When the old altar in St Joseph's Church was constructed in 1909, it resembled those churches found in Sicily. The whole front wall of the church was devoted to the saints with St. Joseph, the patron saint of the church, the prominent figure. His large statue was located in an apse high above a very ornate altar, with two saints on both ends of the altar and two other ones in the left and right corners of the front wall. The only reference to Jesus was a large crucifix hung above the confessional to the right of the altar.

From 1907–1924, the pastors of St. Joseph's Church were either of Italian or Hispanic descent. Compared to American standards, the altar looked like a mix of pagan gods with Catholic rites and saints rather than a Christian church devoted to God as the center of focus. It was during the pastorate of Father Ormsby from 1941–1949 that massive renovations were made to "modernize" the interior, which veiled the real intent behind these actions: to bring the Sicilians in line with the doctrines of the Diocese.

The renovations of the church interior, in conjunction with the transferring of non-Italian priests to run the parish, was a way to gradually bring the congregation of St. Joseph's Church into the American Catholic mainstream. The Buffalo Diocese used these two mea-

St. Joseph's Church, 1920. LeRoy Historical Society.

The original altar St. Joseph's Church 1908–1941. LeRoy Historical Society.

View of renovated altar from the choir. 1950s. LeRoy Historical Society.

sures to sanitize Sicilian Catholicism in LeRoy by infiltrating the parishes with either Irish priests, who would put an end to this nonsense, or they sent Sicilian-American soon-to-be priests to American seminaries for indoctrination in proper American Catholicism. As Rudolph Vecoli wrote in his article, "Cult and Occult in Italian-American Culture," when Italian priests were schooled at diocesan seminaries, "they underwent a process of assimilation to the dominant Catholic model from which they emerged enthusiastic Americanizers."[26] From 1924–1964, the parish was sent two Irish priests and one English priest to serve as pastors. The system worked, and the Sicilian mystic practices were watered down and now have mostly disappeared. This ingenious plan ultimately brought the Sicilians under control, and once and for all tried to end the friction between the different ethnic groups. Italian priests were sent to seminary school and indoctrinated with the American brand of Catholicism. Over time, Italian priests started weeding out the mysticism that Sicilian immigrants brought with them from Sicily. Unlike Hispanic Americans, who have kept their culture alive, the Sicilians sacrificed who they were to become "good Americans" to "fit in."

St. Peter's Church, January 4, 1943. LeRoy Historical Society.

The end result of the renovations produced a church interior that looked more Protestant than Catholic. Gone are the saints on and above the altar; they were replaced with the large image of Christ that was once over the confessionals. In fact, Father Ormsby removed the large, carved, wooden statues of saints that adorned the altar since the beginning of St. Joseph's Church and burned them in a bonfire behind the church to complete the "sanitation" process that he implemented to rid the church of its Sicilian heritage and, therefore, undesirable influences. In their place, new smaller subdued statues of the Blessed Mother

---

26 Vecoli, "Cult and Occult," 9.

and St. Joseph are introduced off to the left and right of the altar, each fronted with banks of devotional candles—one concession to the Sicilians.

The interior of St. Peter's Church, on the other hand, retained its "Catholic" look. The altar remained ornate and as in other Catholic churches: there were statues to the various saints, such as St. Patrick and the Blessed Mother, but to my recollection there was not a statue dedicated to the patron saint of the church, St. Peter. It was very curious that elements like the ornate altar and the multitude of statues of saints throughout the church was fine for the Irish parish but had to be purged from the Sicilian parish. Through the years, the transformation of the interior of St. Joseph's Church from a fusion of "magical-religious" beliefs to a very sedate and mundane Protestant-esque one became a symbol of assimilation and the erosion of Sicilian culture in LeRoy.[27]

After the death of Monsignor Zupa, the longtime pastor (1964-2008) of St. Joseph's Church, on February 6, 2008, the two dioceses were joined together due to the shortage of priests. The Buffalo Diocese wanted to combine the churches a few years before his death but the Monsignor fought hard to keep his parish separate. The Bishop of the Buffalo Diocese made a deal with the parish that in effect said as long as the Monsignor was alive he could keep his parish separate. As a compromise, the parishioners of St. Joseph's Church were able to keep their identity. Today, the diocese uses the church as an oratory to hold daily Mass and uses the rectory, where the priests lived, as a convent for the Sisters of Mercy. Old St. Peter's Church is used as the main area of worship on Sunday and the finally reunited parish is called The Church of Our Lady of Mercy. As a concession to the parishioners of St. Joseph's Church, there are now devotional altars in the side altars where worshippers can light candles to the Blessed Mother and to Jesus, but these areas are really scaled down to only one small bank of candles compared to the endless rows of candles that serviced the parishioners in St. Joseph's Church. Even today, the two parishes find it hard to be together and tensions still exist. Recently, my Aunt Dorothy was at the beauty parlor and overheard a life-long member of St. Peter's Parish remark that when she "enters her church to go to Mass on Sunday, it is like being in Little Italy." One can understand how the Italian members of the new reunited parish feel as much like outsiders as their ancestors did at the turn of the twentieth century, even after one hundred years of coexistence in the community. Remarks like this are a flashback to the times when non-Italians felt superior in every way to the lowly Sicilians. Some things haven't changed since 1907.

While the Protestants' reaction was predictable, one might have expected a more sympathetic response from the Catholic Church. The bigotry of the American Catholics equaled or even exceeded that of the Protestants. Evidently, the Italians did not live up to the ideals of American, that is, Irish, Catholicism.[28] Those strange, almost pagan, beliefs and festivals associated with Sicilian immigrants were too much for the established parishioners to accept. This clash of traditions ended up alienating two different worlds.

In addition to the hostility they encountered with the Irish Catholics at St. Peter's Church, the Sicilians were also met with an unbridled bigotry from the town. An example of this alienation happened in the late 1930's just before World War II, which demonstrated how intense the bigotry was in LeRoy that targeted Sicilians. At this time there was a Ku Klux Klan

27   Vecoli, "Cult and Occult," 2.
28   Vecoli, "Cult and Occult," 8.

chapter with its headquarters in the Northern Lights District on the outskirts of the northern part of the village. It was called the Northern Lights District because so many crosses were burnt in effigy aimed at the Mediterranean population that people thought it resembled the aurora borealis. An African American teenager incredibly attended one of the cross burnings at a Klan rally intended to intimidate the Sicilians. When he got home and told his father where he had been, his father emphatically ordered him never to go to one ever again. It seems that African Americans were more accepted in LeRoy than my Sicilian ancestors.[29]

During World War II, the federal government was not convinced of the loyalty of the Italian-American citizens in LeRoy. An undercover FBI agent lived in the town during the war and kept files on the Italian community to make sure that there was not any un-American activity and sympathy for Mussolini.[30] Prior to the war, some Italians, such as my grandfather's cousin, sent money in support of the dictator, so the decision to closely watch the Italians wasn't totally unwarranted. It wasn't until after the war that the climate in LeRoy started to get better for my family, as the Italian population skyrocketed and they became the dominant ethnic group in the town. In addition to the increase in population, when Italian-Americans served with their fellow Americans in Europe (including in Italy as well as Sicily) and in the Pacific, the stereotypes started to disappear and we were looked at in a positive light. Now we were seen as brave, loyal, and patriotic.

During the tough times before the war, Italians were either forced by economics, bigotry, or by social restrictions to buy the worst, most run-down houses in the poorest section of town—many of which were falling apart and in some cases had all of the windows busted out. In response, they did what many other immigrant groups did: they banded together and created a community where they could speak Italian and try to assimilate into American society at the same time. Because of the spirit of *campilismo*, they lived together in communities like they did in Sicily. Neither of my great-grandparents spoke English well, but since they lived with other Italians in a close-knit community, they were able to survive very well without learning much English. One of the great strengths of these hearty immigrants was their tremendous work ethic, and over time they fixed their run-down houses, which became homes they could take pride in. They debunked the stereotypes that Italians were dirty, lazy, and avoided hard work at all costs. They actually transformed the face of LeRoy in a very positive way by buying dilapidated houses in the least desirable part of town and fixing them up into beautiful old homes. They were essentially practicing their own form of urban renewal in the Italian community without government assistance. Trying to bring a part of Italy with them and to supplement the table, they planted beautiful flower gardens, fruit trees, grape vines and bountiful vegetable gardens. On a recent trip to Italy, as I was traveling through the countryside, I noticed the striking similarity of the homes of my childhood and the country homes in Italy.

---

29   This incident was told to me by Lynne Belluscio, Director of the LeRoy Historical Society, on June 23, 2011.

30   These events went told to me in an interview with Lynne Belluscio, Director of the LeRoy Historical Society on June 23, 2011.

Great-Grandfather Calogero (Charles) Barone

Born: October 25, 1862, Valledolmo, Sicily
Died: January 22, 1942, LeRoy, New York

Great Grandpa Calogero Barone was a very handsome man and very friendly. He was thin and relatively tall, around five feet eight inches and towered over his wife Maria, who was barely four feet nine inches. In his youth, he served in the Italian army so he learned how to read and write Italian. He was thirty four when he immigrated to America from Valledolmo, Sicily, a small remote mountain village in the state of Palermo. Calogero, like many of his fellow countryman, lived a life of poverty in Sicily with no chance of escape; consequently, he decided to immigrate to America. To make the move possible, he received financial support for the passage from his brother who had already made the journey to the "Promised Land." From documents found at Ellis Island, he arrived in the United States with $30.00 in his pocket. When an immigration agent asked him where he got the money, he replied that his brother in America sent it to him.

Great Grandma and Great Grandpa were very religious and went to church every day and sat in the third pew next to the confessional. Sicilians in general are very devout worshippers, with my great-grandparents fitting perfectly into this mold. "Sicilians of the lower class are devout worshippers, and conform scrupulously to all forms and ordinances of the Church differing much in this respect from their brethren of Northern Italy."[31]

My great-grandfather was naturalized in 1902 and was an industrious, hardworking member of society, debunking the stereotype of the day that Italians were lazy and unproductive. He worked for the railroad as a laborer until he retired, like most Italians in my hometown. Through hard

My great-grandparents, Maria and Calogero Barone, in front of their house in the 1930s.

---

31   Caico, *Sicilian Ways and Days*, 76.

work, he was able to buy a house on lower Lake Street, just south of the Northern Lights section of town, with some sizable property. From family accounts and photographs that I've seen, it was a beautiful house in its day with a large front porch with a swing.

My great-grandparents' house on 130 Lake St. in LeRoy, 1930s.

After moving to LeRoy from Avon in 1903, he and my great-grandmother lived in a series of apartments until they were able to save enough money to buy a house. On August 31, 1915, they bought a house at 130 Lake Street for $2,650. The property that Calogero and Maria purchased had room for a chicken coup, a large vegetable garden, and on the back of the property a hill overlooking the Oatka Creek. This was the place where Great-Grandpa grew his grapes to make red wine for himself and white wine that Great-Grandma preferred. They always had wine with their meals, and he was considered to be an excellent winemaker. On the border of the property, they had a large quince bush from which Great-Grandma made quince jam. The house had a fence around it so that Great-Grandpa's dog could have free rein to roam around the yard. There was also a large barn with a hayloft and, since they had no car, this is where he kept all of his tools.

They were well liked and relatives from Buffalo would travel the one hundred miles round-trip to visit them on Sundays. For the big meal to celebrate their visit, he would kill a chicken and Great-Grandma would roast it and make chicken soup, pasta, and sometimes her famous chocolate cake made with sour milk.

After suffering a stroke early in 1942, Great Grandpa Barone died at his home several weeks later due to complications. He was seventy-six years old.

Great-Grandmother Maria Orazia Guzzetta Barone

Born: July 11, 1871, Valledolmo, Sicily
Died: January 30, 1944, LeRoy, New York

Maria Orazia Guzzetta Barone came to America when she was twenty-five years old. She spoke very little English, and according to my grandma and aunts, she was not very hospitable. In fact, Grandma told me that her own mother didn't treat her nearly as well as her mother-in-law, Florence O'Geen, although Maria treated Grandma's sister Mary and her children much better. My cousin Rita, Great-Aunt Mary's oldest child, told me that Grandma Barone would give her birthday parties and that her brother and sisters were treated wonderfully. Grandma's children were not as fortunate and did not have the same warm relationship.

My Aunt Dorothy told me of a time when she was at Grandma Barone's house with her cousins and Great Grandma offered them some cookies. When she came back with the snacks she offered them only to Rita and Rita's siblings and not to Dorothy. I asked Dorothy why she thought she was left out. Dorothy said that none of Grandma's children learned Sicilian and that was an affront to Great-Grandma Barone; therefore, she wanted nothing to do with them. Since my aunt's father, Frank O'Geen (Gugino), did not insist on his children learning Sicilian because he wanted them to assimilate as fast as possible, Grandma Barone did not like him and therefore extended her dislike to his children. Not learning Sicilian was a repudiation of the culture and way of life they left behind in Sicily. Old world Sicilians felt that if their descendants became more American by learning English and not Sicilian, then the parents would have less influence over their children and grandchildren's lives. Discipline and control is central to the culture of the Mediterranean.

A family friend and my Grandpa's godson, Benny Joy, who lived next to Calogero and Maria on Lake Street, told me his recollections of my great grandmother. He said that she was a large woman and would always wear a big white apron with pockets in it. Since she was corpulent, it was difficult for her to bend over to tie her shoes and she would ask him in Sicilian to tie them for her. There was an old pear tree stump that was on the border between the two houses and she would place her foot on it. After he tied her shoes, she would reach into her pocket and give him one of her freshly baked cookies for a reward. Since Benny spoke Sicilian, they got along fine and he remembered her fondly. He also said she made the best cookies he ever had.

Things changed somewhat for the next generation. Having grown up in a beautiful, orderly, and well-kept home, it must have been quite a shock for Mary to leave it when she got married. She married a young man who had limited resources and the house she moved into was very rundown in comparison.

On November 23, 1942, ten months after Great-Grandpa died, Great-Grandma sold the house and first went to live with Grandma's sister, Mary, but soon wore out her welcome. She then moved in with Grandma. Again, it fell to Carrie to sacrifice for her family who took her in out of her sense of duty, regardless of what had been between them before. Aunt Dorothy said that Grandma's relationship with her mother did not improve and that Maria was always critical of everything Grandma did.

Great-Grandma Barone died at the home of her daughter, Carrie, after several months of failing health. She was seventy-three.

CHAPTER 2

The First Generation

The nine children of Calogero and Maria Barone are:

Calogera (Carrie) Barone

> *Born: February 12, 1893, Valledolmo, Sicily*
> *Died: January 28, 1992, LeRoy, New York*

Santo (Jimmy) Barone

> *Born: March 23, 1894, Valledolmo, Sicily*
> *Died: August 1985, Baltimore, Maryland*

Giacomo (Joe) Barone

> *Born: October 27, 1895, Valledolmo, Sicily*
> *Died: September 10, 1975, Buffalo, New York*

Peter Barone

> *Born: October 28, 1897, Avon, New York*
> *Died: September 11, 1977, Baltimore, Maryland*

Petrina (Mary) Barone

> *Born: May 8, 1900, Avon, New York*
> *Died: January 14, 1993, LeRoy, New York*

Anthony (Tony) Barone

> *Born: June 13, 1902, Avon, New York*
> *Died: November 6, 1978, Rochester, New York*

Rosalino (Ross) Barone

Born: September 12, 1904, LeRoy, New York
Died: March 24, 1993, Ulster, New York

Samuel Barone

Born: October 16, 1906, LeRoy, New York
Died: January 31, 1986, Rochester, New York

Cosmo (Moxie) Barone

Born: April 25, 1913, LeRoy, New York
Died: November 7, 1962, Rome, New York

The first generation, 1946. Left to right: Cosmo, Sam, Giacomo (Joe), Petrina (Mary), Santo (Jimmy), Calogera (Carrie), Tony, Pete, and Rosalino (Ross).

These first generations of my family to live or be born in America turned out to be a collection of well-to-do businessmen and professionals along with a few shady characters, and, of course, homemakers. Three of Cologero and Maria's children were born in Sicily and the rest were born in America. Some of my great-uncles retained their Sicilian heritage at home, even if it was behind a façade of naturalization the outside world could not penetrate, while others became Americanized to the point that they didn't seem Sicilian at all even to us and changed their Italian names. The only two women in the family, Grandma and Great-Aunt Mary, remained essentially peasants their whole lives. I was able to grow up in an environment that allowed me to view them practically unnoticed and to witness firsthand the dynamics of their relationship to one another. I could become immersed in the Sicilian customs they retained, and when I left home I saw how different my family was compared to the rest of American society.

The differences between Old World customs, particularly the practices in Sicily, and the urbanized American family were striking, especially when it came to marriage. The expectations for a marriage partner for the first generation followed very strict guidelines. An individual with parental consent could make the selection of his or her own mate. An ideal engagement would be to select a mate from your village, but marriage to someone from the same region could be tolerated. Under some circumstances, very reluctant permission would be granted to someone outside the nationality but not permission for anyone outside the religion.[1] Both my grandmother and my great-aunt married Sicilians from their village in Sicily. All of my great-uncles eventually married, but only two of them married Italian women. All of my great-uncles moved away from the small provincial town of LeRoy to find a better and more prosperous life moving to big cities, where they were able to fit in better away from the vicious bigotry of a small town. My great-uncles married non-Italians as symbols of their Americanization, further distancing themselves from their peasant parents and the Old World. It is a telling statement of the upward mobility the men had with opportunities to mingle with and marry non-Italians and to conduct business and take advantage of educational opportunities. This contrasts with the lack of education and the relegated roles as homemakers destined for the women because of their gender. The men were allowed to graduate at least from high school while education for the women seemed unnecessary, since they would go to work at a young age and then eventually get married and be supported by their husbands. Sometimes these marriages would be arranged, depending on how much control and influence the Sicilian born parents had over a child.

It is amazing to see how fast my family became assimilated into American society. Environmental and social pressures conspired to Americanize them away from the Old World peasant pattern. They, and others like them, broke down the stereotypes through their tremendous work ethic and the realization that "to remain associated with the Italian way of life in the American community means low status, social and economic discrimination and prejudice."[2] In Sicily, the concept of upward mobility did not exist, but in America the opportunities were there for the taking. Their message to me was to work hard and overcome any obstacles.

---

1   Paul J. Campisi, "The Italian Family in the United States," *The American Journal of Sociology* 53, no. 6 (1948), 443–449.

2   Campisi, "The Italian Family," 447.

CHAPTER 3

Grandmother Calogera (Carrie) Barone

Born: February 12, 1893, Valledolmo, Sicily
Died: January 28, 1992, LeRoy, New York

My grandmother, Carrie Barone, immigrated to America with her family when she was three years old. Her godmother, not wanting to be forgotten, presented the family with a picture of herself so that Grandma would not forget her. That picture was the only keepsake my grandmother had from the Old World.

When I was in high school, I asked Grandma what her Sicilian name was since Carrie didn't seem sufficiently Italian to me. She actually didn't know and never learned her given name since it had been anglicized at Ellis Island. Calogera, her actual name that I learned much later, is a distinctly Sicilian name and does not appear in other parts of Italy. Her parents were trying to assimilate into a hostile environment, so they accepted the name she was given in America and they never told her what her real name was. Carrie left school at the end of third grade to take care of her six brothers and her sister so her parents could work. Consequently, she never learned to read or write.

LIFE WITH GRANDMA

When I was eleven years old, because of dire financial circumstances, my family moved to live with Grandma and Aunt Franny. In true Italian fashion, Grandma came to our rescue by remodeling her large house so that we would each have a large apartment and semi-privacy. In this way, I had a front row view of life in an Italian immigrant household. It was at this time I was introduced to all of Grandma's culinary delights, since up to that time, my Scottish father, who hated Italian food, and my mother, who wanted to be more American than Italian, cooked only the food my father liked. I never had anything Italian except pizza. It was in this setting that Grandma would repay me for shoveling her sidewalk and never-ending driveway of snow after a

Grandma in her fifties, 1940s.

big storm by making me a large plate of warm *sfingi* (Italian donuts) to devour. I was also a spectator when the multitude of relatives made their pilgrimage to the house to visit their beloved sister, also known as Aunt Carrie to many.

Grandma was very short, approximately four feet nine inches tall, but she ruled the roost over all three generations. Grandma was a kind woman and loved all children. She really didn't seem to see the differences in people. One weekend when I was home from college, Grandma heard that I was bringing Linda, my future spouse, home to meet everyone. She cornered me one day and interrogated me.

"Tommy, I hear you're bringing home a girl from college."

I replied that I was, and she continued her investigation.

"Is she Italian?"

"No, Grandma, she isn't."

"Is she Catholic?"

"Ah, no, Grandma. She isn't."

"Is she a gypsy?"

"No, Grandma."

"Then she must be very nice!" she replied very enthusiastically.

She spoke with an accent, and those who met her for the first time had a hard time understanding her. When Linda came to my house in 1970 for the first time to meet my family, she really didn't know what to expect. Even though she had heard stories about my family, she thought I was exaggerating. As we were sitting in our side of Grandma's house watching TV, she overheard Grandma talking on the phone to one of her old Sicilian friends. Linda's family had immigrated to America from England in the 1600s, and she thought all families were like hers in that they only spoke English. She never heard any language but English spoken in the house. As was Grandma's routine, she would start the conversation in English and then when she got excited or got to the good parts of a story, she switched to Sicilian to keep everyone else in the dark. When Linda heard this, she asked me, "What is wrong with your Grandma?" I didn't know what she was referring to since this seemed normal to me. I replied, "That is just Grandma talking on the phone to one of her friends." But Linda, more confused than ever, said, "Yeah, but what is she saying? Does she have something wrong with her?" Then I realized for the first time that we had grown up in totally different cultures. In the 1970s, diversity had not become the accepted norm, and different cultures were still looked upon as being somewhat un-American. I got the feeling of how my relatives must have felt many years ago when they first came to America, and their customs were looked at with suspicion.

Through the years, Carrie became very fond of my wife, the non-Italian who wasn't even Catholic. Grandma liked people if they were "good inside." I think she remembered the hard times when her family was considered to be outsiders and they only wanted to be given a fair shake in life. Since she essentially raised her brothers, they visited her often and sought her approval. Her brothers became pharmacists and prosperous business owners and thought of her as their mother. When they came to visit her you could see the utmost respect and love they had for her. She was a peasant woman from the nineteenth century, but these sophisticated and worldly travelers never acted like they thought they were better than her. Even the brothers who lived a hedonistic lifestyle cared about what she thought of them. She seemed to give them latitude when they came to visit her since she allowed them to smoke and drink in her house, a vice she forbade the rest of us.

I was especially struck by how strong she was mentally and physically. Even in her late seventies, she was still weeding her flower garden and working part time at Hickey Freeman making custom suits. I can only imagine the struggles she endured throughout her life. I was fortunate enough to hear some of the stories and to see the emotion they stirred in her. On days when she felt "too lame," she would pay me one dollar to weed her beloved flower garden. The first time I did that for her, I was very proud of all the nasty looking roots I had dug up. I can't describe the look of horror on her face when she saw that I had laid waste to all of her beautiful tulips and peony bushes. She still paid me the dollar and then spent the following week replanting all of them. The next time I weeded it was under her watchful eye.

Grandma was an excellent and resourceful cook, as all Italian grandmothers are, particularly those who start cooking at an early age as she did. On Easter Sunday, we would meet at my Aunt Helen's house and Grandma would make homemade ravioli using macaroni made from scratch. One time I "helped" her, which meant that she let me watch her make it. Since she was so short, she couldn't easily roll the pasta out on the countertop so she put a wooden board on a kitchen chair and this became her workspace. She would mix the ingredients by feel or intuition, never measuring anything. When she added seasoning, she would place the right amount in her hand or grab a pinch between her fingers. Grandma was a more resourceful cook than a totally Italian cook. Life on the farm during the Great Depression meant that she often had to invent meals from virtually nothing. Just like in Sicily, much of their food was derived from foraging for native plants in season, and even after the hard times passed, she still went out to the fields with her brother-in-law, Tony, to find *cardunis* (burdocks), bittersweet mustard greens, or dandelion greens. I remember one day Great-Uncle Tony drove into Grandma's driveway, screeched to halt and rushed into the house. We thought something was wrong. He said, "Carrie I found the best patch of bittersweet I've ever seen. Get your bushel basket and let's get there before someone else finds it." And off they went.

Burdocks (*cardunis*), considered annoying weeds by many, are a delicacy to the Sicilians in Western New York. Before they grow burs, the stalks look like rhubarb and are edible but taste similar to artichokes. This could be a source of embarrassment if non-Italians knew what we were eating, so we hid the truth. In fact, the exact content of Grandma's large pan of what she called "asparagus" was a carefully guarded secret that was kept especially hidden from my father and my German uncles. I remember a family picnic where some of my aunt's friends from work were attending. My aunt was horrified when she saw that Grandma had made *cardunis*. After some discussion, us grandchildren were sworn to secrecy, but Grandma was fuming. "What! You think they are better than us?" At the meal my aunt's non-Italian friends asked what was in the pan that smelled so good. My aunt said, "Asparagus! Try it." We held our breath as they put the first morsels in their mouths. After a moment of absolute quiet they enthusiastically exclaimed that this was the best asparagus they had ever had and they wanted her recipe. Grandma answered them, "I can't tell you, it's a family secret!"

After I was married and had my own family, my wife and children and I would visit my mother and Grandma every Sunday. I realized then that there was something special about Grandma, and I wanted to save her legacy, so I started to videotape and photograph her. As it turns out , Grandma really liked the attention. The first time I asked her if I could videotape her and she saw the camera, she asked me to explain to her what a videotape was. I explained to her it was like making a movie, except when I got through you could watch it on TV. Surprisingly, she agreed. I guess she liked the thought of starring on a TV show, but before I could do anything she had to have her hair combed. My wife volunteered. This started a ritual, when every Sunday or whenever we came to visit, Linda had to comb her hair and Linda had to do it the way she did it the first time: French braiding the sides and then putting her hair in a bun. After that, no one could comb Grandma's hair except for Linda. As Grandma got older and her hair became brittle, it started getting thinner and breaking off so then the bun had to go, but the French braids remained. From the first time I did a videotape, she was perfectly comfortable in front of a camera and was never self-conscious. The tapes reveal all of her mannerisms and hand gestures that display all of the emotion she felt on various subjects. My aunts thought that she had no clue about the technology and that was why she felt so comfortable in front of the camera, but I thought differently. She would ask me the next time I visited, "Did the pictures come out good?" I believe that she enjoyed all of the attention, since she really never got any growing up from her parents or from my grandfather. At times when she would get mad at one of us she would say, "What's going to happen when I die? You'll all starve!" And, "Nobody remembers the tough days. Everyone has it easy now!" I think the implication was that she was proud of the fact that she "made it" despite all of the hardship she endured, and proud that someone wanted to hear her story. Above all, I think she wanted to be remembered and to know that she had not lived in vain.

CHILD LABOR AND TRUANCY

Poor families often rely on the labors of their children for survival, and sometimes it is their only source of income. Child labor was widely employed in subsistence agriculture, in the household, or in factories in this country in years past. As an eight-year-old, my grandmother left school to take care of her brothers and sister in the winter, and in the summer she helped supplement her family's income by working as a farm laborer. Trucks picked up Italian workers (adults and children) on a street corner in town and they were loaded into the back of it like cattle. At this young age she was responsible for her six-year-old brother Joe, four-year-old brother Pete, and one-year-old sister Mary. In 1902 she became responsible for her brother Tony, and in 1904 brother Ross was born. As the brothers got older, they went to school and some received their high school diplomas, but Grandma either took care of her ever-increasing family or went to work. She told me of the times when the truant officer would come around the house to check on her because of her absenteeism. She would take her brothers and sister and hide under the bed so he wouldn't see her through the windows. Grandma was able to elude him for years. When she got older and her brothers were in school, she went to work full time at various factory jobs, and her sister Mary took over taking care of the younger brothers. By the time her brother Cosmo was born in 1913 she was already married to my grandfather. Her life up to that point was bleak, to say the least.

When Grandma was twelve years old, she had a factory job at the LeRoy Cotton Mill and was so short that she had to stand on a wooden box so that she could reach her workspace to make cotton yarn. When she was in her teens, Grandma worked at the LeRoy Salt Company where she filled, weighed and sewed ten-pound bags of salt and was paid ten cents per one hundred bags. Grandma thought that this was easy money because she could sew up the burlap bags faster than anyone. By the time she got married, all she had known since the age of eight was that she had no choice in life but to work hard at any job she could get. Life was not fun. At this time in history, Italian immigrants were given the jobs that no one else wanted to do or they were exploited because of their poverty. America was a place that considered them less than equal; they were regarded as low-class, stupid, and inferior.

MARRIAGE

Grandma was married on November 24, 1912 to Frank O'Geen (Chapter 12), whose surname Gugino was anglicized to O'Geen at Ellis Island. Grandpa also came from Valledolmo, Sicily. It was an arranged marriage and Grandma had no say in the matter. According to my

grandmother, her parents thought she was getting too old and should have been married and out of the house. Grandma's parents had a large family—eight children at the time, with number nine on the way. Frank, being much older, was looking to start a family, so they seemed like a good match. Since the families knew one another in Sicily, the deal was done. Their courtship and marriage followed the strict guidelines that were set down by generations of southern Italian peasants. Since my grandparents were from the same village in Sicily, the requirement that they both had to be from the same village was met. Grandma was only alone with him two times before they were married and both times it was in the parlor of her parents' house while the adults were in the next room acting as chaperons so the chastity rule was enforced.

Sacred Conversation, 2014. Egg tempera on panel. Santo (Jimmy), Calogero (Carrie) and Giacomo (Joe), 1902. This is about the time Carrie left school to work as a seasonal farm worker.

In fact, she had never been on a date in her life.

In the painting, *The Arranged Marriage: No One Saw the Magpie,* I kept the deer-in-the-headlights look that Grandma has in the wedding photograph since it conveys the feeling she must have experienced marrying a complete stranger. There is no visible sign of tenderness or love between them. I asked her one time if she grew to love him and she replied, "He was my husband." That was all she had to say on the matter.

The imagery in the painting above reflects the life they had together. The pendant she is wearing is a heart with seven swords, referring to the Virgin of Sorrows in Catholic iconography and the seven daughters that survived during their years of marriage. According to folklore, a lone magpie signifies sorrow, but this sorrow can be counteracted and turned to joy by saying, "Hello, Mr. Magpie. How is your wife today?" Since Grandma doesn't see it, the magpie becomes a symbol of her hard life. The grouping of angels at the top of the painting is from Botticelli's *The Mystic Nativity* and represents the idealistic hope they shared at the beginning of their life together. The appropriated painting in the background is Bartolomeo di Giovanni's *The Marriage of Peleus and Thetis* and was chosen for its hedonistic subject matter

and as a source of a wedding celebration. I like the way these two paintings act as opposites and create a sense of conflict between religion and the temptations found in life.

The frame is based on an egg tempera painting by Michelangelo entitled *The Donni Tondo* that I saw in the Uffizi. After looking at that painting, I saw the expressive possibilities that a frame could add to the total conception of a painting. For this painting, I made casts of a doll's head and bird wings and placed them in the four corners of the frame. I wanted these objects to represent the children my grandparents lost at childbirth or infancy, as well as to be a heavenly reference.

Grandma and Grandpa had nine children with seven surviving to adulthood. They were all delivered at home with a midwife. The first, Florence, died at

The Arranged Marriage: No One Saw the Magpie, *2007. Egg tempera on panel.*

birth, and Tony, the only son, died of pneumonia with complications from measles at six months twenty-nine days. It was not uncommon for poor people during the early twentieth century to lose one or more children to diseases that have since been all but eradicated by modern vaccines. I found a family photograph of the three of them and based a painting on this life-altering event.

On Christmas Day 1987, I was interviewing Grandma, and I don't know if it was because my two children were there or not, but she started to reminisce about her life, and in particular the day Little Tony got sick. Grandma and Grandpa were visiting her parents when he got a fever. As she was telling me what a beautiful baby he was and that he "looked like a little peach," she started to cry. She said, "We were visiting my parents and he got a fever and then he died." It was very touching that even after his death ninety years ago she had such vivid memories of him. She ended the subject with her favorite saying: "Whadda ya gonna do? I've been through hell, but God's been good to me."

The painting *The Short Life of Little Tony* depicts my Grandma and Grandpa with little Anthony just before he died of measles in 1916. I combined the photo of them with two adorations of the *maji*—one by Gentile da Fabriano, and the other by Domenico del Ghirlandaio. Behind my grandmother's head is the infamous farm workhorse that dragged her about a mile one day while she was unhitching it, acting as a reminder of her unpredictable and tough life on the farm. My grandfather can be seen smiling—this is the only photograph I have that depicts him happily engaged with one of his children. Out of nine children, Anthony was the only boy they had, and being a farmer and Sicilian, his heartbreak when Anthony died must have been unimaginable. This painting shows them at the beginning of their life together before the Great Depression crushed their hopes and dreams. Compared to her unsure demeanor at her wedding, here Grandma looks very self-assured and confident with her son and husband.

The Short Life of Little Tony, *2007. Egg tempera on panel.*

LIFE ON THE FARM

My grandparents bought an eighty-acre farm on the outskirts of LeRoy, New York, on 9522 Asbury Road and worked it from December 1, 1915, until February 11, 1939, when the Great Depression became too severe and the farm became unprofitable. Apparently, Grandpa and Grandma did not have enough money to buy the farm outright, so his brother, Joe, and sister-in-law, Lena, put up a portion of the money and the four of them became co-owners of the farm. The house was built in 1883 and had seen better days. The exterior was weathered, with the shutters falling apart and there was no indoor plumbing. On the farm at one time or another, they had a wide range of farm animals: a horse, cows, chickens, goats, sheep and pigs. They also grew wheat, potatoes and corn. A typical day would find Grandma waking before dawn to make breakfast for the family as well as bread for the day, and later making lunch and supper. In between she often worked in the fields helping my grandfather plow and harvest their crops in addition to doing all the housework. My grandfather's godson, Benny Joy, told me of an instance when the three of them were cutting hay. He told me that my grandfather was a hard worker but was most impressed with Grandma. My grandmother drove the team of horses, and when the wagon was full of hay, she drove the wagon to the barn and then threw the hay up into the loft. When the wheat was ready to harvest and the threshers came to the farm, Grandma had to cook for and feed the crew of threshers on top of her regular chores.

It was at this time that the family made a conscious effort to become Americanized, particularly with regards to food. Grandma was not entirely an Italian cook, but certainly she had her Sicilian specialties. One of the "American" neighbors that Grandma always talked about was a woman named Gert Snider. It was Gert who taught Grandma to expand her culinary offerings to include dishes like scalloped potatoes and turkey with dressing, recipes that reflected "American fare." In fact, when Grandma made scalloped potatoes for her sister Mary and brother-in-law Tony for the first time, she created quite a stir. The new dish was a rousing success, and so "American" cuisine was added to the menu. For Thanksgiving meals when her German sons-in-law came for dinner, Grandma had to make a casserole dish full of extra dressing because they thought hers was the best they ever tasted. By moving to the farm, my grandparents moved out of the Sicilian neighborhood and tried to forge their own way in an attempt to assimilate. Grandma had a hard life and got little or no appreciation for all of her backbreaking work. One evening after Grandpa and the hired man[1] came from town, they

Florence and the farm dog that chased the gypsies, 1920s.

were sitting in the hired man's bedroom talking. Grandma heard the hired man tell Grandpa that, "Frank, you gotta damn good wife." Grandma told me, "Frank never told me anything like that." Her contribution to their survival apparently was taken for granted and compli-

---

1   Grandpa had a series of hired men over the twenty-four years he worked his farm. One was even an African American man and some were non-Italian, and all of them seemed to be liked.

ments were few and far between. She was expected to do whatever needed to be done without complaint.

One of the hired men got into a tough spot and brought a touch of drama and intrigue to the farm. Throughout the twentieth century and even up through the 1960s, groups of gypsies would descend on the small towns in Western New York. Sicilians in particular were suspicious of them, probably due to unsavory encounters in the Old World, and so they were on their guard to protect their property and in some cases against kidnaping. As soon as a gypsy was spotted walking the streets of town, word would spread like wildfire and then everyone would be ever vigilant. One of my favorite stories that she told over and over was the story of when the gypsies tried to kidnap the hired man. Grandma was making supper one day when she heard their dog barking. Grandma knew it had different barks for different

The farm horse that dragged Grandma, 1920s.

situations, so she was able to tell if friends and strangers were coming down the driveway. This bark was an angry bark so she ran out of the house and saw the dog bolting out toward the road where she saw a carload of gypsies trying to stuff the hired man into the back seat of their car. Grandma rang the dinner bell and Grandpa came running from the barn, saw what was happening, and ran toward the car. The dog had reached the gypsies by this time and started biting them, and the hired man broke loose and ran toward the house. Since the gypsies saw Grandpa running toward them and had the dog biting them, they took off in the car. Grandma said that their dog saved the hired man's life.

I asked, "Why were they trying to kidnap the hired man?"

She replied, "That's what gypsies do!"

During the winter months, the only way they could get around was by horse and sleigh since the town did not plow their road. One Sunday after they got home from church, Grandma was holding the reins of the horse while Grandpa was unhitching it. Something spooked the horse and it took off running through the fields with Grandma still holding onto the reins, bouncing up and down behind the horse as it fled. Grandpa and the kids chased after them, and after about a mile the horse came to halt. When Grandpa and the kids saw them from the distance, Grandma was just lying on the ground. My aunt who was listening to the story told me that they thought she was dead because she was just lying there and not moving a muscle. The next day she was so bruised and sore that she couldn't get out of bed to make breakfast but she managed to get up later in the day to help out around the house. When I asked her why she held onto the reins and allowed herself to be dragged as opposed to just letting the horse go, her response was, "He was the only horse we had. We would have been goners!"

THE GREAT DEPRESSION

During the 1930s, life on the farm became unbearable until finally Grandpa had to sell the farm. Prices for crops hit rock bottom and it became impossible to make a living. By this time, they had seven daughters and no sons to help him with the hard work. Grandma had had enough. In an act of bravery when circumstances became dire and they were on the brink of starvation, Grandma challenged Grandpa's absolute authority by announcing to him that she was packing up the kids and moving to town to find a job. At that time, when women were considered second-class citizens and men were the heads of households, she was strong enough to stand up to her husband. It was the right decision since my grandfather died of cancer a few years later. He could have gone with her if he wanted to but she had had enough of that life and was going to find a job. They all moved to town with Grandpa traveling back and forth to the farm every day to tend the livestock until it was finally sold. This was only the first blow.

With the grip of the depression getting worse and very little money coming in the household, Grandpa went to the town hall to ask Mr. Heaman for "relief" (the equivalent of welfare). Grandpa asked for only three dollars a week and was denied his request. Times for Italians in LeRoy had not gotten much better since the first families settled there in the late 1800s. The discrimination continued even into the 1950s, when they became the dominant ethnic group. Grandma, in an interview in the early 1990s, referred to the town officials as a "bunch of stinkers!" This was the worst language I had ever heard her use, if you don't count what she said in Sicilian when she was mad. They were able to get through these hard times through the generosity of her neighbor, Gert Snider, who heard of their plight and gave them a 50-pound bag of flour. Grandma made it last until they could get back on their feet and find some jobs. Grandpa at this time was sick from cancer and couldn't work.

After they left the farm, they moved into a series of apartments until the farm sold. In 1940, they finally bought a house at 36 Lake Street for three thousand dollars in the village of LeRoy. The house allowed my family to turn their life around in a neighborhood that reaffirmed their culture because they now lived among other Sicilian families. It was a house that was built in 1846 and had seen its better days. There were holes in the floor and walls but it had a large backyard that had fruit trees and a place for a vegetable and flower garden. With Grandpa sick and dying of cancer, the move to town allowed Grandma and my mother and aunts the opportunity to find work and turn their lives around.

FOLK REMEDIES

Being poor and living in a remote part of the town of LeRoy, Grandma had to be resourceful when it came to administering cures for her sick children. One of the cures she swore by was using onions for earaches. On Christmas of 1975, my wife and I were home from graduate school and I had a very annoying ear infection. It was so bad I couldn't get off the couch. My mother had nothing for it, and of course it was a Saturday evening when drug stores weren't open. Grandma heard that I was in pain so she came over and said to me, "An onion will fix you up." I was used to her riddles by this time so I asked her to explain how an onion can cure an earache. She replied, "It will take a little while but I'll show you." She left and came back in about ten minutes with a thin washcloth wrapped around an onion she heated up in the oven and instructed me to put it on the ear that hurt. I did and she left. In a matter of minutes the ear started popping and with each pop the pain subsided until it was gone. My mother, who had been watching this, went and got Grandma, who came in with another one for the other ear. I was amazed. Grandma told me she used onions and other plants for a number of ailments when they lived on the farm. Sometimes these folk remedies worked and sometimes they didn't; since the doctor was so far away and they had no telephones, one could be dead before medical assistance was able to get to his/her house, so families had to be resourceful. For the rest of the evening the conversation centered on how Grandma had saved the day and how thankful I was.

My mother, at various times in her life, looked to Grandma when she had no answers. For the most part, my mother looked at Grandma as if she were old fashioned and way behind the times (which she was). She couldn't believe that someone as uneducated as Grandma could compete with the findings of modern society. My mother considered herself to be a modern woman and always thought that anything new was better than anything old, so second-generation parents like my mother deferred treatment of all childhood illnesses to a physician, especially using the latest developments in medicine. Sometimes emergencies occurred supplanting logic and science, so for those instances, the territorial borders between the generations came down. "For the Southern Italian peasant family in Italy, child illnesses were treated by folk remedies and only in emergencies or a crisis was the local physician summoned. The first-generation parents treated childhood illnesses with a combination of folk remedies and the family doctor."[2] The dynamics between mother and daughter constantly ebbed and flowed, with my mother trying to be totally American and not be drawn into the world of Grandma. But when the modern world had no answers, then just maybe the old ways would work and my mother would resort to the way she was brought up in the Southern Italian folk-peasant culture. In the struggle between the first and second generation, "the parental way is not wholly repudiated although there is some degree of rejection."[3] I was surprised when my mother stepped aside and allowed Grandma to call the shots on our side of the house.

ROSIE THE RIVETER

During World War II, many women replaced men working in factories while they served as soldiers. Carrie was one of these women who stepped out of their roles ordained by the male- dominated society and found work in a factory making insulators. Like other women of the era, she lost her job when the soldiers came back home. It was hard for her to take a step backward after getting a taste of working a real job and making real money. Like other women in her situation who stepped forward in times of need, she was expected to return to her "rightful" place in the home even though she had done exemplary work. With jobs scarce for women, this was an extreme hardship for my grandma since the pay was the most she ever made and there were still children living at home to support. But the response was the same: she was let go so a returning soldier could have her job.

---

2   Paul J. Campisi, "The Italian Family in the United States," *The American Journal of Sociology* 53, no. 6 (1948), 446.
3   Campisi, "The Italian Family," 446.

EDUCATION

The Italians knew that the only way to escape prejudice, poverty, and the isolation of being in a strange and unfriendly country was through education. Even though Grandma never attended school beyond the third grade, she understood the importance of a good education and sent one of her daughters to college, and another to a professional school. She was very proud of her accomplishment of getting all her daughters through high school and two of them beyond. In typical Italian fashion, the extended family of her brothers helped her out financially to make this happen since they understood that their parents had sacrificed Grandma's education so that they, her brothers, could become successful as pharmacists, a marine surveyor, and a businessman. Similarly, my aunts who were successful career women extended their support to the sisters who sacrificed for them. However, in a reflection of their upbringing, my grandfather insisted that her eldest daughter, my Aunt Florence, forgo her dream of being a nurse in order to go to work in the bean fields to help support the family.

VOTING RIGHTS

Women received the right to vote in 1920. I can remember Grandma exercising her right to vote in all of the elections, local and national. She took this right very seriously and voted with a social conscience. Throughout the years, I heard her express her views on the Presidents who she thought had helped out poor people the most. At the top of her list was FDR. In the late 1980s we were visiting and my aunt walked by, so Grandma asked her if she had a check in the mail. I asked her what check and she replied, "Oh the check that that nice President Roosevelt sends me every month even though I don't work any more." My aunt, who was exasperated, said to her, "Ma! He's been dead for 40 years! It's your Social Security check." To make her point, Grandma said, "Yes I know, but it was that nice man in a wheelchair who saved us when we were goners." The other great president in her mind was JFK, mostly because he was a Catholic. She always voted Democratic because she thought Republicans "couldn't care less about poor people." She hated President Nixon because "he was a crook!" In order for her to vote, my Aunt Franny would get her an absentee ballot and Grandma would tell her for whom she wanted to vote and my aunt would dutifully record her preferences. Grandma would then put her "X" at the bottom of the page and my aunt would sign her name.

The painting *La Mia Vita* is based on a photograph of Grandma that I took when she was in her late nineties. I was visiting her one Sunday and she was reminiscing about her life. Stories about life on the farm and life in an inhospitable environment were the main subjects and became the basis for this painting. To express her hard life, I borrowed a mourning saint from Luca Signorelli's *Lamentation* and the screen of fabric behind her with the fruit is from an enthroned Madonna by Carlo Crivelli. The gloomy farm scene in the background is based on an actual photograph of the farm they worked during the Depression. This scene of a sunset in winter contrasts dramatically with the warm mountainous region of Sicily where she was born. Since she thought President Roosevelt was a saint and said a prayer for him every day, I depicted him in a panel mounted on top in his touring car and signature cigarette and holder riding around heaven doing good deeds.

LIFE AS A SEAMSTRESS

Grandma went to work as a seamstress for Hickey-Freeman in a small workshop in her neighborhood making custom suits, and stayed there until she was in her late seventies when she finally retired. She could make anything and could hem up a pair of jeans to make them look like they just came from the factory. When her sister Mary was making a dress, she would bring the cloth and pattern to Grandma to cut it for her because they all agreed that cutting the cloth was the most important part of a sewing project. The shop was a place where she and her other Sicilian friends/acquaintances worked, and it was like a big social club with lots of gossip, of course, all spoken in Italian. In the winter when the sidewalks were slippery, my job was to go to the shop and walk Grandma home. When I opened the door of the workshop, the cacophony would immediately cease and the sea of black dresses would turn in unison and glare at my intrusion. My grandma would assure them in Italian that I was her grandson and that I came to help her walk home. Their piercing expressions turned to smiles and they exclaimed over my virtues, or so Grandma said, and then the noise soon resumed. This was a place where they were able to practice and preserve the Italian way of life.

La Mia Vita, *2011. Egg tempera on panel.*

RELIGION

The religion my great-grandparents brought with them from Sicily was a blending between *La Vecchio Religione* (The Old Religion), which predates Christian European religion that is based on Etruscan and Roman mythology and the Roman Catholic faith. "The two most obvious [differences] are the reverence for Mary (as the 'Mother of God'), and the belief in the intercession of the saints (a remnant of Pagan worship related to specific spirits who have power over various aspects of life)."[4] Both religions used incantations, fetishes, amulets and

---

4   Raven Grimassi, *Italian Witchcraft: The Old Religion of Southern Europe* (St. Paul, Minnesota: Llewellyn Publications, 2000), 57.

petitioned spirits for special favors.[5] Each generation passed on the ancient traditions until the origins were forgotten. Grandma never identified herself as being a member of *La Vecchio Religione*, but like other Italians she "employed various prayers to a host of saints, lighting candles and placing assorted objects as required by tradition."[6] I know that she believed in evil forces, like the *mal'occhio* or evil eye that only *stregheria* could control, but she was secretive about it. There was a family member by the name of Mananna, who was a *strega* and "cured" one of my cousins. Grandma took me to a *stregone* to cure a skin disease when I was a teenager (see Chapter 7) so there was a whole other world of which I only got a glimpse.

Grandma was a devout Roman Catholic and went to church literally every morning. I would often find her sitting in a chair "reading" her prayer book upside down since she couldn't actually read, and saying her rosary so fervently that she wore many of them out. My family heartily and enthusiastically lit candles and prayed to the saints with vigor. She firmly believed that the only way I got through undergraduate and graduate school and was successful in my search for teaching jobs was the fact that she spent a small fortune on candles to light to the Blessed Mother. I remember as a child whenever there was a particularly violent thunderstorm, my mother or Grandma would light blessed candles to ask the Blessed Mother to watch over us and protect us.

Grandma prayed and talked to the saints on a daily basis. She believed that her relationship with the saints was so intimate that she could ask them for special favors. For example, while a member of an Irish-American Catholic church might pray to the Blessed Mother for strength to overcome adversity, my grandmother felt that her relationship with the Blessed Mother was sufficiently close and personal that when our cat disappeared for three days, Grandma took my sister to church, and through prayer and lighting candles, they petitioned the Blessed Mother to bring her home. And it worked! While reading Lousie Caico's book, *Sicilian Ways and Days*, I was struck by this passage as she describes the Sicilian peasant's relationship with their Creator and their favorite saints: "St. Joseph, the Virgin Mary, and the Child Jesus are human beings, as familiar to him as the old man, the women, and the babies he sees around him; the impression of past centuries is not felt, for to him they live today, such as they think, live, and speak in his primitive village."[7]

Grandma believed in the power of the scapular and wore one every day of her life as a symbol of her devotion. She believed, as many Catholics do, that the power in these two small-blessed pieces of wool joined together by strings and worn over her shoulders would keep her from the fires of hell. She insisted that every one of her relatives had a medal of St. Christopher, the patron saint of travelers, attached to the sun visor of their car, or a magnetic statue attached to the dashboard. In the 1960s, the Vatican decided that St. Christopher was not really a saint, which created a major uproar in our house. Grandma could not understand how he couldn't be one since he had answered her prayers for years. The Vatican had just put in her in an awkward situation since now she had one less saint to watch over us. Who would pick up the slack? She had put her faith in St. Christopher's hands for decades, and the "proof" was that no one had been in an accident or even gotten a speeding ticket. After many impassioned conversations with her sister Mary, they decided to fill the vacuum of

---

5   Grimassi, *Italian Witchcraft*, 57.

6   Grimassi, *Italian Witchcraft*, 58.

7   Louise Caico, *Sicilian Ways and Days* (New York: D. Appleton and Company, 1910), 197.

St Christopher's demotion with a magnetic Blessed Mother statue on the dashboard of their car. Grandma never really got over it and still prayed to him when someone went on a trip.

When Grandma donated part of the land around her house on Lake Street so that an addition to the parochial school could be built, it was the demise of her extensive flower gardens, fruit trees, and vegetable garden. It was another step toward assimilation and away from the customs brought from Sicily. From the beginning, St. Peter's Parish did not allow Sicilian children to attend the school. In 1941, the pastor of St. Joseph's Parish, Father McQuire, decided that enough was enough. He felt that there should be children from his parish attending the parochial school since we are all the same in God's eyes. He made a call to his counterpart, Father McCoy, at St. Peter's Church down the street and made his case. He must have been very persuasive because not long after his conversation, Father McQuire contacted our neighbors, Ida and Ross Martina, and suggested that their daughter Annette should be the first Sicilian child to attend the elementary school. In 2011, Annette relayed her experiences to me. One instance that she remembered vividly was a day when Father McCoy visited her class. He asked Annette in front of the whole class if she could speak Italian and asked her to translate various words. Annette, who was around eight years old at the time, did not pick up on the fact that she was being made a spectacle in front of her classmates and was singled out for being "different." She just replied that she would have to ask her grandmother. After the new addition was built and many more Italian children went to the parochial school, those who did felt that the nuns and priests from St. Peter's Church made their lives particularly miserable.

The adults did not feel very welcome either, even in the church. I never remember Grandma regretting her decision to give up the land, since it was going to help Italians as well as the rest of the Catholics in the town. In her mind, this was for the church, and God would look down favorably on her. In the fall of 2012, Holy Family School closed because of low enrollment. In all of the years of its existence, however, although there were commemorative plaques in the classrooms that honored the generous contributions of parishioners for blackboards, classroom furniture, etc., nowhere was there any mention of the most important contribution of all, one that made it possible for the school to exist: the donation of my grandmother's land for a school in which her children were not welcome.

When Monsignor Zupa was transferred to St. Joseph's Church, he replaced the beloved Father Flynn in 1964. I was an altar boy by then, so I came into contact with him on a regular basis. He was a friendly and outgoing person and a sports fanatic, so we hit it off. It helped that my Aunt Franny was the parish secretary. Grandma had her suspicions of him from the first day she saw him. There was something she didn't like about him, but couldn't put her finger on it. Grandma went to church every day. There was a mass at 6:10 a.m. every Sunday morning that only the old Sicilians went to, and that was the way Grandma preferred it. Sometimes Father Zupa slept in, and Grandma would have to go to the rectory to wake him up. She would come home from Mass steaming. In the early days, he didn't make many points with her. One day she asked me to do her a favor. She wanted me to ask Father Zupa where his family lived in Italy because she suspected he was a Neapolitan. I asked her what was wrong with Neapolitans. She said, "They're the scum of Italy because they're a bunch of backstabbers!" The next time I saw Father Zupa I asked him the question. "From Naples," he said proudly. I thought, "Oh boy."

When I got back from Mass, Grandma asked me, "What did he say?"

I told her that I forget to ask him.

She was not pleased. She said, "The next time you see him don't forget!"

On my aunt's advice, I kept putting her off and was able to do so for about a couple of weeks. I thought she would forget, but eventually I had to tell her because I didn't want to get on her bad side.

Her eyes got big and she shouted, "I knew it!"

She never warmed up to him and seldom invited him over to her house. (Whenever Monsignor Zupa was invited for supper, he was lukewarm about her cooking, especially her sauce. He said her macaroni was like mush and he would rave about his mother's cooking. That didn't go over very well. I did have the opportunity to taste his mother's spaghetti on occasion, and I didn't understand all of the fuss he made over it.) In Italy, northern Italians look down on those from the *Mezzogiorno*, and everyone looks down on the Sicilians. I'm sure this played into my Grandma's distrust of Neapolitans. Since Sicilians who immigrated to America first sailed to Naples and then to America, there might have been instances of Sicilians being swindled at the hands of the Neapolitans. Neapolitans, like Sicilians, do not have the best of reputations among other Italians. In fact, the most violent of all the mafia is based in Naples.

In a bit of irony, the parish of St. Joseph's Church does not exist any longer. Because of the shortage of priests, when Monsignor Zupa died in 2008, the two Catholic parishes were combined to form one large parish with everyone attending mass at St. Peter's Church just like it was prior to 1907. My aunt who attends mass says she feels like she is not welcome by the members of St. Peter's Church and many Italians wish they had their parish back. So in the twenty-first century, relations between the Italians and non-Italians in LeRoy still exhibit an undercurrent of prejudice.

GRANDMA AS A PARENT

Since Grandma never had a childhood, she was a no-nonsense type of parent. Being Sicilian, where the tradition is of a male-dominated society, she deferred mostly to Grandpa's wishes. Since both of my grandparents were born in Sicily, Grandpa had the highest status and he had the right to punish his children severely if he so chose.[8] When they worked the farm, there was no time for anything else but work, and it was expected that the children do their share of the work. Consequently, their children felt neglected by them. A strict code of conduct was in place for all of her daughters, and they weren't allowed to go on dates until they were much older. It helped since they all lived on a farm outside of town and boys didn't have cars in those days.

In any case, Grandma didn't understand the concept of having fun. When my sister and I first moved to live with Grandma, there was a period of adjustment for all of us. My mother was strict and overprotective just like Grandma, and didn't allow us to go outside and play in the yard unless she was home. Consequently, my sister and I would engage in roughhousing

---

8   Campisi, "The Italian Family," 445.

activities in the living room, which sent Grandma to banging on the wall shouting at us, "Behave! You're acting like a bunch of wild Indians."

She was domineering and very strict. She laid down the law to her children and there was no compromise. I asked my Aunt Dorothy, Grandma's youngest daughter, if she ever let Dorothy go to social events when she was in high school, since by this time they had moved off the farm and into the town and Grandpa was gone. She said yes, but then qualified her answer, noting that she felt free, but their mother intimidated her sister, Franny. "Well, I think I just did what I wanted to do and ignored her. Franny let Mama get away with too much."

Franny was the sixth daughter of my Grandparents and lived with her mother her whole life, sixty-five years. At times Grandma bullied and intimidated Franny into doing what she wanted. Franny always wanted to avoid conflict and always relented. When Franny went out on dates, in her forties, Grandma gave her a curfew. Much of the time she didn't like her date very much, so she used Grandma as an excuse, but it sent Grandma the wrong message. Grandma bossed her around even more because she could.

Sometimes the events in our house felt like a three-ring circus. Franny worked two jobs. She was a cashier at a local drug store and a church secretary. One day, Franny was getting ready to go to work and Grandma asked where she was going. She answered, "To work at the rectory and then to the drug store." Grandma must have been in a bad mood, because out the blue she accused Franny of not really going to work when she went to the rectory. The implication was obvious, and Franny got so mad she told Grandma to take it back and apologize. Grandma refused, and Franny went to live with her sister Helen who lived across town. Grandma was beside herself and kept calling Helen's house to talk to Franny and tell her to come home. Using Helen as an intermediary, Franny made it clear she was never coming back home. This went on for about two weeks, until Grandma started driving everybody nuts. Finally, Franny relented and came back home to Lake Street. Nobody really understood why she came back, because Grandma was always watching Franny like a hawk. No one really knows why Grandma made such an accusation, either. Franny's behavior was beyond reproach, and she never did anything in her life that could be considered immoral. Maybe it was that Grandma didn't trust the Neapolitan priest. Old beliefs die hard.

When it came to her children, Grandma's code of ethics had to be followed to the letter, and she cut the children no slack. My grandparents were old school Sicilians and were brought up with the belief that family members should not bring any shame onto the family. Both Grandma and my mother lived with the fear, "What would the neighbors think?" But Grandma had a double standard. She allowed her brothers to do what they wanted without much interference. Even when I got into trouble she never said anything to me, although my mother did her best not to let Grandma ever find out. My mother used to say, "If Grandma ever finds out about this, she will get mad." That was enough of a deterrent for anyone.

As my friend, fellow Italian, and social worker Lyndia Radice, explained it to me from her observations based on years of living with her Italian family in Queens:

1. Sicilians from this era were still very tribal, meaning they kept strict codes of behavior that were based on more ancient ways of thinking and acting. Sicilians were the most conservative, I believe. Women and men had very different roles, and there were also assigned roles for family members, such as the "good son"

and the "bad seed" and the "good daughter." As people get more assimilated into American culture, this is less apparent on the surface; but if you look deeper, you can sometimes see the old ways coming out.

2. Usually there is at least one female child who is sort of the spinster caretaker for the family—I know this because I lived through it with my family and I believe I was sort of designated into that role (although I worked hard to get out of it). The girl was given unclear (and sometimes very clear) messages that she was to be the one who stayed and took care of Mom or Pop. When she tried to date or go to school, for example, they would work to prevent her from doing those things.

3. Usually there is a give-and-take dynamic between the parent and the child, where they play this game back-and-forth of letting the child go a bit (like Franny dating) and then pulling in the reins if it looked like the child might escape. It could get very, very warped.

4. As for the double standard, bad behavior is expected from men, but is usually just overlooked. I grew up in a house where my grandmother lived downstairs with the two spinsters. My father, mother, sister, and I lived in two rooms upstairs and across the hall, my aunt and her husband lived in two rooms. Every so often, one of my father's five brothers would get kicked out and come to stay with my grandmother—it was expected and not condemned.

Grandma always had a couple of aces in the hole. At one time or another there were three of her unmarried daughters living at home into the early 1960s, but that ended when Aunt Helen announced that she was engaged. Grandma was opposed to the marriage. One day before their marriage, I asked Grandma what she thought about Helen's fiancé. She made a face and said, "He's nothing but a social climber." Her other unmarried daughter, Aunt Dorothy, left LeRoy to live in Delaware on a career-related move, which left Franny, until we moved in and my parents separated, and my mother then joined the mix. Poor Aunt Franny was the constant through everything, and I remember her saying to me how it was her duty to take care of Grandma since somebody had to do it.

CHRISTMAS AT GRANDMA'S HOUSE

It wasn't until we moved to Lake Street in the fall of 1961 that I experienced a good old Sicilian Christmas. On Christmas Eve, Grandma would start cooking for the feast that followed Midnight Mass. She would make one of her famous Sicilian-style pizzas that had a thick homemade crust that was seasoned just right with a combination of oregano, garlic, onions, cayenne pepper, and her fabulous sweet tomato sauce topped with Romano cheese. There would be homemade pies, apple and pumpkin, plus all of the Italian cookies one could eat, and of course some Asti for toasts. Sometimes Aunt Ida from next door would send over a plate of breaded veal cutlet or her delectable *cannolis* with little bits of chocolate and almonds in the custard filling that everyone would fight over. But the treat of all treats was Great-Uncle Tony Argana's homemade Italian sausage, both sweet and hot. He would only make his special recipe sausage during the Christmas season, and he always sent Grandma her ration. His secret was that he used only the leanest meat: a blend of beef and pork all seasoned with fennel seed and Romano cheese. When it was fried, someone had to add a little bit of olive oil in order to keep it from sticking to the pan.

As soon as Mass was over, my aunts, relatives, and friends made their way to Grandma's house, where a fabulous feast would take place. When I got to be a teenager and really understood the value of good food, Christmas with all of its trappings was a real let down. The presents were nice, but Christmas Day couldn't hold a torch to the good cheer and feeling of goodwill that was felt in the house. By 2:00 a.m., the party would be winding down and the dishes would be finished. As people got old and others past on, the tradition was abandoned to the detriment of all. There was a feeling that the Christmas season just wasn't the same anymore, and it wasn't.

All Grandma knew throughout her life was hard work for very little pay. Grandma used to tell people, "If you lived my life you'd be dead." As I think back to conversations I had with her, they always seemed to end on the fact that she was so proud that she survived. Her life spanned the beginning of the Italian immigration at the end of the nineteenth and early twentieth centuries. She grew up in a world where women and Italians were second-class citizens, and she succeeded in spite of the prejudice and discrimination. She lived a humble life and was a source of great strength and inspiration to the people who knew her. She was a working mother who became the matriarch of three generations. Her life literally spanned the horse and buggy age to the computer age, though she could not conceive of men walking on the moon and never quite believed it. She would say to me, "Tommy, how could they fly to the moon? There are no gas stations on the way!" To her last day, Grandma was that little old peasant woman named Calogera from the remote mountains in Sicily.

Aunt Franny died on January 6, 1992, after battling breast cancer for a year. When she was diagnosed, all of the sisters agreed to keep it quiet and hid it from Grandma since they felt she would not be able to take it. She had already lost my mother, Lena, to the same disease years earlier and her death had shaken Grandma. She told me parents are not supposed to outlive their children. When Franny had her mastectomy she convalesced at her sister Helen's house and then returned home when she was better. After about a year, she began to fail and was in and out of the hospital with stints at Helen's house. My aunts made up stories, saying Franny went on a trip or that she was helping Helen clean her house. Grandma, who was beginning to fail herself in her ninety-eighth year, never believed any of it, and kept saying that Franny was sick and to have her come home, but the charade continued even up to and during Franny's funeral. Nobody told Carrie that her daughter had died. By that time, Grandma rarely got out of bed. She told me that she knew Franny was dead so what was the point of getting up. As the days after Franny's funeral moved on, Carrie never got out of bed. I visited her regularly, and on some days she knew who I was and other days she thought I was my cousin Bob, who lived in Maryland. She asked me questions like, "How is Franklin?" Franklin was Bob's father and had been dead since 1986. We knew she wouldn't last much longer. She died a "happy death," in her sleep, on January 28, 1992, two weeks before her ninety-ninth birthday and twenty-two days after Franny's death.

CHAPTER 4

Great-Uncle Santo (Jimmy) Barone

Born: March 23, 1894, Valledolmo, Sicily
Died: August 1985, Baltimore, Maryland

Great-Uncle Jimmy (Santo), circa 1914.

Great-Uncle Jimmy was Grandma's favorite brother and second oldest in the Barone family. He was a devout Catholic (like Carrie), was a short, portly man, around five feet two inches, and he was very intelligent. He was a no-nonsense, unforgiving person who was quick to judge us, and if he was ever disappointed in one of us, then we ran the risk of being shunned forever. Nobody ever remembers him smiling. This was probably the result of his hard childhood and the extreme poverty he experienced as a child. His parents worked all of the time, and like Grandma, he had to grow up fast. He was very religious like his sister Carrie and attended mass faithfully. Jimmy helped Grandma take care of their younger brothers and sister and was a role model by his example as an honest and hard-working man. It is incredible to think that he was born in a small, isolated mountain town in Sicily, a place where there was no upward mobility, and that he was able to immigrate to America and rise to become a very respectable member of society in a country where southern Italians were considered barely human by some people. The odds that any of the Barone children would rise to the level they did in the course of one generation were incredibly small. His parents, like most Sicilians, had nothing when they arrived, but their children beat tremendous odds and were able to achieve the American

Dream. He was the first of Calogero and Maria Barone's children to leave LeRoy and move to another part of the country (in his case, Baltimore). He showed the way for his brothers to assimilate and become Americans by getting an education and rising above the stereotypes of the day. He worked and managed to get enough money to get a degree in pharmacy at the University of Maryland, and for many years he worked for Hynso, Westcott and Dunning pharmaceutical company in Baltimore, Maryland. It is staggering to think that he was able to achieve all of this on his own.

THE LOSS OF JIMMY'S HERITAGE

I never thought of Jimmy as being Italian like Grandma was. He spoke proper English without any accent and didn't have the mannerisms that are common among Sicilians. He

Jimmy and Pauline on their fiftieth wedding anniversary, September 25, 1976, Baltimore, Maryland.

seemed like he wanted to be an American at the expense of his culture. When he left to live in Baltimore, his brother Pete went with him. Jimmy and Pete were very close, but they were complete opposites. Great-Uncle Pete enjoyed life, got divorced, had girlfriends, traveled the world, was the life of the party. Great-Uncle Jimmy never told a joke, never drank any alcoholic beverages except for a glass of wine now and then and was married to same woman, Pauline, his entire life. There must have been a special bond between them, since they got together and had lunch once a week. I remember Great-Uncle Pete mentioning to Grandma that he would rather see Jimmy alone than go to his house, since Pauline would drive him crazy with her opinions about his lifestyle.

Jimmy married Pauline Lammers on September 25, 1926. She was a non-Italian from Baltimore and spoke with a Southern accent. They were married for fifty-nine years. She was very prim and proper and came from a respectable family, so they were perfect for one another. Great-Uncle Jimmy must have gotten rid of all of the traces of his Italian ancestry by then to marry a person of her stature. They were both very sophisticated and dressed well for dinner, with Great-Uncle Jimmy wearing a coat and tie and Great-Aunt Pauline wearing a fashionable dress. Great-Aunt Pauline had an interesting brother, Hy Lammers. He played clarinet and was a member of John Philip Sousa's orchestra in the early twentieth century.

When Great-Uncle Jimmy came to LeRoy, we noticed that he was trying to be somebody else. It was as if he didn't want to be linked to Italian culture anymore. He might have been a little embarrassed of his family when he compared it to the Lammers. He seemed to want to have a different heritage and didn't want to act or look Italian. During his youth, he lived in extreme poverty and did not want to be associated with his upbringing. When he left his parents' house and moved to Baltimore, he changed his persona. He married Pauline, and she became the symbol of his new life.

Most of the family didn't like Jimmy and Pauline very much since they had no sense of humor. Since Jimmy wasn't a sports fan and he didn't have any hobbies that anyone knew of, there was not much to talk to him about. He mostly talked to the adults to find out whether their children were being good and studying hard, and if any of us weren't, we got a lecture from him on how important it was to do so. Jimmy and Pauline couldn't keep from giving advice to my aunts and cousins on how to straighten out unruly children, even though they never had any. It wasn't that the cousins and I were a particularly unruly bunch, it was just that we were kids and when we got together, games like dodgeball, football and hotbox would break out. When they came to visit Grandma, the children had to be quiet and not run around or have any fun. They were very critical and much too serious for anyone to be around. Never having children of their own, they probably never really understood how to deal with real young people.

My cousin, Marie Argana, worked and lived in the Washington, D.C. area, so she saw Great-Uncle Jimmy and Great-Aunt Pauline frequently. The first year she moved to Washington, they invited her to have Thanksgiving dinner with them, and it became an annual event until he died. Great-Uncle Pete also joined them while he was alive.

Jimmy (left) and Pete (right) at Conlon Park in Baltimore, Maryland, June 4, 1923. They were an odd pair. Jimmy was a very straight-laced and proper man, and Pete was the life of the party.

Like the rest of us, Marie had some unpleasant memories of them when they visited LeRoy, but when she visited them at their house in the suburbs of Baltimore, they were gracious hosts. They always went out to dinner since I don't think Great-Aunt Pauline cooked very much. The restaurant they chose was very well known and it was filled with photographs, paintings and sculptures. After dinner they would drive back to their house for dessert, with my great-uncles stepping outside to smoke their cigars.

Great-Uncle Jimmy was generous, although it came with a price. For Christmas he would send all of my aunts, his nieces, presents. To the married ones he would send packages of scented soaps or vanilla and the unmarried ones got five dollars. It was without fail that they would get a package from him and all they had to do was sniff a little bit and they knew what it was and who sent it. Obviously, it was right to thank him for his gift, but he was exacting in his standards about a response to those gifts. He expected a thank-you note within a week of Christmas, and if someone didn't send one, he would call Grandma and she would chastise you for him. If he was upset enough, he never sent that person anything else and when he saw him/her next he wouldn't talk; all over a bar of soap. He did not extend his gift-giving to my generation; however, he did send me one hundred dollars for college every year because he understood the value of an education and we were not well off financially. I really appreciated his generosity and wrote him sincere thank-you letters within a week of receipt.

Even though Great-Uncle Jimmy didn't seem Italian to us, he knew how to use the tried-and-true method of coercion that Mediterraneans sometimes use with impunity to control behavior—guilt. After my sister, Mary, left her first husband in 1980, Great-Uncle Jimmy sent her in 1982 a Christmas present of soap and included with it a long letter to counsel her, i.e., make her feel guilty to make the right decision and go back with him. The essence of it was that since my mother, Lena, was dying of cancer and did not have long to live, Mary should go back to her husband; when Lena died, then it would be all right to leave. My sister had been separated from her husband for almost two years by then and already started a new life in Pittsburgh when she got the letter, so the request was ridiculous. My sister never responded and never heard from Great-Uncle Jimmy again.

Jimmy died in 1985. Upon hearing of her brother's death, Grandma remarked, "She (Pauline) killed him making him wait on her all the time!" He had stipulated in his will a certain sum of money that was to be divided among all of his living nieces at the time of his wife's death. All six of my aunts shared this sum, but my mother had died of cancer long before. Pauline died in 1994.

CHAPTER 5

Great-Uncle Giacomo (Joe) Barone

Born: October 27, 1895, Valledolmo, Sicily
Died: September 10, 1977, Buffalo, New York

Great-Uncle Joe Barone was the third oldest in the Barone family and the last to be born in Sicily. He was about five feet six inches and a very quiet man, since it was hard for anyone to compete for the floor with his wife, Rose. He mostly sat in his chair puffing on his cigar. Great-Uncle Joe had a very pleasant singing voice, and on occasion, he would surprise everyone and spontaneously serenade us with a love song or a popular hit.

Rose and Joe, June 12, 1930.

Whenever I went to greet him and shake his hand, he would size you up with squinty eyes and puff on his cigar so that smoke would come out of his mouth like a chimney. Joe went to the University at Buffalo to become a dentist, but he had epilepsy and had to quit college, since at that time there were no effective seizure-control medicines. Great-Uncle Joe's wife, Rose Jerris, was actually his cousin, although she was born in Buffalo, New York, and no one now remembers how removed they were. Gerace, her family's Sicilian name, had been changed in order to fit into American society. Joe and Rose's relationship underwent a change when Great-Uncle Joe went on a trip to Fresno, California. While he was on the West Coast he wrote his cousin letters and their relationship to each other evolved through their correspondence. After he came back east, he started courting her. He married her on June 12, 1930. Great-Aunt Rose's family was fairly well off, and the wedding they had was a very stylish and extravagant affair with all three attendants carrying gigantic bouquets of white roses, with the bride's being the biggest. The wedding dress had a long train and her veil was full length and flowing. She was a beautiful bride.

When Great-Uncle Joe married Rose, he became a member of a well-to-do family and entered the family business. The Jerris family owned a grocery store on West Ferry Street in Buffalo, and after Joe and Rose were married they too opened their own store. Joe and Rose's first apartment was on Elmwood Avenue across from the grocery store. Later when they were able to save some money they bought a large three-story house on Bidwell Parkway with a large enclosed sun porch in the front and a smaller open porch in the back. The living room was large with old and elegant furniture and tall ceilings. Great-Aunt Rose had good taste and collected antiques before doing so came into vogue. When my great-grandmother, Maria Barone, sold her house after Great-Grandpa died, Rose took the old chairs that were in the house since no one else wanted them. She reupholstered them in the same green velvet that was the original color and fabric. Today I have one of those chairs in my home, and the ornate carving and the curved lion-footed legs make it a treasure not only from the past, but from my family's past.

Joe and Rose had three children, two boys and a girl, the last two being twins named Gerald and Geraldine. After they grew up and left home, their parents made an apartment on the third floor. Great-Aunt Rose was a very short woman—she was so short her feet couldn't touch the floor when she sat in a chair, so she always sat on the edge of it. Rose was about the same height as Grandma at about four feet nine inches, but was much heavier. By the mid-1950s, when I knew Great-Aunt Rose, her ankles hung over her orthopedic shoes, and she spoke with a gravelly voice that sounded like a frog croaking, but she was beautiful inside. Whatever she lacked in physical appearance, she made up for in being a thoughtful and generous woman who was well liked by all of my cousins and aunts. Great-Aunt Rose was very magnanimous, and when she visited, she never came empty handed, always bringing "bushels" of food with her, according to Aunt Dorothy. Great-Aunt Rose loved antique dishes and gave them to us as presents. When I got married she gave me and my wife a little antique vase with roses painted on it and a bright orange enameled lasagna pan.

I remember the first time I met Great-Aunt Rose, when I was four. I couldn't wait to meet her, since she had bought me my favorite book that my mother read to me, *The Contented Little Pussycat*. I liked the story so much that I asked for it to be read to me constantly until I could recite it by heart. When I walked into Grandma's parlor, there was Great-Uncle Joe smoking his cigar and Great-Aunt Rose leaning on her chair. I followed my mother into the room, and when Great Aunt Rose saw me, she said I was so handsome and tall and made a big fuss over me. My mother told her that I wanted to "read" her the book she gave me, and I pretended to read the book to her. When I was through, she told me to come over to see her so she could give me a big kiss. I was used to this kind of treatment because all of my aunts expected a kiss from me, but I wasn't ready for what followed next. When I got close to her she grabbed both cheeks with her hands and shook my head back and forth telling me how nice it was to meet me and how much she liked the story and that she hoped I was a good boy and listened to my mother. Then she enveloped me into her bosom and I disappeared. After a few minutes I came up for air and made my escape. Both of my cheeks stung like crazy and I kept my distance from her the rest of the day. From that day on, whenever we went to see her, I tried to get out of having to give her a kiss so that I could avoid her overly enthusiastic greetings. Every time I saw her, the same ritual of the pinching of cheeks was replayed anyway, even when I grew and up and was in college. Then I had to bend over as far as I could or get on my knees so that I could get down to her level for my kiss. That must have looked quite comical.

Great-Aunt Rose's reputation as a cook was legendary. Whenever we were invited to her house for a meal, it was quite a spectacle. It was a real Italian food orgy. First she would bring out a salad, followed by a pasta dish (usually spaghetti and meatballs or ravioli) with her homemade bread or rolls, then a roast or ham with all of the fixings would follow, and then a light dessert—a choice of pies, including her famous cheesecake. If we were lucky, sometimes she would whip up a plate of spare ribs with her special barbeque sauce or a Sicilian-style pizza that closely rivaled Grandma's. Whenever I finished eating, I could hardly move from the table because I was so full. As a teenager I could handle everything she brought out and maybe have seconds, but I paid the price of not being able to move for quite a while. It was all right because then I could sit in the dining room around the table with the family and listen to all of the lively chatter and goodwill that was flying around. Great-Uncle Joe would talk to the men about how business was, and Grandma would be talking to Great-Aunt Rose and Great-Aunt Mary about the latest gossip with flourishing hand waving and gestures. It was a wonderful way to spend an afternoon.

My Aunt Dorothy, Grandma's youngest daughter, told me that if I stopped for a visit, even if Great-Aunt Rose had worked all day in the grocery store, she could whip up a four-course meal in what seemed like a matter of minutes. Even though Rose was a heavy woman, Dorothy said that when she got into the kitchen a transformation took place, and she became light on her feet while making food at break-neck speed, and the next thing we knew, the food was on the table.

Great-Uncle Joe was at times a sarcastic man, and often his sharp words were aimed at Rose. Great-Aunt Rose would complain to Grandma about some of Joe's social activities, such as spending time drinking with his friends. Every time Great-Aunt Rose talked to Grandma about Joe an ocean of tears would follow. I cannot remember a visit when she didn't cry several times while they talked. I don't think it was so much that Great-Uncle Joe was so mean, but I think that Great-Aunt Rose was very sensitive. This melodrama played out time and time again with end-of-the-world histrionics over the smallest incidents with the all-important sympathetic audience of Grandma as an ally to set her brother straight.

One lazy, hot summer afternoon when I was around nine years old, Great-Aunt Rose and Great-Uncle Joe came to visit Joe's brother, Pete, who was staying with Grandma on a visit from Baltimore. The women were visiting in the living room and Great-Uncle Joe, Great-Uncle Pete and I were on the front sun porch. Great-Uncle Joe was telling Pete about the baseball game he had been to and heard Rose start to cry in the other room. "Oh Pete," he said, "You don't know what I put up with. She is always complaining about something I've done." He then said to me, "Tommy, go in the other room and find out what she is talking about! And don't let them know what you are doing." So I went into the other room and sat in a chair and listened.

Great-Aunt Rose was crying and telling Grandma, "What a beast Joe is to me! He goes to ballgames and goes out drinking with his friends." Grandma was shaking her head very sympathetically. I went back onto the porch to give my great-uncles my report. Great-Uncle Joe said to Pete, "Let's go down the street and get a beer." There were two bars down from Grandma's house by the railroad tracks. As they departed, Great-Uncle Joe warned me, "And don't tell them where we are going. If you do, you will never be allowed to sit with the men ever again." Well, on their way to the bar, they had to walk in front of Grandma's large front window, so when they passed it, Great-Aunt Rose and Grandma saw them. Great-Aunt Rose said to me, "Tommy where are they going?" I replied, "I don't know." My great-aunt told Grandma, "Well, I do!" When they finally came back a few hours later, Grandma and Great-Aunt Rose read them both the riot act. We all ended up back in the same rooms again with Great-Aunt Rose telling Grandma, "Wait till I get him in the car!"

The men weren't amused, and I got blamed for telling the women of their excursion. I tried to explain to them that when they walked in front of the window everyone guessed where they were going. I don't think they believed me. I tried to be helpful and gave Great-Uncle Joe a heads up about how Great-Aunt Rose couldn't wait to talk to him on the way home. He didn't seem amused.

The Visions of Great-Aunt Rose, 2009. Egg Tempera on panel.

My painting *The Visions of Great-Aunt Rose* is based on stories like the one I just told. I truly believe that Great-Aunt Rose saw herself as a Christian martyr and Great-Uncle Joe was her cross to bear. Like her cousin Carrie, my grandmother, the angels in the painting attend to her and weep for her trials and tribulations. As I was preparing studies for the painting, I was looking through my Renaissance resource books and surfing the Internet to find a suitable painting that would expand the meaning of the family dynamics in the photograph. I found one that portrays a classic Great-Aunt Rose look and gesture. I was stunned at the resemblance when I found the painting *Mourning the Dead Christ* by Ortalano, c. 1522. The saint in *Mourning the Dead Christ* is shown wringing her hands in a manner identical to Rose's familiar pose, and the sympathetic saint is on her knees with her arms spread out, perfectly representing the empathy my grandmother felt for her friend and cousin. Rose saw herself as suffering great indignities at his hands. It was Catholic culture at work in a dysfunctional marriage.

For Great-Uncle Joe I found the perfect foil for his wife's animated gestures in the Fra Angelico egg tempera painting, *St. James Frees Herogenes.*[1] In it, St. James is shown touching Philetus with his staff empowering him to loosen the ropes, metaphorically absolving Herogenes of his sins, while in the background there are demons snorting, farting, and raising hell. When I was working on the studies, I had to figure out what Great-Aunt Rose was so upset about. I got the idea to use the demons from the Fra Angelico painting to represent the trials and tribulations that the world inflicted on her over and over again, which she had no control over.

Every family photograph that I have found has Great-Uncle Joe wearing the same black suit and red tie, sitting in exactly the same pose puffing on a cigar. I have to look twice to make sure that I'm not looking at the same photograph. One might almost think that he is tied to the chair—a prisoner in a situation that he is trying to escape. Grandma is sitting opposite Great-Aunt Rose, and as always, was her sympathetic ally, taking sides against Joe.

In the 1970s, the neighborhood around the grocery store on Elmwood Avenue declined and became dangerous. The store was robbed, and my great-uncle was even mugged several times walking to his car to take money to the bank by junkies. One time I was home from college, and my mother got a call from a hysterical Great-Aunt Rose telling my mother that Great-Uncle Joe had just been mugged again. He had lacerations on his head and had just gotten out of the hospital. We were all very upset, and I told my mother that I would go to Buffalo if they needed me to help them, especially when money had to be taken to the bank. They declined my offer, retired, and sold the business.

After Great-Uncle Joe died, Rose sold the house and moved to Williamsville, New York to live in an apartment in an assisted living senior citizen house. Of course, it had a kitchen where she cooked her delicious meals to the delight of everyone in the place. One day after I was married and living in South Carolina, my mother called to tell me that she had just visited Great-Aunt Rose in her Williamsville apartment, and my great aunt was inquiring if my wife Linda, who is of English and German ancestry, had learned how to cook good Italian food for me. She particularly wanted to know if Linda was making use of the lasagna pan she gave us and of course my wife was. Shortly after that, Rose passed away.

---

1   Hermogenes was a magician who was bound by the very devils he sent to destroy St. James.

CHAPTER 6

Great-Uncle Peter Barone

Born: October 28, 1897, Avon, New York
Died: September 11, 1975, Baltimore, Maryland

Great-Uncle Peter Barone, the fourth child of Maria and Charles Barone, was the first to be born in America. He was one of the taller members of the family, standing five feet seven inches. He was a heavy man and had a large stomach from the good life he liked to live. He enjoyed wine, women, and song, as well as a nice cigar after a meal. He was a warm and congenial man who was my favorite among all of Grandma's brothers. He was the life of the party. Some years, he would visit LeRoy at Christmas, and I remember him at the kitchen table laughing and telling stories with his brothers. When I made my confirmation, I chose Peter as my confirmation name in honor of him. He was very pleased. He lived in Baltimore and visited Grandma every summer for about a week. I was very excited when he came to visit, and even before we lived with Grandma, my mother would bring me over to Lake Street to spend the day with him. He would take me for rides to the country club to get lunch, or we would sit on the front porch and talk baseball and he would tell me stories about his life. Great-Uncle Pete was a happy man who enjoyed life.

LIVING LIFE TO THE FULLEST

Pete spent part of his life in the Merchant Marines after having earned a certificate as a Ship Chief Engineer through correspondence school. During World War II, his ship was part of a convoy from New York to Murmansk, Russia, one of the most dangerous routes in the war. After World War II, he first consulted for the shipping firm that he sailed with during the war and then he opened his own company as a marine surveyor. I remember he had ballpoint pens with his company name, Pete Barone, Inc., imprinted.

Consequently, he was a world traveler and he used to tell me stories of some of the places he had visited. One such story took place during the height of the civil war in China during the 1930s. Great-Uncle Pete's ship was sailing on the Yangtze River and he said it was not uncommon to find dead bodies floating down the river or to have people killed before his eyes. In one such incident a man was shot and fell into the river; almost simultaneously, men in nearby boats jumped in and fought over the dead man's shoes. This was history brought to life for me by Peter Barone, who had lived it.

He was an avid baseball fan and followed his beloved Baltimore Orioles. I thought he had the coolest situation since he lived in the neighborhood of old Memorial Stadium and so he could walk to the games. He would bring me Oriole autographs trying to make me change my allegiance from the Yankees.

Grandma and her brothers had a special relationship; she essentially raised them when they were young and they looked to her as their mother, and, to her, they could do no wrong. So, like his other brothers, Great-Uncle Pete visited her often, especially at Christmas. When he did visit, he made the rounds to visit his childhood friends—especially a cousin who owned a bar. On one particular Christmas Eve, before I was old enough to be there with them or to understand, he talked my Aunt Helen, one of Grandma's daughters, into going out to have a few drinks before midnight mass. As they were leaving, Grandma, who wasn't pleased with this excursion, reminded them to get home in time to go to church. Both Great-Uncle Pete and Aunt Helen liked to have a good time, so the afternoon turned into evening and they barely made it home in time to get to mass. Great Uncle Pete was inebriated. Of course Grandma blamed Aunt Helen for getting Great-Uncle Pete drunk. Off to church

they went through the ice and snow—Grandma and Great-Uncle Pete arm in arm with Grandma probably holding him up rather that the other way around.

Up they marched to Grandma's pew in the front row. As the mass went on, Great-Uncle Pete became drowsy, fell asleep and started to snore right in the middle of the sermon. Grandma gave him a well-placed elbow to the ribs that stirred him, but before long he started up again. When the altar boys started ringing the bells at the altar, he jumped up and shouted, "Where the hell am I?" Needless to say Grandma was mortified and Great-Uncle Pete made a hasty retreat back to Baltimore.

Great-Uncle Pete, Chief Engineer, 1940.

ADVICE ON WOMEN

I remember on one of his summer visits when I was about eleven years old, we were sitting in Grandma's kitchen and he asked his sister if he could use her phone to call his friend, Mrs. Oliver. I thought this was a strange way to refer to a friend so I did what I did best at that age; I eavesdropped. Great-Uncle Pete said, "Hello Mrs. Oliver, this is Pete." This must have been code to convey that he was at his sister's house and he couldn't talk. The conversation was fairly inane. He told her when he was going to be back in Baltimore and that he would call her. After he got off the phone he told me never to write a letter to a woman; always call her. I asked him why, and he told me that way they can never hold anything against you. If you promise them something in writing, then they have you right where they want you. It is much cheaper to use the phone since that way you can always deny anything you said. I guess he was speaking from experience since he had a wife named Hazel that he divorced around the time I was born. He must have lost his shirt when they parted company and he was trying to give me some man-to-man advice.

The egg tempera painting, *The Adventures of Great-Uncle Pete*, portrays his days as a merchant marine. The photograph of him, upon which I based the painting, shows him on the deck of his ship with his ever-present cigar in his hand. The top portion is an oil painting by Piero di Cosimo entitled *Pericles and Andromeda* appropriated for its fantastic quality and which relates to the stories Great-Uncle Pete used to tell me of his adventures traveling the world. The cityscape located in the lower right corner is a scene of the Tiber River in Rome, one of his favorite cities and a place he loved to visit.

The Adventures of Great-Uncle Pete, 2009. *Egg tempera on panel.*

CHAPTER 7

Great-Aunt Petrina (Mary) Barone

Born: May 8, 1900, Avon, New York
Died: January 14, 1983, LeRoy, New York

Great-Aunt Mary was the fifth child of my great-grandparents and Grandma's only sister. Mary surpassed Carrie's education by graduating from the fifth grade. She was also short, around five feet tall, full of energy, talked fast, and was very feisty. I was told that when she was young, she had auburn hair. She was the disciplinarian of her nuclear family and ruled her household with an iron fist.

Mary had six children: five girls and one boy. One of the girls, Marie, died tragically in 1936 at the age of four. The tragedy happened when my Great-Aunt Mary was mopping the floor. In those days, people heated water on the stove and then mopped the floor with very hot water. She had just taken the boiling water off of the stove and put it on the floor and started mopping when little Marie fell into the bucket. The doctors said that Marie didn't die from burns of the scalding water but rather from the shock. Rita, my Great-Aunt Mary and Great-Uncle Tony's oldest child, said Marie had been a beautiful child with blond hair and blue eyes; a

Great-Aunt Mary, 1920s.

rare occurrence among Sicilians. "A real Barone" is what they said about her. I think what she meant was that the Barone Family were all fair skinned. Rita told me that her parents never talked about the incident, but after my great-aunt died, it was discovered that Great-Aunt Mary had kept all of the sympathy cards people had sent many years ago. She must have thought about her Little Marie every day.

All of the rest of Mary's children went to college and became respected professionals. Great-Aunt Mary and Great-Uncle Tony were very close to my grandparents, her sister Carrie and brother-in-law Frank, visiting them every Wednesday driving the six miles from Le-Roy to the farm. When my grandparents sold the farm and eventually moved to Lake Street, the visits continued every Wednesday evening (and some weeks more often) up until Mary and Tony died. They were inseparable. When I was around eight years old, I couldn't understand why my cousins found her to be such a no-nonsense parent, since I saw her as a friendly and generous old relative who made me feel special every time I saw her. Since she only lived a few streets away from us, I saw her more than any of Grandma's brothers. She always remembered my birthday and sent me a birthday card with a stick of gum and a dollar "to get an ice cream cone." She did this all through my college years and up to the year she died.

Great-Uncle Anthony (Tony) Ross Argana (Gargano)

Born: May 25, 1893, Valledolmo, Sicily
Died: October 30, 1972, Batavia, New York

Great-Aunt Mary married Anthony Ross Argana (Gargano) on July 25, 1920. He was born in Valledolmo, Sicily and immigrated to the U.S. in 1900. My Great-Uncle Tony was a little taller than Mary, around five feet four inches. He was a handsome man with shocking white hair and a perpetual tan. Tony Argana was a gentle man, and I never remember him losing his temper. Mary was more demanding, unafraid to express her opinion, and the disciplinarian of the family. Tony catered to Great-Aunt Mary and gave her anything she wanted. She never did any of the shopping, and when Great-Uncle Tony went to the grocery store, he always brought his sister-in-law Carrie, my grandmother. For years, people in town thought that Grandma and Great-Uncle Tony were actually married, since they went everywhere together.

Mary and Tony's marriage was the perfect partnership. The division of labor was mostly drawn down traditional gender lines. For example, Mary was responsible for the cooking, the dishes, the laundry and the house cleaning, while Great-Uncle Tony loved to go downtown and socialize when he paid the bills or went grocery shopping and did the yard work. He was always running errands for her or driving downtown to pick up whatever she needed. If she needed a ride, he drove her, since she didn't have a driver's license. My recollections of them were that, for a married couple of their time, when averaging everything they did for each other, they had an equal say about how things were done in the marriage. My great-uncle catered to my great-aunt, but she also took very good care of him. Sicilian fathers were consciously feared by their children and had the reputation for being chauvinistic and not afraid to use corporal punishment. Tony was different. He was very compassionate and considerate of his wife and children. My great-aunt and great-uncle worked well together as partners, as demonstrated by the fact that they ran the Eagle Hotel starting in 1937. One aspect of their gender-line partnership was that Great-Uncle Tony made the important decisions when it came to finances. According to my cousin Rita, their oldest daughter, my great-uncle bought the hotel before he told my great-aunt. When they moved out of the hotel and bought their first house, again he bought the house without telling her first. He did what he felt was best for the family on his own when he felt it was necessary. Great-Aunt Mary and Great-Uncle Tony were in many ways opposites, but they made a wonderful team and eventually succeeded in living the "American Dream."

The egg tempera painting, The *Wedding of Mary and Tony*, depicts them at the start of their life together and symbolizes the admiration I had for them. They are standing in front of their ramshackle house located in the poorest section of LeRoy. From these humble beginnings, through hard work they were able to live a comfortable life, becoming well respected in the Italian and American communities. Above them are three angels from the egg tempera painting, *The Ecstasy of St. Francis*, by the Renaissance artist, Sassetta. They represent the virtues Chastity, on the left, Industry, in the middle, and Poverty, on the right, ideals that served my great-aunt and great-uncle well during their life together.

Tony Argana was a butcher by trade, and there is an interesting story that has been handed down through the years of how he became one. When he was fifteen years old, his mother gave him a dollar to purchase something at Miller's Meat Market. On his way, he lost the money. Upon confessing to his mother, he was told to go back to the market and ask for work to earn what he had lost. Mr. Miller was apparently so impressed with Tony's story that he agreed to his request by having him sweep the floor. Since $1.00 was a significant sum in those days, we assume it was for a period longer than one time. As the story goes, Mr. Miller tested Anthony's honesty more than once by dropping paper money, as much as $20.00, on the floor prior to the sweeping. Tony returned all the money to Mr. Miller and was rewarded with a full-time job, eventually working up to manager of Mr. Miller's shop.

World War I interrupted Tony's civilian life when he was reg-

The Wedding of Mary and Tony, *2012. Egg Tempera on panel.*

istered into the Army in Batavia, New York, on July 27, 1918. His enlistment record notes that his character was "excellent" and he was "honest and faithful" with no AWOL or absences. While in the Army, he worked as a butcher and was honorably discharged on December

21, 1918. Upon returning to LeRoy, he resumed his association with Mr. Miller for another nineteen years.

My great-uncle was a man of goodwill, serving as a trustee of St. Joseph's Church and a very active member of the Knights of Columbus.[1] He worked for Miller's Meat Market for twenty-nine years and later owned the Eagle Hotel for another twenty years, so he was very well known among the "Mericans"[2] and was one of the most respected persons in the Italian and American communities. When his daughter Marie died, the most prestigious family in LeRoy, the Woodward family, known for starting the Jell-O empire, sent their condolences. In the Italian community, Tony's reputation for honesty and intelligence was beyond reproach, so *paesani*[3] asked him to interpret important papers for them, write letters, and asked his advice on important matters. He was the "go-to" person in the community. Even though

Mary and Tony, 1970.

he only went to the third grade, he learned to read and write. His oldest daughter, my cousin Rita, believed he would first listen to the radio to educate himself and stay abreast of current events, then buy the evening paper on his way home from work and spend the evenings reading about them to improve his reading skills.

Another example of the incredible esteem that Great-Uncle Tony commanded in LeRoy was illustrated when Rita was old enough to attend public school in the 1930s. Each class was divided into three groups of students. The first group contained all of the smartest non-Italian children from well-to-do families; the second group contained the slower children; and the third group contained all of the "others," that is, the "ethnic" children—African-American, Hispanic, and Italian. Except for Rita. She was placed in the first group with all of the offspring of the socially prominent families in LeRoy. She was smart, but so were other Italian children. What made her different was Great-Uncle Tony and his impeccable reputation.

THE EAGLE HOTEL

My great-uncle left Mr. Miller's butchering business in 1937 and became an entrepreneur when he purchased the Eagle Hotel. In those early years of ownership, Tony and Mary had an apartment in the hotel, and through hard work and with the help of his brother and

---

1   The Knights of Columbus are a fraternal and beneficent organization of Catholic men that was formed in 1882. The purpose of the society is to promote Catholic education, give financial aid to the needy and scholarships to Catholic colleges, and provide homes and education to Catholic orphans and temporary financial assistance to families of deceased members. Columbus Day was instituted largely through the efforts of the organization.

2   A slang term that was used by the Sicilians in LeRoy.

3   *Paesani* are people from the same country, especially other Italians.

family, he became very well off and eventually bought his own home. They owned the Eagle Hotel from 1937 until early 1958. Great-Aunt Mary did the cooking, washing, and ironing with the help of her children, and kept the books while Great-Uncle Tony tended the bar, did the buying and also helped with the cooking. When they became financially comfortable, they hired someone to do the washing and ironing.

Great-Aunt Mary made an incredible spaghetti sauce in the Sicilian tradition—a sweet tomato sauce seasoned with olive oil, tomatoes she canned, some puree, sugar, garlic (whole cloves), basil, beef, and pork. She always used both beef and pork. Her sauce was in such demand with the boarders at the Eagle Hotel that one summer she and her daughters canned fifty bushels of tomatoes just to keep everyone happy. After that year, my Great-Aunt Mary realized she could buy canned tomatoes and tomato puree to make her sauce for hotel guests, and no one was the wiser.

Great-Uncle Tony was a very good cook in his own right. As I mentioned in Chapter Three, he made an Italian sausage that was admired by all of his customers (see Appendix for recipe). It was a family tradition that he would make it for our Christmas Eve parties, which everyone celebrated after Midnight Mass. If we were lucky enough, he would stop by the house a few days before Christmas Eve and drop off a few pounds. It was so lean that we would have to cook it with some olive oil just so it wouldn't burn in the skillet. It had such a unique combination of spices and meat that I have never tasted anything close to it. Commercially made sausage, when compared to it, is bland and too fatty.

GREAT-UNCLE TONY THE SAINT

When my sister Mary was eight years old, she found a stray kitten across the street from our house on Lake Street. Since Lake Street is a main thoroughfare through LeRoy, it has a lot trucks and cars traveling on it day and night. My sister was worried the kitten would be hit, so she brought it home. She hid it in our apartment, since Grandma would not let us have any pets, and when Mom came home she pleaded with her to let her keep it. Our mother said she would ask Grandma, so we went over to her side of the house. As it turned out, it was a Wednesday and Great-Aunt Mary and Great-Uncle Tony were visiting and sitting in the living room. We asked Grandma if we could keep the kitten and of course, she said, "no." My sister started crying and begged Grandma to let her keep it, but nothing was going to change her mind. Just then, Great-Uncle Tony intervened. "Carrie" he said, "let Katie keep the kitten." He always called my sister, Mary Catherine, Katie although no one actually knew why. He said, "It will catch the mice that live in your cellar. You had cats on the farm. What harm will it cause?" Well, Grandma was a hard case, but Tony was persuasive, and she let us keep it. It was a tortoise shell cat named Tiger. Grandma grew to like the cat, since it spent much of its time in the cellar catching mice. We always liked our great-uncle, but after that evening we thought he was a saint.

During the first year or so that we had Tiger, Grandma would chase her out of her apartment with a broom, but eventually she warmed up to the idea of having a cat. She would talk to her while canning tomatoes. She even had her own special name for Tiger, calling her Snoopy because Tiger liked to sleep on the furnace down in the cellar and hide in Grandma's kitchen closet. Tiger often disappeared across the street on hunting trips, and one time she was gone for several days. In times like this, Grandma would light candles for Tiger. One particular time when the cat was gone for longer than usual, Mary went with Grandma to church and lit a candle and said a prayer to the Blessed Mother for the safe return of Tiger. Tiger always came back, and Grandma would be so proud that her petition to the Holy Mother worked once again. That cat was either very smart or had more than nine lives, since we lived on a busy truck route to the New York State Thruway (Interstate 90). Tiger would hide in our bushes in the front of the house, and when the coast was clear she would make a beeline for the woods across the street. Several times she almost got hit, but Grandma believed the Blessed Mother was looking out for her.

My cousin Mike Cinquino told me another story that demonstrated Great-Uncle Tony's kindness and compassion. One day Great Uncle-Tony, who was Mike's grandfather, brought home a stray dog for his grandchildren without asking his daughter, Rita. She was not too happy about that because she didn't want a pet. He told Rita that all kids should have a dog and convinced her to keep it, ultimately bringing home several dogs for his grandchildren over time. Whenever one dog died, Tony would show up with another black one. One time when the Cinquino kids needed a new pet, Tony brought home a white puppy and all of his grandchildren were in an uproar. Since the dog was white, not black, how could they name it "Blackie"? So, Tony took the white puppy back to the farm and got a black one. Because of Great-Uncle Tony, many puppies got a good home and became important members of the family. Today the Cinquino kids look back on those days with "Blackie" with fondness and still talk about him.

The year before he died, Tony got Great-Aunt Mary a little pug named Buffy, which she babied. When we used to go see her, Buffy would greet us at the door, setting up a ruckus and then running around the house looking for some toys for us to use to play with him. The similarities between my great-aunt and Buffy were striking. They were both short and extremely bowlegged, and when Great-Aunt Mary walked, she waddled back and forth just like her dog (I used to watch her walk up the aisle in church in wonderment). Looking back, the thought occurred to us that maybe Great-Uncle Tony knew his time was short and that his wife was going to need some companionship when he passed on. At first, Great-Aunt Mary resisted getting a pet, but eventually warmed up to the idea. Whatever his motivation was, it worked out incredibly well, because the two were inseparable and I'm sure Buffy got her through a lot of lonely nights without her husband of fifty-two years.

Great-Aunt Mary constantly told Great-Uncle Tony what to do; so much so that we felt sorry for him. We thought he was "hen pecked." One evening there was a family gathering at my Aunt Helen's house. Since my mother didn't drive, Great-Aunt Mary offered to drive us home. My mother, my sister and I got in the back seat and Great-Uncle Tony started driving. Every second of the way, Great-Aunt Mary was telling him to put on the brakes, put the blinker on, turn the wheel, straighten it out, and so on. Finally, my mother couldn't take it any longer and said, "Aunt Mary! Leave Uncle-Tony alone. He can drive." We were stopped at a red light so when the light turned green he stepped on the accelerator and headed through the traffic light. To get to our house, we had to turn left and go over a bridge that went over a wide creek in the middle of town. So Great-Uncle Tony turned left and we started to approach the bridge. Great-Aunt Mary kept quiet. Well, Tony never straightened out the wheel and we were headed for the sidewalk and the railing of the bridge with the creek below. Finally my mother yelled, "Uncle Tony, turn the wheel!" He did, avoiding disaster, and we continued home with Great-Aunt Mary giving him verbal instructions all of the way. After that incident we never interfered in their relationship again.

THE RIVALRY

There was a strong sibling rivalry between Great-Aunt Mary and Grandma, centered around who was the best cook. Whenever Great-Aunt Mary would make some of her home-made manicotti, she would always send me a dish to taste since she knew I liked it so much. When I would call her up to thank her, she would always ask me whose sauce was better, hers or Grandma's? I would tell her, "Aunt Mary, you make the best manicotti and spaghetti sauce in the world." She would say, "Oh I thought the sauce was a little runny but I'm glad you liked it. Don't tell your Grandma. It will be our little secret." Grandma, knowing that Great-Aunt Mary had sent me something to taste, would ask me, "How was it?" Of course I would tell her that it was excellent but not as good as hers. She would reply, "I thought so, but let her think she makes the best sauce." This would play out time and time again, and there was never a downside for me to their little competition because I was in the middle and got to do all of the tasting.

As is typical of sisters, Mary and Carrie would occasionally clash. Both of their personal-ities were such that they both were used to being in control and not used to backing down to anyone. There might have also been a little jealousy involved in the relationship over the fact that when the out-of-town brothers visited LeRoy for a vacation, they preferred to stay with Grandma, the older sister. One summer, two of Mary and Carrie's brothers from Baltimore, Pete and Jimmy, and Jimmy's wife, Pauline, visited LeRoy at the same time. Both brothers wanted to spend the week with Grandma, but she didn't have enough room, so Pete was chosen to stay with his younger sister Mary. About midway through the week, Pete called up Grandma begging her to let him come stay with her since Mary was driving him crazy. From then on, they never came up at the same time so that no one had to draw straws.

One Wednesday evening, when I was a teenager and just starting to become interested in Grandma and her world, I walked into Grandma's apartment to hear her say, "Chi mi muor!" (Hope you die!) under her breath as Great-Aunt Mary and Great-Uncle Tony were leaving. Something had happened to make Grandma livid. There was no contact between them for weeks, not even a phone call. Wednesday came and went and no Great-Aunt Mary and Great-Uncle Tony. Grandma was miserable, but she would not tell us what had hap-pened. My Aunt Franny called Great-Aunt Mary to find out what had happened, but she was tight lipped as well. Finally, after several weeks, Great-Uncle Tony and Aunt Franny got together and planned to stop the lunacy by forcing the sisters into the same room. When the next Wednesday came along, Great-Uncle Tony packed his wife in the car and set out for Grandma's house. Once they got there, they tried to get them to talk. They were cold to one another, but by the end of the evening they were beginning to talk to each other. After they left, Grandma was still mad, but the thaw had begun; by next week things were back to normal. Nobody ever found out what precipitated the disagreement.

Great-Aunt Mary liked to crochet and make clothes. She spent the winters making af-ghan blankets for all of her great niece and great nephew's children so that after she died, they would remember her. My son instantly loved his blanket because it had "nice thumby holes." He still has the one she made for him, although it had to be made into a pillow from the wear and tear over the years. He became so attached to it that he even took it to college with him.

Great-Aunt Mary had a special place in her heart for my mother. The feeling was mutual, since my sister was named after her. I think she felt sorry for my mother, since my father proved not to be a very good breadwinner and my sister and I grew up without a father for a role model like Great-Uncle Tony was to their children.

TRADITIONAL BELIEFS AND STREGHERIA

Grandma, Great-Aunt Mary, and Great-Uncle Tony represented a link to the culture and way of life in Sicily. Grandma's brothers assimilated into American culture very quickly, mostly because they were men and had many more opportunities to become professionals and to move up the social ladder, even though they were Italian. But Grandma and Great-Aunt Mary remained *contadini*, steeped in southern Italian culture with their gender holding them back. Both factors conspired to keep them in very traditional roles as women. Grandma and Great-Aunt Mary, along with Great-Uncle Tony, carried with them a glimpse back in time to the life of the *contadini* (peasants), except in this country they were able to improve their circumstances and live a (generally) better life. They never totally integrated into American society, but were always in a world between two cultures. They watched television, rode in cars, and modernized their houses, but still clung to many Old World Italian beliefs, such as the idea that there was "a sense of magic in religion" and "a sense of religion in magic."[4]

There is a long tradition of blessing rituals, ancient pagan beliefs, and magical practices in southern Italy. Along with the cult of the saint, the immigrants from the *Mezzogiorno* (southern Italy) brought with them their occult beliefs and practices. Emigration could not help a person escape from the power of witches. Events and tragic circumstances that affected their lives, that even the police, the priest, or a doctor could not cure, required the help of a *strega* (a female magician) or *stregone* (male magician) to remove the evil eye, or *mal'occhio*. The evil eye could be a curse that a bad witch or an enemy casts upon someone, or one could be possessed by evil spirits just by walking down the street.[5] When an evil spirit is cast out, *strege* do not destroy it, but just send the evil spirit on its journey, "and unloads its evil on the rest of the world."[6] To Americans, this appeared to be a ridiculous response to the events of life, but to the Sicilians, this was the only way they knew to how cope with unexplainable events. Each crisis was faced with the support and love of family and *paesani* and increased the sense of community.[7]

It was through the experience of these traditions that I was exposed to the traditional Italian side of our culture. My cousin Mike Cinquino told me the story how Great-Uncle Tony's sister, who everyone called Aunt Mananna (her real name was Marianna), performed the evil eye removal ritual on him. He had been sick for three days and was not getting any

---

4   R.J. Vecoli, "Cult and Occult in Italian-American Culture: The Persistence of a Cultural Heritage," in *Immigrants and Religion in Urban America*, ed. T.D. Marzik and R.M. Miller (Philadelphia: Temple University Press, 1977), 33.
5   Vecoli, "Cult and Occult," 7.
6   Thomas Hauschild, *Power and Magic in Italy* (New York: Berghahn Books, 2011), 22.
7   Vecoli, "Cult and Occult," 7.

better, so Aunt Mananna did the ritual and the next day he was "cured" and felt fine. This impressed him so much that he never forgot it.

I also experienced this belief in Italian folk medicine firsthand. I suffer from a foot malaise that I have had since I was very young, called dyshidrotic eczema. When I was thirteen, I had a bout that was so bad that my feet became infected to the point that I couldn't walk. At the time, doctors could not figure out what was wrong with them, so I suffered through frequent periods where my feet really bothered me. Great-Aunt Mary was very concerned, and one evening talked to my mother about taking me to an Italian folk doctor or *stregone*.

The next day I was told by Mom that Grandma, Great-Aunt Mary, and Great-Uncle Tony were going to take me to a doctor in the nearby city of Batavia. They were sure he could help my foot condition. Above all, I was not to tell my father anything about where I was going because he wouldn't have understood and would have caused trouble. My parents were having marital problems at the time, and he was still living with us in an apartment in Grandma's house. My father was also trying to convert my sister and me to become Jehovah's Witnesses, which was just increasing the tension and stress in the house.

So off we drove with Grandma and I in the back seat to a part of Batavia that was not familiar to me. Finally, coming to a block with old houses, we stopped at a run-down apartment house and went up to the second floor. It was dark and smelled old. Great-Uncle Tony knocked on the door and a short little man with an aquiline nose let us inside. We sat in his living room with Grandma sitting next to me on the couch. I was thinking, "What kind of a doctor is this guy? This looks like his apartment, not a doctor's office." Then Grandma told me that this was the man who could help me. The four of them started talking in Sicilian, so I had no clue what they were talking about, but I got the feeling that the conversation centered around my foot condition. The old man told me in a heavy Italian accent that doctors haven't been able to help me because they are not treating the right thing and that there were demons causing the infections.

Since I was brought up not to be superstitious by my parents, I thought the man was crazy. He bragged to me about all of the amazing cures he had performed on people, like mending broken bones that wouldn't heal. He told me I had to believe that he could cure me, and then Great-Aunt Mary asked me to take off my shoes and socks. He looked at my feet for some time, turning them over, looking between the toes. With great ceremony, he gave them the sign of the cross while reciting some prayers in Sicilian, and then, to my complete horror, started spitting on them. By summoning the proper saint through prayer and incantations for each specific malaise, healers used tears and saliva as a way of conquering over evil forces.[8] Since a *stregone* cannot exterminate a spell, he lets his saliva "flow so that the evil forces could be transported to their next stop."[9] He repeated this ritual several times on both feet and then he was through. My first reaction was to jerk my feet back, which obviously annoyed the *stregone*. He chastised me for not believing in his powers and told me there would be no hope for me if I didn't change my attitude. Grandma paid him and we left.

I was totally stunned by what had happened. Nobody had mentally prepared me for this ordeal, and as a typical thirteen-year-old, I felt incredibly embarrassed. I was thankful

---

8   Hauschild, *Power and Magic in Italy*, 115.
9   Ibid., 137.

none of my peers lived in Batavia, so I could sneak in and out of the building without being recognized.

My mother was not particularly superstitious and spent her life trying to be more American than Sicilian. So in hindsight, when she agreed to let me go, I knew she had lost faith in traditional medicine and as a last resort put her faith into a blessing ritual hoping for a miraculous cure. I went back three times before I was able to talk her out of making me go back. She agonized the entire week trying to figure out a way of telling Grandma. I told her to tell them that my feet have never felt or looked better than they do now, so I must be cured. For years, Great-Aunt Mary would ask me how my feet were and of course I always said, "Great!" Then she would tell Grandma what a good thing they had done for me. I realized that what they did, they did out of love.

In a bit of irony several years later, I did have another bout of this foot ailment, and this time I actually did go to a foot specialist in Batavia. When I got to the office and saw the name on the door, I realized it was exactly the same name as the *stregone* I had gone to a few years earlier. When the doctor came in the examining room, I told him I thought my Grandma had taken me to see an old man with the same name in an effort to find a cure for my foot ailment. His face turned red and he looked embarrassed. Then he got testy and told me that, indeed, that was his father. In the end, he couldn't help me either. I guess the family had no cures for feet.

During September of my junior year in undergraduate school, Great-Uncle Tony was hospitalized with cancer. My mother called and told me he wasn't doing so well and that I should visit him before he got worse. My girlfriend and future wife Linda and I drove from Oswego to the hospital in Batavia and found his room. When I walked in, there was the family all gathered around him engaged in spirited conversation. They all stopped and the conversation turned to my unexpected appearance. Great-Aunt Mary was pleased that I had made the trip from college. I greeted Great-Uncle Tony, and when he turned to look at me, I saw a look that I had never seen before. It was the look of shock on his face and I realized that he knew he was going to die. I could tell he wasn't ready because he had a far-away look on his face; I don't think he was really listening to me. He obviously wasn't his usual happy self. He was a man who really enjoyed life, and I suspect he felt he still had things to accomplish; there were more *gardunis* to find and hot and sweet sausage to make for Christmas. He died of cancer a month later.

Great-Aunt Mary lived just a little over ten years longer, and died of congenital heart disease. A few months before she died, she mentioned to her daughter Rita that she was near the end. Rita told her we are all going to die and didn't think much of it. Great-Aunt Mary felt sick on and off, and one day she was feeling particularly under the weather. Her grandson Louis was just back from a semester of going to school in England, so Great-Aunt Mary invited him to supper and cooked him one of his favorite meals, her special meatloaf made the Italian way. She felt sick after the meal so he stayed overnight to be with her. Great-Aunt Mary got him up several times during the night, and the last time as he was helping her, she said to him, "You won't have to get up to help me anymore." With Louis at her side, she passed away that night.

CHAPTER 8

Great-Uncle Anthony (Tony) Barone

Born: June 13, 1902, Avon, New York
Died. November 6, 1978, Rochester, New York

Great-Uncle Tony was the sixth out of nine children in the Barone family and one of the tallest. He made his living as a bookie and was arrested more than once for illegal activities, causing great turmoil in the family. One day after collecting on the bets, he noticed that the cops were tailing him so he tried to evade them. Since he did not want to be caught red-handed with any incriminating evidence, as he drove down the road, he started throwing the money out of the window. It didn't work and he was still arrested. This incident was a very symbolic image of his life; easy come, easy go.

Tony's obituary states that he worked as a waiter and as a bartender in different restaurants in Rochester until his "retirement" in 1965. This is the first time I ever heard that he had any sort of profession other than his illegal activities. Tony was loud and a braggart; the proverbial "Big Shot." He talked in a raspy voice that was not pleasant on the ears. Compared to his other broth-

Great-Uncle Tony, late 1940s.

ers—Jimmy, Joe, Pete, Ross, Sam, and Cosmo—he was crasser and less sophisticated. When he visited us, I got the feeling that he really wanted to impress us and was trying to compete with his more conventionally successful siblings. Tony especially craved having his big sister Carrie be proud of him, but he went about this in the strangest way, by constantly trying to impress her with his shady dealings. Obviously, this approach did not endear him to her.

Tony was married once but never had any children that anyone knows about. He met his wife, Patricia, at the racetrack and was married only for a short time. One cousin told me an unsubstantiated story that on his wedding cake was written, "I just won the Daily Double!"

My sister, Mary Catherine, kept her distance from Great-Uncle Tony, always feeling a bit uncomfortable around him, but I thought he was an interesting character. Whenever he saw her, he would reach out his hands and walk toward her saying, "Mary Kay" and grab her cheeks with both hands and give her a wet kiss. Mary said it was disgusting. He was certainly a "man's man." He visited my grandmother often, usually with an absolutely beautiful girlfriend of the moment much younger than him. I thought at the time that he visited because of his love for his oldest sister, but I think in hindsight it was more to use her phone. Imagine the scene: a gorgeous woman dressed to the nines sitting at the kitchen table with my grandmother, who looked like a peasant from the nineteenth century. What in the world did they have to talk about?

Whenever he visited, Great-Uncle Tony wore only the most expensive clothes, and his outfit usually included the same spectator shoes that his brother Cosmo favored. He smoked cigarettes and cigars in Grandma's kitchen, and sometimes she even offered him a beer or a mixed drink (she allowed her brothers the transgressions that she would never allow her children or grandchildren). He liked to brag about all of his money, the new cars he drove and the places he had been, always traveling first-class. Like all the Barone brothers, Tony had a streak of generosity. When his brother Sam's son went to Purdue University, Uncle Tony jumped in to pay for his tuition.

Great-Uncle Tony had an office in Rochester that had only one piece of furniture in it: a desk with a phone in each drawer. On a fall Sunday afternoon in the early 1960s, while visiting my grandmother, Great-Uncle Tony came over to our side of the house to ask me to write down the scores of the football games. I thought he was a devout fan like me. After I delivered them to him, he got up to use Grandma's phone. With appeals to San Antonio,[1] Grandma begged her brother not to get her involved in his business, to which he said, "Carrie, don't worry; your phones aren't tapped." After he made his calls, telling each bettor what they owed him, he turned to me and said, "Tommy, never bet on football games; I'm a rich man because of these *schifozzos* [from "*schifozz*," Sicilian for a disgusting thing]." All I could think about for the rest of the day was that I got some people in trouble with Great-Uncle Tony and God knows who else. To this day I still don't bet, so I guess in his own way he had a positive impact on my life.

Another time, when he was in his mid-sixties, he brought two beautiful younger women on a visit to see Grandma. After the visit, she came over to our apartment fuming and swearing in Sicilian about him. My mother, who didn't actually speak or understand Sicilian but knew that Grandma's words weren't good, asked what was wrong. Grandma replied, "He thinks I'm stupid! He told me he was going on a Caribbean cruise with those two women who he said are his nurses! I know what he's really gonna do!" After this incident, she said he was banned from her house forever. She told him, "Don't bother coming to see me anymore."

About a month later, I saw Grandma getting ready for company, and I asked her who was coming over. She replied, "Uncle Tony."

"I thought he was banned forever!" I exclaimed.

Her response was, "He's my brother. Whadda ya gonna do?"

As Great-Uncle Tony reached his seventies, he became insulated and alone. His younger brother Sam would bring him to his house and feed him. Great-Uncle Sam had a son named Chuck. One day, when Great-Uncle Tony was over for dinner, Chuck was trying out his new lariat. He saw his uncle sitting on the sofa so he threw it in his general direction. As fate would have it, the rope went around Great-Uncle Tony's neck, and Chuck, in his excitement, pulled it tight. Poor old Tony started choking and struggled to get the lariat off his neck, but

---

1 Frequently, Grandma invoked the help of Saint Anthony (or another saint) to overcome some transgression by saying his name and blessing herself.

in doing so, he knocked over the glass coffee table, smashing it into pieces. Chuck told it me this was the first and only time he was able to rope anything.

Grandma forgave all of Tony's transgressions until near the end of his life, when he was too old to live by himself and he was starting to lose his mind. He wanted to move in with her and Aunt Franny. She didn't know what to say until one evening at supper he accused her of trying to poison him. That was it; nobody insulted her cooking and got away with it. She had put up with all of his activities that had for years caused her great humiliation. At times, such as when she heard his name on the radio for being arrested, she was so embarrassed about him that she wouldn't even leave the house except to go to church. But this time Tony had insulted her cooking, and that went to the core of her identity. It was the only thing for which she was appreciated and got accolades all her life. Her decision was made and it was final. She gave him her signature gesture: the sign of the cross and cut him off at the knees. It was off to the old folk's home for Tony.

The retirement home was just one mile down the street from Grandma's house in Le-Roy. Great-Uncle Tony never adapted to his new life. He was beginning to "lose his mind" and thought that he was being poisoned by the cooks at the home. He would sneak out of the facility at night and walk the mile to Grandma's house and sleep in her front porch. When she opened the door and walked out into the front porch to go to church, which she did every morning, there was Great Uncle Tony waiting for her and giving Grandma the start of her life. He would plead with her to let him stay, but he was too much for her to take back.

The painting of my great-uncle, *Great-Uncle Tony Needs a Nurse*, is a microcosm of the life he enjoyed living outside the law. He loved the racetrack, since it was one of his lucrative sources of income; hence, the inclusion of the horse race scene at the top. Connected to this scene is an appropriated fragment of Luca Signorelli's *The Damned* from the *Duomo di Orvieto*, where the devil is running against *The Damned* in a race to hell. The women placed behind him refer to his many "nurses" that gave him succor over the years.

Great-Uncle Tony Needs a Nurse, *2007. Egg tempera on panel.*

Great-Uncle Tony died at Monroe County Hospital in 1978 after eight years of failing health. He lived life the way he wanted to and in the end he died alone.

In retrospect, Great-Uncle Tony fit the stereotype most Italians have had to overcome: that Italians are gangsters. Italian families like the Barones had to put up with the stereotypical image portrayed in Hollywood movies and novels that compared us to the likes of the Sopranos or the Corleones. My family worked hard to become accepted as hard-working, honest citizens, and Tony, unwittingly, did his best to sabotage their strenuous efforts. As much as his exploits are humorous, they also caused much embarrassment to Grandma and the other family members. Deep down inside, he was a generous and a friendly individual who did his best to help his family members who needed help, but above all he was an enigmatic figure.

CHAPTER 9

Great-Uncle Rosalino (Ross) Barone

Born: September 12, 1904, LeRoy, New York
Died: March 24, 1993, Ulster, New York

Great-Uncle Ross was the seventh child of Charles and Maria Barone, and the last surviving of Grandma's siblings. He was very short and rotund in his early years, but as he aged he got thinner. I remember him telling stories with his raspy voice and laughing. He was extremely intelligent and the most sophisticated of Grandma's brothers, and with impeccable manners, he gained widespread respect.

Great-Uncle Ross graduated from the Albany College of Pharmacy with a degree in pharmacy; for many years he owned and operated a very successful drugstore on Monroe Avenue in Rochester , New York. He married my Great-Aunt Ede (Edette Hartznetz) and built a wonderful house in the plush and upscale suburb of Pittsford in the 1950s. Ede was a self-employed interior decorator, and created the most beautiful home my family had ever seen, complete with an in-ground swimming pool in the backyard. I remember the excitement that stirred in our house when Great-Uncle Ross and Great-Aunt Ede came to visit. They were

Great-Uncle Ross, 1922.

always dressed impeccably, and Great-Uncle Ross's incredible turquoise 1962 Ford Thunderbird Italia T-bird made him the height of hip in the eyes of an eleven-year-old boy. He would actually let me sit in it, but my mother insisted that I not touch anything in it. Invitations to their house were treasured, and after visiting, everyone would talk for weeks about the great time they had there and what a great hostess Great-Aunt Ede was. I remember her as being a little bit taller than Great-Uncle Ross, very friendly, approachable, and glamorous.

The contrasts between Great-Uncle Ross and Grandma were striking. They were both from the same family and grew up essentially during the same time, but culturally, Grandma remained a peasant woman from the nineteenth century, while her little brother Rosalino moved on and lived in an upscale community surrounded by the symbols of the American Dream he had achieved. He was able to escape the negative stereotypes that he had encountered as a youth and became a well-respected professional who served as a role model for all of us. He was wealthy beyond our wildest dreams.

My great-uncle had a mustache for most of his life that was a real curiosity to me when I was young. Of course, he was the only one who could get away with facial hair in those days; that "he always had one" was the defense Grandma and my aunts used when I wanted to grow one. There was also the fact that Ross had done so well that he could do no wrong in Grandma's eyes, so she often let him get away with activities that would have been forbidden for the rest of us, such as smoking. In the pocket of his shirts he always had a pocket protector filled with pens and cigars. To this day whenever I smell cigar smoke I smile and think of the times when my great-uncles would visit our house.

In the 1970s, when my mother got cancer, she had incredibly expensive prescriptions that were not covered by her health insurance, and she was denied any help from the United Way and other community organizations. She did not qualify for any government aid because her minimal income was considered too much money. That was very ironic to us, since without Grandma's help we would have been destitute. When she found out how much the prescriptions would cost, she went into a deep depression since she couldn't afford them and was worried what would happen to my sister and me. Her anxieties centered on the marital problems she was having with my father. They were separated, but not divorced, and her fear was that my father would gain custody of my sister and ruin her life. Since I was over eighteen and in college, I was essentially on my own; but Mary was still in high school. I'll discuss this situation in depth in both my parent's chapters, but, basically, my father did not have a steady job and was a religious fanatic. Lena, my mother, agonized daily about the possibility that my father would force Mary to become a Jehovah's Witness.

When Grandma found out, she said, "Let me make a phone call." She called her brother Ross and told him the story. "Ross, Lena 's got the cancer and can't afford the medicine. Can you help her?" He told Grandma that since Lena worked in Rochester, if she came to the drugstore the next day he would help get her set up with her medication. After much arguing with Grandma, the next day Mom went to see Great-Uncle Ross and told him that she couldn't accept his offer because it was way too much of an imposition on his generosity. My mother was concerned how much money it was going to cost Uncle Ross and didn't know how long she had to take the prescriptions. He insisted that if he couldn't afford it he wouldn't have offered to do it. So every time she needed her prescription filled, she would stop in to see him and he would give her the medicine she needed. She did this for a long time and then one month she didn't show up. Ross called Grandma and wanted to know where Lena was. Of course, Grandma came over to our apartment and read my mother the

Great-Aunt Ede and Great-Uncle Ross, early 1950s.

riot act. He continued to help my mother until he retired; then my Aunt Franny picked up the slack, since she also worked in a drugstore.

I remember that when I would go to the city with my mother to shop for clothes for school, we would always stop in to see Great-Uncle Ross at his store. She said that he wanted to see me, so I should look presentable and make sure I spit out my gum before we went in to see him. He would come out from behind the counter and shake my hand, and then ask me questions about school and if I was being good. Before we'd leave he would let me choose whatever candy bar I wanted. He was a kind-hearted person.

Even though he was a man of wealth and style, he never forgot his roots. He loved *gardunis* (burdocks) and said he "liked them better than meat." I have a picture of him sitting at the kitchen table with my aunt serving him a big plate of *gardunis*, a staple of immigrant Sicilian families. The symbolism of that photograph is touching, considering that Grandma was more like a mother than a sister to him. She was nine years old when he was born, and already she was working in the fields and taking care of her siblings. In the photograph, they are at the end of their lives and we see them reverting back to the roles of their childhood.

At Grandma's funeral in 1992, the eighty-eight-year-old Ross made the trip from Ulster, New York , where he was living with his daughter, to pay his respects to his beloved sister. Everyone was surprised that he wanted to make the long trip since he was not in the best of health himself. After the funeral,

Great-Uncle Ross being served cardunis by Aunt Franny , 1991.

there was a big dinner at the American Legion, where he was treated like the Godfather. All of the cousins, aunts, uncles, and family friends took turns going up to greet him. I hadn't seen him for years, since I had moved to South Carolina to attend graduate school and start my first teaching job and my family. He had moved away from Pittsford and was now living down by New York City. I hadn't had the chance to thank him for his generosity during our time of need. I figured I probably wouldn't see him again, so it was now or never. Of course, after I thanked him, he started asking me questions like he always did. I was proud to tell him that I was a college professor and he seemed to be impressed. The next year he died. He was the last link to a bygone era.

The painting *No I'm Not Colonel Sanders*, is based on a photograph of Great-Uncle Ross that I took at my sister's first wedding in 1974 when he looked his most flamboyant. I'm sure Aunt Ede had something to do with it. He sported a mustache and goatee that made him look like the fried chicken magnate Colonel Sanders. Behind him is his drugstore, turquoise Thunderbird Italia and one of his pet boxers. The painting attempts to capture his outgoing personality, as if he is getting ready to say something witty. The angels above him are from the tempera painting *Madonna with Child and Saints* by Fillipino Lippi as they shower him with roses because of his kindness to others.

No I am Not Colonel Sanders, *2009. Egg tempera on panel.*

Great-Uncle Samuel Barone

Born: October 16, 1906, LeRoy, New York
Died: January 31, 1986, Rochester, New York

Great-Uncle Sam Barone was the eighth of Colgero and Maria Barone's nine children. He was around five feet seven inches tall and talked in a loud voice, so we always knew when he was visiting his sister Carrie, my Grandma. Sam was the brother who came to see Grandma more than any of her other brothers, since he lived only a short distance away in Henrietta, New York, and his sister-in-law lived next store to Carrie.

Great-Uncle Sam put his family above all else. If a family member needed his assistance, he would drop everything to help them. When his brother Tony (Chapter 8) became incapacitated in old age, Sam brought him his meals or let him stay at his house until he got back on his feet. He was a kind soul. On the weekends, he traveled either to LeRoy to see Grandma and his in-laws or to Buffalo to visit his brother Joe (Chapter 5), or they would come to his house. He did say that the only drawback about visiting Joe was that he had to see Joe's wife, Rose, who drove him crazy because she cried so easily.

Great-Uncle Sam in the 1930s.
He was a fun-loving man.

Uncle Sam wanted to be accepted by his other siblings, especially his sisters, but had a hard time getting close to them. He just couldn't express how he felt to them. When he went to visit his sister Mary, he would come back and say she was tough to talk to because she was so direct and uncompromising in her opinions. He seemed to get along better with Grandma since she was the oldest and helped raise him. One of his nieces characterized him as being an outsider and not as polished as his brothers. Despite this, the younger members of the family all have fond memories of him and liked him very much.

I think that part of Great-Uncle Sam's feeling of isolation was due to his the odd sense of humor. To give an example, when his son Chuck was born, he weighed only three and a half pounds. When he finally gained enough weight to go home, Great-Uncle Sam exclaimed,

"Get the roll ready, the wiener is coming home." This unusual sense of humor in part caused him to be seen as an outlier to the rest of his family.

According to family members, in his youth, Great-Uncle Sam was a bit of a hellion and spent some time in a minimum-security facility for petty theft. Since his mother Maria could not speak English well, much less write, her granddaughter Rita wrote letters to Sam while he was in prison. With his parents, my great-grandparents, working full time and being supervised only by his older sisters, he was left to his own devices and drifted into minor trouble.

Sam made his living working for the most prestigious men's clubs—such as the University Club of Rochester—so he knew some of the well-to-do patrons and TV celebrities in the area. My great-uncle worked hard all his life and built a nice home for his family in the town of Henrietta, a sprawling suburb of Rochester.

When World War II broke out, Sam joined the Army, and by the end of the war, he had reached the rank of Technician Third Grade, working as a supply technician. Technician Third Grade was basically a non-combat rank the equivalent of a sergeant. Great-Uncle Sam spent the war working at a supply depot making sure the fighting men had what they needed for combat. He was thirty-six when he enlisted, too old for a combat role, so he made his contribution in this way. I'm sure his civilian jobs prior to the war made him a natural for this role.

Great-Uncle Sam married Mary Riso on October 2, 1948, when he was forty years old. Coincidentally, one of Mary's sisters, Ida Martina, lived in an apartment house next door to us, so when Great-Uncle Sam and Great-Aunt Mary came to visit Ida, Sam naturally came over to visit us. In fact, he really didn't have any choice. If he came to visit his sister-in-law next door and failed to visit his sister, then there would have been hell to pay. It is, however, another example of his attempt to bond with his big sister. He was a good-natured, congenial man who always seemed to be in a good mood. On every visit, he stopped over at our apartment to pay his respects to my mother, who truly enjoyed his visits. He was my sister's favorite Great-Uncle and she remembers him as always smiling and being a kind man.

One summer afternoon in 1956 when I was five, Sam's intervention in my life changed it forever. I was in Grandma's front lawn with my Aunt Helen trying to hit a baseball. Helen, one of my mother's sisters, was pitching to me. My mother had just bought me my first baseball uniform, of which I was very proud. Great-Uncle Sam had just arrived at his sister-in-law's house and stopped in her front yard to watch me hit. After a few minutes, he came over to me and greeted me in his usual engaging way. He asked me if I had a favorite baseball team, to which I replied the Dodgers. I had just gotten my first pack of baseball cards as a present, and I had fallen in love with the style of the Brooklyn Dodgers uniforms. Great-Uncle Sam frowned and told me that the men in our family were all Yankee fans (I think he forgot about Great-Uncle Pete and his passion for the Baltimore Orioles). He went on to tell me that the Yankees had all of the good players like Joe DiMaggio and Phil Rizzuto—good Italian role models. My Aunt Helen, who was listening, agreed with Great-Uncle Sam.

I spent the rest of the summer wrestling with the idea of trying to like the Yankees and soon became a die-hard Yankees fan just like Uncle Sam. One day my mother came home from shopping with a present for me: a t-shirt with the Dodgers' logo on the front. I was a Yankee fan and I would rather have had a Yankees shirt, but I was stuck with that damn

Dodgers shirt until I grew out of it. Uncle Sam saved me a lot of grief and heartache given that the Brooklyn Dodgers only won one World Series and left Brooklyn for Los Angeles in 1958.

Sam died at the age of seventy-nine in the V.A. Hospital in Batavia, New York after being ill for a long period of time.

CHAPTER II

Great-Uncle Cosmo "Moxie" Barone

Born: April 25, 1913, LeRoy, New York
Died: November 7, 1962, Utica, New York

Left to right: Cosmo, Tony Argana, Sam Barone, and Ross Martina, 1961.

Great-Uncle Cosmo Barone was the youngest of Grandma's siblings, standing about five feet nine inches tall, making him the tallest of the first generation. He took after his father, Calogero, in that he was handsome, very tall, and stayed trim his whole life. Sicilians have a tradition of giving each other amusing nicknames. In LeRoy, some of the more unusual ones were "Nunni," "Acey," "Spike," "Iggy," "Mokey," and "Spotty." Cosmo's friends and relatives called my great-uncle "Moxie." Some say he got the nickname because he drank Moxie soda and others say it was because he had guts; maybe it was both. Cosmo was well liked but was always "working on something," according to a cousin on my father's side of the family who went to high school with him. Whenever one of the family members mentions his name, one of two reactions occur. Either they roll their eyeballs and say he wasn't one of the nicest of Grandma's brothers, or they smile and say, "What a character!" He was engaging and charismatic, so it is little wonder that he that he had many friends, and especially girlfriends.

Like his brothers, Cosmo looked up to his sister Carrie as a mother figure. Whenever he was in Rochester he made sure that he visited her and his nieces, who, like everyone else, loved his visits. Since Carrie was poor and struggling in life and did not have money for such luxuries as Christmas presents, Cosmo stepped up and bought them for everyone. His lone surviving niece still remembers his generosity and kindness. The one present that still stands out in her memory is a large dollhouse that showed up under the tree one year. She said there always seemed to be presents even though they were poor, and credited her uncle for his generosity. For all of his worldly ways, Cosmo had real sense of family and never forgot his roots and his sister.

From what I can tell, he wasn't very religious, and I never remember him visiting his older sister Carrie, my grandmother, during Christmas or Easter like his other brothers. By all accounts, he was outgoing and people he met remembered him long after he died. My cousin Rita and her husband Louie were on a senior citizens' trip in the 1990s and they stopped at a restaurant in Rome, New York, the city where Moxie had his last job and died in 1962. Rita thought that maybe some of these old people would remember Cosmo so she asked a group of old Italian men hanging out if they knew Cosmo Barone. They said that they hadn't heard that name in years, but of course they remembered him. They told Rita that he was full of stories of movie stars and famous people. They said that sure they missed him. Cosmo seemed to be more transient and restless than his other brothers, who, after settling down, lived in one place all of their lives. Cosmo moved around the country and never stayed in one spot for very many years. He had a house he built in Henrietta, New York that he used like a home base. From there, he moved from job to job from Reno, Nevada to Rome, New York. He was probably looking to get a better deal. If one compares the life that Grandma lived to the life that Moxie lived, their contrasts are striking. He was the youngest of nine children and twenty years separated him from Carrie. I'm sure that their parents, Maria and Cologero Barone, were worn out after establishing themselves in a new country

so they were more lax with Cosmo than their other children. Carrie, as a woman, certainly had limitations concerning what she was allowed to do as a child and teenager. She was very moral, but Cosmo, possibly because of the laissez-faire approach to his upbringing by their aging parents and the greater freedom he experienced because of his gender, grew up more hedonistic and had free reign to live his life on his own terms. And he did.

During the Depression, Cosmo worked for the Civilian Conservation Corps and helped build electric power plants in Tennessee. During World War II, he served in the Merchant Marines as a steward and was stationed in the Pacific. On his return from serving in the Merchant Marines at the end of World War II, he stopped in to see my Grandma. During his time in the war he grew a full-length beard that he neglected to shave before visiting her. As he was walking down the sidewalk to the

Cosmo home from the War, 1945.

front door, Grandma and my aunts were startled at the sight of this scruffy man approaching their house, and all of them went into a tizzy. They thought he was a dangerous beggar. After repeated knocks on the door, Cosmo finally yelled from the porch, "Carrie! It's Cosmo!" She peered through the window next to the door and replied, "You don't look like Cosmo!" After she stopped being scared, she got angry and told him that she would not let him in the house looking like a bum and that he should shave and come back when he was presentable. He did that and then he got a lecture from her about looking like a beggar. After hearing this story, I asked her, "Great-Uncle Ross has a beard, so why couldn't Great-Uncle Cosmo have one?" She replied, "Eh, Uncle Ross always had one." Later in life he did grow a tasteful, pencil thin David Niven-type mustache that made him look like a real rascal that I've been told the ladies adored.

Later, beginning in the late 1940s, Cosmo made his living as a head waiter and maitre d' in restaurants in Rochester, New York and Reno, Nevada. During his long tenure, he served many celebrities (he was acquaintances with "Bud" Abbot of Abbot and Costello) and was known to hundreds of customers/friends as the best in the business. Great-Uncle Moxie was sophisticated, an immaculate dresser, a great storyteller, and he enjoyed life to the fullest. One lasting memory I have of him is the image of him sitting in Grandma's kitchen smoking cigarettes, drinking Canadian Club and wearing brown and white spectator shoes. In general, I remember him as the life of the party. He was married twice. Nobody I ever spoke with remembered anything about his first wife, which was probably because he was divorced from her. All I know about his second wife, Yvonne, is that she was born in France. Cosmo also divorced Yvonne, who then also almost entirely disappeared from the memories of the family. My Aunt Dorothy remembers her as being very quiet, and when she did speak, she did so with a thick French accent that was hard to understand.

One day my Aunt Helen told me a story that I think puts Cosmo's life into perspective. She was going to Rochester to shop with a few of her girlfriends and Aunt Helen suggested that they stop into her uncle's restaurant, surprise him, and have lunch, assuring them he would treat them right. This was in the early 1950s, and in those days, going to Rochester from LeRoy was going to the "City," where you took the bus and dressed in your finest clothes including mink stoles and stylish hats. They found the restaurant and the waitress who met them said, "Oh, you must be friends of Cosmo. I'll go get him." My aunt was beside herself. She couldn't figure out how he knew they were coming. Her friends were thoroughly impressed with him and with the service they got and the fact that Cosmo picked up the bill. I tried to tell my aunt that nice good-looking young ladies coming looking for Cosmo was probably a regular occurrence. After all, the rumor was that he was a "ladies man." Aunt Helen defended him and wouldn't hear of it.

One summer I was staying with my Sicilian Aunt Florence and her husband, Uncle Joe, who was of German descent. Florence was only one year younger than Cosmo, and I found many family pictures that she saved of them playing together when they were young—they were very close. She was showing my cousin Joey and I one of her family albums. She showed us a photo of Cosmo and some her friends who were his guests at a restaurant where Cosmo was tending bar. In the photo he was serving them drinks and everyone was laughing, probably at one of Cosmo's jokes. Aunt Florence was telling us what a great time she had and what a great storyteller Cosmo was, relating all of his adventures mixing with movie stars and other celebrities. Just then my Uncle Joe interrupted her and insisted that Cosmo was in the mafia. Joe said he never wanted Florence to have anything to do with him ever again. He continued, "Look at the way he dresses, the cars he drives and the people he knows and the places he works." Aunt Florence turned blood red and went on the offensive. "Don't you ever say anything like that about my uncle again! I'll see him anytime I want!" She did, and that was the last time my uncle ever brought up the subject of Cosmo.

Cosmo, like my Great-Uncle Tony, was a character shrouded in mystery. Most of the family members thought he was involved with organized crime in some capacity like his brother. But whereas Tony had a flamboyant lifestyle, Cosmo was very discrete. He never brought any of his girlfriends to see Grandma nor was he ever arrested. He was like Teflon; nothing stuck to him. Many of my older cousins who also knew him have said the painting, *Cosmo Barone in Paradise* that depicts him as the ladies' man of his Reno days, cap-

tured his personality, as they knew him. The painting at the top is part of *The Agony in the Garden* by Andrea Mantegna. This represents the devout, pietistic Catholic way he was brought up, and the lower section represents the hedonistic lifestyle he chose as an adult. The showgirl over his shoulder symbolizes the glamorous world that surrounded him at the casinos in Reno and the high life that he relished. Cosmo met a violent end in the early morning hours of November 7, 1962, when he died in a car accident after closing up a restaurant in Rome, New York. Apparently, he fell asleep and crashed into a tree, suffering massive chest and head traumas. He died en route to the hospital. The funeral was held at St. Joseph's Church in Le-Roy, and since I was an altar boy

Cosmo Barone in Paradise, 2009, Egg tempera on panel.

by then, Grandma asked Father Zupa if I could be one of the servers in the mass. It was a solemn ceremony with a lot of people in attendance that I didn't know, but I felt very honored to be a part of it. After the funeral, my cousin Chucky and his father, Cosmo's brother Sam, were cleaning out Cosmo's house. Chucky got the job of packing up Great-Uncle Cosmo's belongings from his dresser drawers, and in one of those drawers he found nothing but silk stockings and contraceptives. So I guess the stories about his being a "ladies man" must have been true regardless of what Aunt Helen thought.

CHAPTER 12

Grandpa Francesco Gugino (Frank O'Geen)

Born: 1885, Valledolmo, Sicily
Died: March 13, 1941, LeRoy, New York

My grandfather, Frank O'Geen, was born in Valledolmo, Sicily and immigrated to America with his family on May 1, 1903 on the SS Sardeana. Though he bore the appearance of a true Sicilian, his surname was changed from Gugino to the Irish-sounding "O'Geen" at Ellis Island. The Irish name was supposed to help them become assimilated into American culture, but I'm sure when he showed up for a job he didn't look or sound the part. He was five feet two inches with dark wavy hair and an olive complexion. Unlike many Italians who were born in Sicily, he learned to speak English while here without much of an accent and had non-Italian friends.

Grandma's parents did not like Frank, possibly because of his personality and his attempts to become American as fast as he could, and the fact that none of his children were taught to speak Italian. He thought it was important for his children to become as invisible as possible, and if they spoke Italian they would be greater targets than they already were from the Americans who looked down on them. Italian was not spoken on the farm for the simple reason that all of the hired men that worked for him were non-Italians, and Grandpa thought that if the family was conversing in Italian the hired men would think the family was talking about them. From stories I have heard about him from my aunts, cousins, and people who worked and celebrated with him, he was a complex and multi-faceted person.

Soon after he married my Grandma, they bought an eighty-acre farm on December 1, 1915, at 9522 Asbury Road in LeRoy that they worked with an array of hired men. In order to buy the farm, his brother Joe and sister-in-law Lena had to be joint owners, since my grandpa did not have all of the money for the purchase of the property. Frank and Carrie had nine children; Florence died at birth and Anthony at six months. (I'm sure the death of little Anthony was something he was never able to overcome. My Grandma talked to me about little Anthony when she was in her mid-nineties, and she still cried over him.) Here he was, a farmer with seven girls and no boys to help him work the farm. Even though the girls were very little help to him on the farm, he very much wanted

My grandfather, Frank O'Geen, 1930s.

all of them to graduate from high school, which they all did. But without family workers he was not able to maintain the farm, and toward the end of the Great Depression he had to sell it.

My mother and some of my aunts remember Grandpa as a strict disciplinarian in the Mediterranean mold where the man is the absolute head of the household. The side he showed the outside world was in stark contrast to what he showed his family. Frank's Godson, Benny Joy, who worked with him on the farm, remembered him as a kind man and enjoyed working with him. Benny also told me that Grandpa didn't particularly like farming and wondered why he became a farmer in the first place. I'm sure the combination of having no sons and a farm where he felt out of place complicated his life to the extent that his situation was too much for him at times, and he was, consequently, hard on his family.

However, Frank could also be a really compassionate man. Grandma liked to tell the story that during the height of the Great Depression, Grandpa would bring home hungry and destitute men to the farm for a good meal. He did this repeatedly even though he wasn't a wealthy man and was barely scraping by himself. It was a great display of charity in the truest Christian sense. One man he brought home had a ring that had a huge amethyst stone of an absolutely beautiful hue that he gave my Grandpa for being so kind to him. Since the ring was old and unusual, Frank tried to give it back to him but the man insisted. My aunt said that for years Grandpa looked for the man whenever he went to town, hoping to give him back the ring; but he never saw him again. The ring is still in the family.

Grandpa liked his wine and loved playing cards, especially euchre, with a man named John Callan. Ironical-

The Italian Grapes of Wrath, *2007. Egg tempera.*

ly, they are buried right next to one another. Other cousins have described Frank as a scrappy little man who stood his ground when life got tough. The painting, *The Italian Grapes of Wrath*, is based on a photograph taken in the 1920s portraying a man taking what the world is dishing out to him. If you compare this painting with the image of him some ten years earlier in *The Arranged Marriage: No One Saw the Magpie*, he appears to have aged tremendously and is much thinner. In the background, you can see the house is falling apart; his clothes are old and torn with his daughters showing no signs of recognizing his struggles. They seem to be in their own worlds. He isn't smiling. This is the image of a man who knows only hard work. I chose a painting by Carlo Crivelli called *The Pieta* and took the mourning figures from this painting to symbolize his trials and tribulations. The border of pears, apples and cucumbers is also from a painting by Crivelli that in a symbolic way represents the life of plenty he aspired to but was never able to obtain for his family. On February 11, 1939 he sold the farm. He died in 1941 after battling liver cancer for several years.

LIFE IN CALIFORNIA: THE FRESNO O'GEENS

My grandfather had seven siblings that included two brothers, Joe and Tony, and five sisters. Great-Uncle Joe was married to a woman from LeRoy named Lena, and he was the first of the brothers to move to Fresno, California. He worked for the Metropolitan Life Insurance Company in Fresno and he made a very comfortable living as an insurance salesman. He became very affluent and assimilated into American society very easily. Since he was well off, he made occasional trips back East to Western New York with his family to visit his relatives.

Great-Uncle Joe hunting in the Yosemite Valley, 1925.

Great Uncle Joe was a very happy and popular man. He was slightly taller than my Grandpa, about five feet four inches, and heavier. He enjoyed hunting and went on hunting trips to the Yosemite Valley in search of jackrabbits. Pictures from family albums show a lifestyle that was in stark contrast to the Sicilian relatives in LeRoy; they actually looked like they enjoyed life. They were well dressed and had very stylish, furnished homes. The O'Geens of Fresno were middle- to upper-middle class Americans and the O'Geens of LeRoy were decidedly members of the struggling lower class.

Great Uncle Tony O'Geen, the youngest of the boys, was a very friendly, thin man who was well liked by everyone. He owned, at one time or another, a series of bars from LeRoy to Buffalo to Fresno. He served in World War I, and during one battle he survived a mustard gas attack. After the war, his respiratory system could not take the warm, humid summer weather in Western New York, so he moved to Fresno, California to be with his older brother Joe. Like his brother Joe, Tony made trips back East to visit relatives during the winter months because of his health issues. The two brothers lived "the good life" in California but Tony never married. Great-Uncle Tony also had an affinity for hunting, and a family photo (below) shows him surrounded by his hunting dogs. It looked like he lived an idyllic life.

One has to ask the question: since Frank didn't particularly like farming, why didn't he move out to California after seeing the success his brothers achieved? There didn't seem to be the same societal and economic barriers for Great-Uncle Joe and Great-Uncle Tony in Fresno that kept Frank poor and destitute in LeRoy. It was probably a combination of several factors. Since Grandpa was the oldest son, I'm sure it was his duty to stay with his parents and the money required for such a move with so many children kept him where he was. One must also keep in mind that he didn't seem to be close to his siblings, so why would he want to move across the country to be with them? Frank must have been caught between two worlds, wanting to be an American but not quite willing to give up his Italian heritage. From family photographs, both of my great-uncles looked like they lived a prosperous life in California, having vacation time to go hunting, join a hunting club, and buy modern houses with all of the amenities while Frank scraped by living on a run-down farm without indoor plumbing and never got a vacation. The contrasts were astonishing. My cousins in Fresno wore fine clothes and lived the "American Dream" decades before their cousins in Western New York. Meanwhile, back in LeRoy, New York, one of my aunts was forced to work in the bean fields just like Grandma did in her youth to help make ends meet. The career choices each of the brothers made took them down totally different paths with affluence on one side and poverty on the other.

Great-Uncle Tony surrounded by his hunting
dogs in Fresno, California, 1920s.

The Fresno O'Geens enjoying the good life in California, 1920s.

CHAPTER 13

Great-Aunt Giuseppa Gugino (Josephine O'Geen)

Born: October 18, 1896, Valledolmo, Sicily
Died: February 12, 1981, LeRoy, New York

Great-Aunt Josephine was the youngest child of Alfonsa and Antonino Gugino (Florence and Anthony O'Geen), my great-grandparents. She was very short, about four feet eleven inches, with a pleasant round face and a very warm personality. Josephine O'Geen married Joseph Micelli in 1921 and they had two children, Mary and John. Great-Aunt Josephine and Grandma became very close friends after the death of my grandfather. It wasn't because there was any bad blood between brother and sister; Grandpa just wasn't particularly close to any of his relatives. In fact, Great-Aunt Josephine thought the world of her brothers, even Frank who was distant. One time during a severe storm, Frank was driving Grandma and another woman to work at the Bean Shop and passed poor Josephine walking in the inclement weather and didn't even stop to pick her up. In fact, there were other times when he could have given his sister a ride but he never did. When Frank was dying of cancer, Josephine

Great-Aunt Josephine Micelli, 1920s.

thought of him and made her brother his favorite dish; stuffed mushrooms with a little bit of tomato. His strange, distant demeanor did not affect her feelings for him.

As the bonds of friendship grew stronger between the two sisters-in-law, Josephine became a frequent and welcome guest in Grandma's house. A recurring memory I have of summer evenings is of Great-Aunt Josephine sitting in the sun porch with Grandma sharing gossip and family stories, half in English and half in Sicilian. Like her brothers Tony and Joe, my great-aunt was a merry person.

Sadly, Great-Aunt Josephine eventually succumbed to Alzheimer's disease. Even though she had a hard time remembering people, she would leave the house unnoticed and start walking down Lake Street. Neighbors would call Michi, her daughter, to report sightings of her mother walking down the street. When Michi would catch up to her and ask my great-aunt where she was going, she would say, "I'm going to see Carrie."

The painting, The Celestial Tilt-O-Whirl, commemorates the close friendship these sisters-in-law had. Both women grew up under harsh and extreme circumstances and literally did not know how to have fun. They both had lost childhoods. The painting of my great-aunt and Grandma is based on a photograph of the two of them sitting in folding chairs at a family gathering. They were sitting on a small incline that made look like they were going to fall over or they were riding on a Tilt-O-Whirl. The Tilt-O-Whirl image also has another connotation. When St. Joseph's Parish had their annual lawn fete in the church parking lot next to our house, Grandma would sit in the yard looking at the carnival rides rubbing her neck. One day I asked her if there was something wrong. She replied to me, "No, but those people are crazy! Why do they want to ride that thing? The next day their necks must be killing them or they are too lame to get out of bed." To miss a day of work due to the luxury of having fun was a concept that she could not grasp.

The Celestial Tilt-O-Whirl, *2007. Egg tempera.*

When I saw the photo I had a flashback to that conversation and got the idea to depict Great-Aunt Josephine and her best friend, Grandma, finally having fun in the afterlife. For the background I used Raphael's *Disputa* and positioned Grandma, Great-Aunt Josephine, and the Tilt-O-Whirl on a cloud with Grandma's brothers, her sister Mary, and her brother-in-law Tony all waiting for a chance to have fun. Grandma's youngest daughter, Dorothy, is playing Italian songs on her violin as the angels in heaven all come out to see this truly remarkable event.

Great-Aunt Josephine kept many of the customs of Sicilian culture alive in her home, among them the Sicilian tradition of hosting a St. Joseph Table. In Lent, during the Feast of St. Joseph, March 19, Sicilians make a St. Joseph Table to ask for favors, to fulfill a promise they made to St. Joseph, and to celebrate their good fortune. My great-aunt prayed to St. Joseph to ask him to protect her son, John, while serving in World War II. She petitioned the saint to protect her son and if John returned home safe at the end of the war, then Great-Aunt Josephine promised to sponsor a St. Joseph Table in the saint's honor. When John came home from the war, she fulfilled her promise to him.

THE HISTORY OF ST. JOSEPH TABLES

The decoration of St. Joseph altars, a Sicilian tradition, began as far back as the Middle Ages in gratitude to St. Joseph, the patron saint of Sicily, for answering prayers for deliverance from a famine. The families of farmers and fisherman built altars in their homes to share their good fortune with others in need. To thank their patron saint, they gave back to him in the form of a feast presented on an altar.

Throughout the centuries, people who have prayed for a favor and were granted it, showed their appreciation by "hosting" a St. Joseph's table. Some common requests are the safe return of a loved one from a war (a very common request during World War II), or that a loved one will survive from a serious illness or accident.

THE ALTAR

The altar features three tiers, representing the Trinity or steps to heaven. A statue of St. Joseph sits on top of the altar surrounded by carpenter tools, flowers, candles, spaghetti, wine, lemons, artichokes, *cardunis fritti*, and of course, St. Joseph bread. Italian cookies and deserts, such as biscotti, canolis, fig cookies, and "meatball" cookies are found on the table in abundance. The finishing touch is to sprinkle breadcrumbs around the altar to symbolize sawdust from the carpenter tools. The altar can be simple or very elaborate, but it is always vegetarian. The table can also be described as a shrine or a place of pilgrimage. After the altar is constructed, a priest visits

Great-Aunt Josephine's St. Joseph Table, 1946.

the table and blesses it. Friends and neighbors are then invited to visit the table and share in the good fortune. In Sicily, after the table is blessed, the food was distributed to the poor or people less fortunate than one's own family.

THE BREAD

After the image of St. Joseph, bread is the most important component of the altar. The bread is braided or shaped into symbolic images and is part of the ancient tradition of shaped celebratory breads found in countries in the Mediterranean. Sicilians are particularly interested in the presentation of food, and St. Joseph bread is a perfect example of such a tradition. When Grandma made St. Joseph bread and shaped it into religious images, I would have to guess which saint or Easter symbol she made—usually St. Joseph or the Madonna and child, but I couldn't be sure. One year she totally surprised me when she shaped the bread into a lamb. Occasionally, I would guess right and she would feel satisfied, but when I guessed wrong she would be so disappointed and pointed out all of the clues I missed. I usually found my aunt and asked her for the right answer ahead of time. St. Joseph bread represents the concept that bread is transformed and transcends its role as food by becoming a way of celebrating the sacred and life itself.[1]

1   Anna Maria Chupa, "St. Joseph's Day Altars," *Houston Institute for Culture,* accessed May 7, 2008, http://www.houstonculture.org/cr/stjo.html.

CHAPTER *14*

The Second Generation

The children of Francesco and Calogera Barone O'Geen are:

Alfonsa (Florence) O'Geen

Died at birth

Alfonsa (Florence) Delores O'Geen

Born: June 27, 1914, LeRoy, New York
Died: April 25, 1995, LeRoy, New York

Antonino O'Geen

Born: September 7, 1915, LeRoy, New York
Died: April 7, 1916, LeRoy, New York

Marian Lenore (Mae) O'Geen

Born: January 29, 1917, LeRoy, New York
Died: January 28, 1998, Buffalo, New York

Concetta Patricia (Connie) O'Geen

Born: January 31, 1918, LeRoy, New York
Died: January 19, 2003, Lancaster, New York

Helen O'Geen

Born: July 28, 1919, LeRoy, New York
Died: April 29, 1994, Buffalo, New York

Antonina Joan (Lena) O'Geen

Born: March 13, 1921, LeRoy, New York
Died: March 17, 1986, Batavia, New York

Frances Anne (Franny) O'Geen

Born: March 25, 1926, LeRoy, New York
Died: January 06, 1992, Batavia, New York

Dorothy Onalee O'Geen

Born: February 29, 1932, LeRoy, New York

The second generation, 1947. Left to right: Florence, Lena, Marian, Franny, Connie, Helen, and Dorothy.

The second generation is composed of Grandma's daughters, my aunts. There were seven of them that survived to adulthood. This generation felt the effects of the constant Klu Klux Klan activity that took place in the town in the 1920s and 1930s, since they were all of school age and had to directly confront the bigotry of teachers and classmates. They all went to public school and they all told stories of being harassed and insulted daily by the non-Italians of LeRoy. In fact, my cousin, Pauline Seekins, Class of 1936, a relative on my father's side of the family, told me that when she was in school, she realized at an early age what was being done to her Italian classmates. The school district divided each class into two groups, an "A" and a "B" group. The "Americans" were group "A" and the Italians, African-Americans, and the "slow students" were in Group "B." She said LeRoy was a tough town to live in, especially if one was different.

My aunts never learned to speak Italian and learned to hide the customs of their parents in order to escape notice, and in the process they all achieved their goal of assimilation into American society. They succeeded in becoming Americans, and in every case they lost some or most of their Italian identity along the way. As was the case of most second-generation children of immigrant parents,[1] my aunts displayed their increasing independence by selecting their husbands with or without parental consent. They married outside of the nationality and even outside of the religion. Of the seven children, five married and two remained single. Of the five that married, only one married an Italian, three married German-Americans, and my mother married into the Methodist/Presbyterian MacPherson family that emigrated from Scotland in 1801 and was one of the original settlers of LeRoy, New York. With the exception of the oldest sister, Aunt Florence, they were spared Grandma's fate and did not have to work in the fields as farm laborers.

Every one of the married aunts, with the exception of my mother, moved out of the Italian neighborhood. As was typical of second-generation children, "intimate communication [was] maintained with the parental household, and the relationships with the parents as well as with immigrant relatives [were] affectionate and understanding."[2] My German uncles didn't think much of Italian culture and they were not too fond of Italian food. When my aunts were coming to dinner, Grandma would make them a traditional American meal of roast beef with potatoes and gravy; nothing "strange." The thought of eating burdocks made them sick, and my aunts catered to their tastes. (They did like and respect Grandma, even if they thought she was a little strange. My father, conversely, really liked Grandma and affectionately called her "Ma.") Consequently, my aunts never learned how to make many of Grandma's delicacies. Much was lost. I remember them asking Grandma to make them food that they had on the farm; she would, but not without some pointed comments about learning how to make it themselves. It was Grandma's legacy towards which they turned their backs.

Rudolph Vecoli, Professor of History and the Director of the Immigration History Research Center at the University of Minnesota for thirty-eight years, challenged the "melting pot theory" in the works of Harvard Professor Oscar Handlin in the 1960s. As the prevailing thought of the time, Handlin talked of a "brutal filter" that had blocked the transit of culture from the old country, which forced the immigrants to melt into American culture rapidly. Vecoli insisted in an article in the Journal of American History that Italian-Americans had in fact maintained many of their values, customs, and practices for generations after the original migration.[3]

My aunts, however, did not maintain the values, customs, and practices from the old country as some other members of the Barone family did. For example, Great-Aunt Mary's children spoke Italian and carried on Sicilian family traditions well into the third and fourth generations, but Grandma's daughters did not pass on our culture. My cousin Nancy Hough laments the fact that her family was not more enthusiastic about their Italian culture like

---

1   Paul J. Campisi, "The Italian Family in the United States," *The American Journal of Sociology* 53, no. 6 (1948), 443–449.

2   Campisi, "The Italian Family," 446–447.

3   Dominic Candelero, "GIovanni Schiavo and Professor Rudolph Vecoli: Their Legacies: Pride vs. Anti-Filiopietism," *The Annotico Report*, May 14, 2005, http://www.italystl.com/ra/2137.htm.

other Italian families. They seemed to fall into the "melting pot theory" and became Americans, but they paid a high price for their acceptance. As Ralph Gardaphe stated in his article, "Whites on a Leash: Italian-Americans and White Privilege in the U.S.,"

[Assimilation] has cost us the language of our ancestors—the main means by which history is preserved and heritage passed on from one generation to the next. For a few generations we have had to trade-in or hide any customs, which have been depicted as quaint, but labeled as alien, in order to prove equality to those above us on the ladder of success. In this way, Italian Americans have become white, but a different kind of white than those of the dominant Anglo/Saxon culture. Italian Americans have become whites on a leash.[4]

My aunts had to respond to the dictates of the dominant culture in order to survive. This description by Gardaphe fit my aunts, the second generation, perfectly. They wondered why I was so interested in this ancient history that to them was insignificant and brought back ugly memories, certainly nothing that they wanted to remember. When I spoke to my second generation cousin about the KKK activity in the area her first response was, "How did you find out about that?" and then admitted that it was frightening and horrible time for Sicilians to live in LeRoy. If I hadn't moved in with Grandma, any record of our family history would have been lost forever.

---

4   Fred Gardaphe, "Whites on a Leash: Italian Americans and White Privilege in the U.S.," I-Italy, June 24, 2008, http://www.iitaly.org/bloggers/3011/whites-leash-italian-americans-and-white-privilege-u-s.

CHAPTER 15

Aunt Alfonsa (Florence) Delores O'Geen (Gugino)

Born: June 27, 1914, LeRoy, New York
Died: April 25, 1995, LeRoy, New York

Aunt Florence, 1934.

Aunt Florence was the first child of Frank and Carrie O'Geen, my grandparents, to survive to adulthood. Florence's birth name was Alfonsa. She was named after my grandfather's mother, following the tradition in Sicilian culture. In Sicily, the first-born son and daughter are named after the husband's parents. The O'Geen's first child, named Alfonsa, died shortly after she was born, so my aunt, Alfonsa (Florence) Delores, was the second child to have this name. Like the rest of the family, she was short, standing around five feet tall, but thin. Aunt Florence was the only one of Grandma's daughters to understand Sicilian, but like the rest of them could not speak it.

Since my aunt was the oldest of the children, she became the daughter that helped out with the housework when Grandma went to help Grandpa work in the fields. As a result, her childhood was a watered down version of Grandma's life, except that as per Grandpa's wishes, she graduated from high school in 1932. As with many second-generation children, Florence "became an economic asset" to her family by working in the bean fields just like her mother.[1] Florence had dreams of becoming a nurse, but they were squelched when Grandpa told her she had to get a job as a farm laborer to help pay the ever-mounting bills—the same circumstances that Grandma went through. So, Aunt Florence went to Main Street in LeRoy and was herded into the back of a truck to work all day in the bean fields with the rest of the women and children. After the family moved into town when my grandparents sold the farm, Florence got a job working at Vitel Hosiery, a local industry where women's stockings were made. Since Florence was the oldest and a very obedient child, she did what she was told without any objections. As a result, she never had a real profession—just a series of jobs to help make ends meet. My aunt grew up before her time and never really had a childhood,

---

1   Paul J. Campisi, "The Italian Family in the United States," *The American Journal of Sociology* 53, no. 6 (1948), 444.

and as a result she was very serious. Yet even still, in all of the years I knew her, she never expressed bitterness about her lot in life or her lost opportunities.

Like Grandma, Florence had a real love of flowers, and she had a garden that people in town would drive by just to get a glimpse of what was in bloom. Of course, like everyone who had a garden of any sort, she had a never-ending battle with the deer that lived in the area. She loved tulips and bought them in all colors and varieties and waited in anticipation every spring to see them bloom, but just about every spring the deer would come into her yard and eat all of the buds before she got a chance to enjoy them. Needless to say, she had a love-hate relationship with deer.

I carried on the tradition of having a flower garden from Grandma and Aunt Florence and at every house I owned. My aunt gave me flowers to start my own garden. When my aunt was alive, we would both place orders for irises and daylilies from one of many flower catalogs she got in the spring, and then swap the bulbs when they grew and spread in our own gardens increasing our inventory. Now every time my flowers bloom I have fond memories of her.

Uncle Joseph Francis Burkart II

Born: November 20, 1910, New York, New York
Died: November 1986, Rochester, New York

Uncle Joe was about five feet six inches tall with a medium build, blue eyes, and was bald. He was of German ancestry from both sides of his family and was very conservative. He was very industrious and continued to do hard physical labor into old age. He might have been small in stature, but he was a fearless individual whose strong personality made up for any physical deficiencies he might have had. This was showcased very clearly whenever he and my Aunt Florence went to buy a new car for her. Unlike most people, my aunt dreaded buying a new car. In her eyes, Uncle Joe was totally rude to the salesman and usually left in disgust, abruptly ending the negotiations, and then waited at home for the expected phone call from the dealership with a better offer. He usually got the car for his price and would be so proud of his horse-trading skills but my aunt was mortified.

Uncle Joe was born in Queens and lived just a few blocks from the Steinway piano company. His family had to move out of the city because the youngest sibling, Bob, had respiratory problems and doctors advised them to move to upstate New York where the air was cleaner. Joe and his father traveled to Western New York around 1918 to the small town of Caledonia to look for a place to live. They spent the first months living in a barn, until they could purchase a house and send for the rest of the family. Eventually they found a parcel with eight acres that had a house, a barn, and a chicken coop located on the outskirts of Caledonia. On the south side of the property, the Rochester, Buffalo and Pittsburgh Railroad had a right of way through their yard (as an adolescent, Uncle Joe worked for the railroad cutting grass at the train depot near his house and knew all of the engineers and brakemen). And so, the Burkarts of Queens began a new life in the countryside of Upstate New York.

Uncle Joe only finished the eighth grade. The closest school in those days was in Scottsville, about eight miles away. Since there were no school buses, he took the train to school whenever he could. The engineer would stop the freight train at the crossing that went through the Burkart property and Joe would get on the caboose, and then when the train got to Scottsville the engineer would stop it and Joe would get off it and walk to school. To go home after school, he waited for the train to pick him up on the run from Rochester to Caledonia, if he was lucky. When he missed it he had to walk home. I thought this was the coolest way to go school except for the eight-mile walk home. He missed the train more often than he caught it on the way home, so he got tired of the walks in the rain and snow and quit school to help support his family. Despite the fact that he had very little formal education, he was a very smart man and could figure out how to do just about anything. He was especially good at figuring out mathematical problems in his head, which never ceased to amaze me since I am so mathematically challenged.

In addition to working for the railroad, my uncle made extra money for his family by trapping mink, raccoons, and foxes. Mink were fairly common around his house since a portion of their property bordered the Spring Creek, their preferred habitat. Uncle Joe had a trap line that he checked daily, and for a while he made good money from the pelts he sold. But the grisly nature of the job and dropping of the price of furs made the enterprise not worth the effort, so he started painting houses.

My aunt began dating Joe around 1932, right after she graduated from high school. They had a seventeen-year courtship that was interrupted by World War II. My uncle served in the army in the European Theater where he built airstrips and roads, and repaired railroads in France and Belgium. He achieved the rank of Technical Corporal (Technician Fourth Grade) and was in the zone of the Battle of the Bulge, the last German offensive at the end of the war. He told me that he was very close to action at one point of the battle and was guarding an ammunition dump. A French Captain was in charge who didn't speak any English, but Uncle Joe said they were able to communicate even though there was a language barrier. Their orders were to blow up the dump if the Germans were going to capture it. At one point, the Germans were in the area and my uncle and the other guards could hear the artillery blasts, so they wired up the dump with explosives, according their orders. The only

Uncle Joe in France during World War II, 1945.

problem was that if they had to blow up the dump, they would in all likelihood go up with all of the ammunition. Luckily, the American line held off the Germans and Uncle Joe came home without a scratch.

After the war, Florence and Joe started to date again, and they finally got married when my aunt told him either they get engaged or she was going to move on. In order for the marriage to take place in the church, Joe converted to Catholicism. By the time they were married on October 30, 1954, he was forty-four years old and she was forty. They had only one child, a son named Joseph Francis III, who was born December 21, 1957. My aunt was forty-three.

After the marriage, they built a house on a lot adjacent to his father's house that Uncle Joe's father gave them. I remember when the house was being built, my uncle doing a lot of the work himself. My aunt was the only person among her sisters to live in a house that was actually built for them. The others either inherited one or bought an old house that they fixed up. While the house was being built, the newlyweds lived on Lake Street with Grandma, so I got to see my new uncle on a regular basis.

When I was young, Florence was not one of my favorite aunts. Unlike her other sisters, Helen and Franny, she did not know how to relate to children. Helen would totally engage us with silly games and Franny would buy us ice cream and spoil us. Florence was serious and kept to the background. I was three years old when she finally married Joe Burkart, and she couldn't figure out why I got so jealous of him. Even though she wasn't my favorite aunt, I was jealous, and whenever I would see Joe, I would kick him the shins as hard as I could. Poor Uncle Joe would hobble over to Florence and say, "He did it again! Keep him away from me!" but I always found him or I begged my aunt to let me see Uncle Joe again with the promise, "I'll be good"; and of course I would kick him again. I was so mean to him. I actually think, however, that I did Grandma a favor because I gave Uncle Joe a lot of incentive to get the house built as soon as possible. It took Uncle Joe years to forgive me, but as I grew up and I treated him with respect, we developed a special bond.

Uncle Joe was a happy person who liked to play practical jokes on people, listen to good stories, and go dancing. He especially liked to flirt with the ladies, and always had a friendly word for my wife. It was innocent flirtation though, and no one ever took offense to him. He was very supportive and would do anything for someone if he liked that person; but, if he/she breached his code of conduct or broke his trust in any way, he would shun him/her. He wouldn't talk to or even look at that person. It would take a superhuman effort to mend any transgressions. I got on his bad side my first year of college in 1970 when I came home with long hair. I eventually cut it to get a job, but he shunned me for weeks. It took my aunt interceding on my behalf to finally break the deep freeze and get us back to normal.

As I stated before, Uncle Joe was of German ancestry and found much of Sicilian culture to be very strange, and he never missed a chance to tell everyone exactly how he felt. He especially wasn't very fond of Italian cuisine, except for spaghetti and meatballs and fried peppers and onions, preferring German delicacies like sauerbraten, sauerkraut, and potato dumplings that my aunt learned to cook for him from scratch. Since Uncle Joe liked spaghetti sauce, Aunt Florence learned to make a sauce very similar to Grandma's but much sweeter to satisfy my uncle's sweet tooth. Of course, the sauce was made from fresh tomatoes grown in their garden. I remember the crocks of sauerkraut in their basement full of cabbage rotting before my eyes. I thought it was really strange that anyone would voluntarily eat rotting food. It was a real challenge trying to eat sauerbraten for the first time. I had never smelled anything like that before.

Because Uncle Joe disliked Italian food, my aunt became less Italian and more assimilated into the unique combination of American and German traditions of my uncle. I remember when Florence would visit Grandma by herself and feast on *carduni*, she would tell us, "Don't let Uncle Joe know that I ate any." He thought that eating them was the most disgusting thing in the world, and for my aunt his reaction was a flashback to all of the rejections she received in high school because of the "peculiarities" of her culture. So as a result, she avoided having to confront my uncle's reaction to things Sicilian by giving up her culture and becoming more like him.

THE CARETAKER

As a teenager, Uncle Joe had a very unusual job that he got under equally unique circumstances. On the north side of his family's property was a fishing club owned by the world-renowned sportsman, George Bonbright (1875–1939). In Hoagy Carmichael's book, The Grand Cascapedia River: A History Volume I, Carmichael wrote, "an austere man with considerable nervous energy no more than 5' 4" tall, George Bonbright was as comfortable gunning for partridge and quail (he had his own large hunting preserve in Florida) as he was fly fishing for tarpon or salmon, or trolling for large sea-fish off the coast of California."[2]

Mr. Bonbright was also an avid trout fisherman, and was known by his peers as an innovator for developing several wet fly patterns that he used successfully on his private trout stream in Caledonia, the Spring Creek. Throughout their sixteen-year relationship, Uncle Joe learned from Mr. Bonbright how to fish for trout with wet and dry flies, and even learned to tie his own flies, and like his boss, devised his own patterns. Some of Uncle Joe's successful patterns did not have the same grace and beauty of Mr. Bonbright's flies, but his bucktails and streamers, unusual as they were to look at, sure decimated the fish population. Their working relationship played an instrumental role in shaping my lifestyle, and was ultimately the greatest gift that he passed on to me.

Joe met Mr. Bonbright under less than ideal circumstances. It was Columbus Day October 12, 1923, and Mr. Bonbright was having a large costume party at an estate named the Bungalow. Joe was walking through the field in the back of his house to go fishing on the 900, a public fishing section on the Spring Creek. As he was walking through the field, he happened to look over at the estate and saw that the cedar-shingled roof of the lodge had caught on fire from a spark that came out of the chimney. He immediately ran over to the lodge and alerted everyone and saved the building. Mr. Bonbright was so appreciative that he gave my uncle one hundred dollars, a large sum in those days, and started a working relationship with him. My uncle was hired to do odd jobs around the estate and help the full time caretaker take care of Mr. Bonbright's hunting dogs.

Joe was eventually hired as the full time caretaker and was put on retainer. He was associated with the estate for sixty-three years until his death, when I took over the responsibilities. Through the years, a syndicate of wealthy men from Rochester, mostly relatives of Mr. Bon-

---

2   Hoagy B. Carmichael, *The Grand Cascapedia River: A History, vol. 1* (North Salem, New York: Anesha Publishing, 2006), 152.

bright, owned the club and came to fish throughout the trout season. My uncle would patrol the property to keep poachers out and keep up the grounds around the lodge, and he was also a streamkeeper in the old English tradition. His job entailed removing trees that might block the flow of the stream, or snag a line or position logs to make the flow of the stream faster. He was always trying to think of ways to create "holes" in the bottom of the creek for the fish. There was also a boardwalk that had to be maintained so that one could fish without getting muddy feet. During the summer, he operated a hydraulic weed cutter that would cut the bottom of the creek like a lawnmower, as well as cutting the grass that grew on the bank so that when members fished their lines wouldn't snag on them.

Uncle Joe took his caretaking job very seriously, and in a lot of ways it was a labor of love. He looked at the Bungalow as his property, and much of the look of the grounds today is a result of my uncle planting peony bushes, lilies, and trees that he bought with his own money. The estate is located on the Spring Creek, with 28.6 acres of land with a lodge built in 1903 and a large dog kennel that later became the storage building for all of the machinery. The buildings were all designed by the nationally renowned American architect, Claude Fayette Bragdon (1886–1946), to fit into an overall plan. The main building is a reflection of Bragdon's progressive architectural style. This style was featured in his residential and institutional buildings during the early 1900s and was based on using geometry and music in proportion; in this case, it was a hip roof with sloping triangles on the ends and a rectangular building as the genesis for his inventive design. Bragdon, like his contemporary, Frank Lloyd Wright, controlled many aspects of the overall aesthetic of the building by even designing the furniture that still are part of the furnishings. The dog kennel, though smaller, has a similar roof design with one major difference: the addition of a cupola on its roof. Between them was a third edifice that was a unique twelve-foot square, sixty-foot high structure that captured the imagination of all visitors to the estate. This building effectively disguised the simple framework of a windmill and had a large cone-shaped, witch's hat roof. This is the building I could see easily from Uncle Joe's house, and when I was young was the building I associated with the property. This structure was torn down after it was struck by lightning in a violent thunderstorm in 2009. Its unfortunate demise changed the flow of the dynamic relationship between the buildings, and it is startling to see the vacant spot where it once stood.

The jewel of the whole estate is the Spring Creek, a spring-fed trout stream that flows through the middle of a heavily wooded area on the property that supports a wide variety of wildlife, including many species of warblers, scarlet tanagers, cardinals, Canada geese, ducks (mallards, wood ducks, and common mergansers), a wide variety woodpeckers, green and blue herons, hawks, kestrels, kingfishers, owls, mink, and red and gray foxes. Bears and coyotes pass through on occasion, and, of course, so do deer. This private estate acts like a forest preserve for the whole area, since the trout in the quarter-mile stretch that runs through the Bungalow's property are protected from overfishing in addition to having a safe habitat, while the posted property also provides a haven for animals during hunting season. It is an oasis in the middle of farming country.

To set foot onto the estate even today is like walking back into time. It would be an understatement to say Uncle Joe's roots ran deep with that place; so much so that at times he lost perspective of his role as caretaker. If an owner came to fish without telling him he would give this person a piece of his mind, since he wanted to make sure that the place looked its best—especially the creek. It was like the owners had to make a reservation to fish at their own club.

Uncle Joe quit at least once a year because of some perceived insult from one of the members. They would call him up on the phone and ask him to come back, but he wouldn't talk to them. My aunt had to be the intermediary, and that made her very uncomfortable. She had been brought up to obey authority and not make waves, so she thought my uncle's stand was petty. Finally, after she got tired of all of the drama, she would put her foot down and my uncle would talk to the owners and a deal was made with new concessions on their part. I think his plan was to make sure that no one took him for granted, so occasionally he would show them what it would be like if he actually left.

My uncle was an expert fly fisherman and had a reputation of being the best around the area. Sometimes the brown trout would grow so large—over thirty inches—that their cannibalistic tendencies put a strain on the fish population, decimating the middle- and small-sized trout. During times when the members were not successful catching these monsters, they would pay my uncle to rid the stream of them. He would go down to the creek at night and use one of his large wet flies like a bucktail or a streamer, and eventually he would catch them.

Joe with his catch of the day, 1959.

The days I spent with Uncle Joe working on the estate were some of the happiest of my childhood. Sometimes in the afternoon during the summer, my job would be to check on the grounds and stream. The main building, referred to as the Bungalow, is a magnificent structure. The main room has a huge dining room/living room area with a large rustic fireplace made of fieldstone that is the centerpiece of the room. On display on the walls are Mr. Bonbright's trophies from his years of traveling the world hunting and fishing. There are stuffed capercaillie that he hunted in Scotland (and which are now extinct), a moose head, a twelve point buck, an elk, an antelope, a water buffalo, his 136-pound tarpon (then the world's record, which he caught fly fishing with "The Bonbright Streamer," a fly pattern of his own design), and many trophy trout. The ceiling in this room is close to thirty feet high, so there is plenty of room for everything. There are stairs that connect to a walkway on the second floor that wraps around the perimeter of the room.

One afternoon as I was checking on the lodge, I walked into the main room and had the distinct feeling that I was being watched. As I turned around, there perching on the railing of the walkway directly behind me was a large hawk-like bird that I had never seen before. After a few moments of stunned silence, I tried to contain my excitement and slowly made my way to the pantry and hurriedly called my uncle on the phone. In a few short minutes, he appeared with a broom and a sheet. He walked up the stairs to try to capture the bird, and of course it started flying around the room, which was quite an image in itself. The majestic bird soared around the room with its large wingspan and ended up in a downstairs bathroom adjacent to the main room. I immediately closed the door. Uncle Joe then coolly opened the door with the broom leading the way. The petrified bird was cowering on the floor in a corner. I was afraid he was going to kill it, but to my relief he extended the broom and the bird grabbed it with its talons, and almost immediately my uncle covered it with the sheet. The bird calmed down instantly, and in a moment we were outside in the front yard. I was amazed at how expertly he captured it, limiting the stress and without any sort of injury to the bird.

My uncle told me the mystery bird was a sparrowhawk or a kestrel, a common falcon. It was a stunning combination of unexpected colors that ranged from slate blue-gray to white, and then rich tawny gold plumage with sharp features. I wanted to look at it forever, but after a few moments, my uncle took the rest of the sheet off to release it. The bird unfolded and flapped its graceful wings, dislodged itself from the broom, and then took off with the speed of a bullet and was gone forever over the trees. I was so captivated with what had transpired that I spent the rest of the day reading and drawing pictures of sparrow hawks from Uncle Joe's bird book.

Uncle Joe explained that every so often birds get in the building by going down the chimney, but this was the first time a bird so large made the journey to the inside of the building. The next day was spent on the roof repositioning the chicken wire that had shifted by the wind during a storm. One of the reasons I loved working and living with Uncle Joe was because I never knew what was going to happen on any given day. Every day seemed like an adventure with him. He was cool under pressure and was never at a loss of what to do when confronted with an unusual situation like the one I just described.

I remember the year I moved back to Western New York after living thirteen years in South Carolina, I mentioned to Uncle Joe that I hadn't eaten a fresh trout in years, and he asked me how big I like them. Before I got a chance to reply, he said, "How about fourteen inches?" That sounded good to me. The next day I came to work with him as I generally did in the summer, and found him fishing. He said, "I got some work for you to do. There are three fish on a stringer in the water that need to be cleaned. I've got to catch one more for you. I had a twenty-incher, but he was too big so I let it go." Then he asked me, "Which one of those do you want me to catch out there?" So I pointed to a trout and he proceeded to cast his line in the water. A smaller fish started to take the fly, but he yanked it out of the water because it was too small. If I was fishing I would have been happy with it, but it was under the fourteen inches he was trying to catch. He continued casting for a few minutes until he caught the fish he was after, and then I cleaned them all. I got out the fish deliar (a tape measure), and sure enough, all of the fish were fourteen inches or just a little bigger. He was such a master fisherman that he made it look so easy.

The worst part of Uncle Joe's job was when poachers came on the property and he would have to confront them. Most of the time they would take off as soon as they saw him coming, but a few were brazen and they would wait for him. Those were the times my uncle's German temper would come to the surface and it wouldn't be long before the poacher would be sent packing. He started carrying a pellet gun that he kept in his work wagon, and if he saw a troublemaker he would take it out. That would usually be enough for the trespasser to get the message. In the late 1950s and early 1960s he had a boxer/Great Dane mix, named Casey, which he had trained to chase any rough characters off the property. On several occasions, I accompanied my uncle when he patrolled the stream only to find a poacher fishing on the boardwalk. If they took off im-

mediately, then we would run to car and catch them leaving the property. Then my uncle would admonish them. Sometimes they would just casually keep fishing, working their way down to the path through the woods they used to get to the creek. These were the times that really infuriated him. The four of us, Uncle Joe, cousin Joey, the dog and me, would just keep walking toward the poacher until he unwittingly walked past his path of escape through the woods, and then Uncle Joe would sic the dog on him. It was hysterical to watch the poacher do a double-take and then try to run and reel in his line at the same time. Many times he got

Uncle Joe with his dogs Casey (left) and Pal (right), 1956.

to the end of the boardwalk and had two choices—either to run through the poison ivy and grapevines or jump in the creek without any waders and try to make it through the ice-cold water to the other side of the creek. Luckily, the dog never bit any of them but the message was sent for them to stay away. Times were different in the early 1960s.

On another occasion, a confrontation with a poacher did not have the same humorous ending. My uncle was an avid bird watcher and one summer he befriended a mallard duck that was unable to fly. Every morning he brought down a handful of feed for the poor bird because he felt sorry for it. It was amusing to see how attached the duck became to Uncle Joe. My cousin and I could not get anywhere near it, but as soon as my uncle started walking on the boardwalk the duck would appear from nowhere and swim around and serenade him.

It was very touching when my uncle would start talking to it as he made his rounds with the duck following him swimming up and down the creek.

Uncle Joe became very attached to the bird and checked on it several times a day, especially during hunting season. One day as we were working around his house, we heard a shotgun go off. My uncle stopped what he was doing and we all ran down to the creek. We heard someone making their way through the woods on the other side of the creek heading back to state land and the railroad tracks that served as the public access to the creek. We made haste to the railroad bridge that crossed the creek, and by the time we got there, we found a man proudly holding my uncle's duck by its feet. I've seen my uncle mad before, but this time he controlled his anger and asked the man where he got the bird. The man started bragging about how difficult a shot it was but that he had finally bagged it. Uncle Joe interrupted him and said to us, "This man shot your pet." Then he turned to the poacher and confronted him in a very cold voice, "I hope you're proud of yourself. What kind of a sportsman are you to shoot a defenseless duck that can't fly? When you go home, make sure you don't leave out that fact when you brag about this story to your kids. Don't lie. I know you trespassed on our property and shot a defenseless animal." The poacher started to get belligerent with my uncle, but Joe cut him off and warned the man that if he ever saw him anywhere near the estate he would call the sheriff, or better yet, get his shotgun and chase him off the property himself. We never saw the man again.

THE SOCIAL CLUB

Since Joe's house was near the Spring Creek, he met all kinds of interesting characters who came to fish on the public section of the creek. Some lived in Rochester and Buffalo and some came from out of state. Some were artists, machinists, engineers, teachers, factory workers and professional hockey players. If he befriended someone, then he/she could park on his property, knock on his door and have a beer before heading down to the creek to go fishing. Fishermen would pick his brain about the fishing, especially what hatches were emerging and where to fish on the 900 (the public fishing area). Joe was top dog in this menagerie of interesting characters. He held court every evening during trout season. My cousin and I would sit on the edge of our seats in the patio listening to the stories that these unique individuals told of their fishing exploits or the interesting lives they led. My aunt good-naturedly put up with all of these unexpected guests, since many of them were so appreciative of my uncle's hospitality that they would bring gifts or sometimes take them out for supper. If a piece of machinery broke on the estate, chances were he knew

Joe the house painter, 1960s.

somebody who could make a part for him or repair it free of charge. It was a great life, and he enjoyed it to the fullest.

My uncle had a great sense of humor and was always teasing people with a quick one-liner. My aunt and uncle had opposite personalities, but they were a good match for each other since my aunt was so serious and he was more of joker. Uncle Joe liked his spirits and especially enjoyed drinking his Genesee beer. He would have the local beer distributor drive a truck up to his house and it would unload as much as 20 cases of beer and ale that he stored in his basement. He believed in being thrifty, and he got a better deal this way. I'm not trying to imply he was an alcoholic since the beer lasted a while, and his place was like a social club. I never remember seeing him drunk. In the fall, he would buy two fifty-gallon kegs of sweet apple cider. One keg we would drink and the other he would make into hard cider or apple beer for himself and his friends. He had a refrigerator in his patio that was filled with beverages from which he and his friends and fisherman would have a few cocktails after work or before heading down to the creek. We never knew what he would have in his refrigerator or who would be visiting him.

THE MAN OF THE EARTH

Uncle Joe was a man of the earth. He was a house painter by trade and had such a good reputation for honesty and quality work that if anyone wanted to have him paint their house, he would put them on a waiting list that would be years long. He was, however, allergic to oil paint, so when his arms broke out in blisters he had to take time off until they healed. This is where the job at the estate came in handy, since he could work there and still get money coming into the house. However, my aunt had to get a job to help pay the bills. Since she did not have any formal training, she got a job working in LeRoy at an Italian grocery store where our family were loyal customers that was run by Agostino Rubino and his family. It was not much more than a minimum wage job, but Florence worked there until 1969 when the store burned to the ground.

Their fortunes changed when my aunt got a job working for Bell Telephone to repair telephones. She got the job because her sister Helen worked for the phone company for years as an operator, and then when the system became automated she took a job in the repair shop. The job was a godsend to Florence since she started to make union wages and got a pension.

Despite the fact that my aunt and uncle were better off financially, they still grew their own vegetables and canned or froze them to use over the winter months. Their garden contained large luscious tomatoes, hot and sweet peppers, green and yellow beans, carrots, beet greens, and Swiss chard. In the late spring, Uncle Joe's rows and rows of rhubarb would be ready to be made into relish and pies. Besides being an ardent fly fisherman and caretaker, he was a birdwatcher and an arborist. Even though he was so different from my Italian-American family, he became the main role model of my life. Since my father was an alcoholic and absent for weeks on end, Joe filled the gap in my life and taught me how to grow up. My mother wanted me to have a male role model, so she let me go to visit them as much as possible on weekends. When I was thirteen and fourteen, I spent summers with them helping my uncle paint houses and work the caretaker job at the adjacent estate. Their house became my home away from home, and Uncle Joe became my substitute father, while my cousin was like a brother; I thought I was in heaven.

Uncle Joe was so supportive of me, and the bonds between us grew so strong, that we forged a relationship stronger than the one I had with my own father. On my weekend visits to my aunt and uncle's house, the days would be filled with walking around his property or the fishing club seeing how many different birds we could identify, or meandering down to the trout stream to see if we could catch the big brown or rainbow trout, since only he knew where they were hiding using just the right kind of fly. In the winter he would teach my cousin and me how to tie flies or make birdhouses. He introduced me to a way of life that was so different than the matriarchal Italian lifestyle on Lake Street that he became a strong influence on my life and eventually the art I produced. When I lived with my aunt and uncle I never wanted to go home.

CAUGHT IN THE MIDDLE

My aunt was a very good cook and always made something special whenever I came to visit—usually pizza from scratch, homemade biscuits for breakfast, or a fresh pie of some sort. Her fresh peach pie was the best I ever had. When I painted houses with Uncle Joe at the age of thirteen, Aunt Florence would send along a whole peach pie and some sandwiches on homemade bread for lunch. Over the course of that day the two of us devoured that pie. She used to say that I only liked two kinds of pie; hot and cold.

Since Uncle Joe was not Sicilian, he could not comprehend the close attachment Florence had with her family. Florence was caught in the middle between two cultures. When my mother got cancer and Grandma's health started to decline, the other sisters took turns giving Franny and Dorothy a break since they were the main caretakers of both of them. When it was Florence's turn to pick up the slack, Uncle Joe did not want her to go to LeRoy. Her sisters thought she was shirking her duties, and some animosity ensued. They believed everyone should do their part. Uncle Joe didn't see the need for his wife to involve herself in these caretaking responsibilities, because when he thought of "family" it just included his nuclear family not the extended family of siblings and a parent. In his eyes, Florence had her own family to worry about. Florence agonized over this situation, and sometimes she just made him mad and went despite his objections. He never understood the bond of the extended family, since the Burkart family, after they married, saw one another once a year (if that), and then went their separate ways. When Joe's father

Aunt Florence in Grandma's sun porch, 1960s.

got too frail and needed extra help, he was sent to an extended care facility. All of my aunts outlived their husbands, and they all found strength with each other and came full circle in their relationships with one another. When they lived on the farm, all they had was one another, and as each one became terminally ill they once again became closely linked to each other, this time as a support group.

Uncle Joe was one of the few relatives who supported me in my quest to be an artist. He encouraged me to draw and he enjoyed looking at my new work, especially when I started to learn watercolor. My earliest works were drawings I did on-site at the estate. After work, I would get my sketchbook and go down to the stream and draw for a few hours. One year in undergraduate school, when I was taking a course in etching, I did a print based on one of the drawings I had completed over the summer, and titled it Burk's Brook as a tribute to him. The print hung in their house until my aunt died and the house was sold. One time toward the end of his life, I painted him a watercolor of a largemouth bass. He was so impressed with it that he showed it to everyone who came to his house. He thought it was so lifelike that it was going to jump off the paper.

JOE'S DECLINE

Joe developed heart trouble and eventually got diabetes. His heart got so bad that he went into the hospital to have a quadruple bypass. The weekend before he was scheduled to have the operation, I went to visit him. When I got to his floor in the hospital I saw him sitting in the lounge with my aunt. He greeted me with, "Why didn't you tell me you sold a print to the hospital! I would have walked around and found it as soon as I got in here!" Above him in the lounge next to his room was the woodcut of a winter scene I had done a few years earlier. My aunt told me that every time he meets a new nurse or receives a visitor he brings them down to the lounge to show them. He was so proud of me, and in his eyes I was such a big success becoming a college professor, and on top of that my gallery had sold one of my prints to the hospital for their art collection. I couldn't believe how fate had intervened to make such a touching moment in our lives.

At the end of our visit, I told him how much he meant to my life and I thanked him for overlooking the fact that I used to kick him in the shins. He told me that he would be home before I knew it. He said, "What, do you think I'm not going to make it?"

On the day of the operation as the nurses and doctors were wheeling him out of his room, my uncle made them take a detour to the lounge so he could see my print one last time before the operation. While there he told everyone that his nephew did that print and how talented I was. My aunt told me that the doctors and nurses were trying to get him into the operation room but that he insisted that they let him look at it for a little while, which they did.

After the operation, the surgeon came to my aunt, my cousin, and I with the news that everything went fine and that we could visit him for a few minutes. We found him in the recovery room still unconscious from the operation. I told him I would visit him the next day and I touched his foot. The next morning I got a call from my Aunt who told me that during the night he had taken a turn for the worse and that he died never regaining consciousness. Then I realized that one of the last thoughts he had was about me and how proud he was of me.

The painting, *He Never Looked at My Aunt That Way*, seen below, commemorates his life as a sportsman. He is holding the largest fish he ever caught, a thirty-six inch brown trout that weighed ten and a half pounds, dressed. The look on his face says everything. I placed him near the spot where he caught it and the place where we shared such wonderful memories that had a profound impact in my life. To make the painting a posthumous statement of his life, to the right of Joe's hat I depicted him as angel in heaven spending all day chasing the big fish. I cast the fish in plaster and then hand painted them in the colors of the three fish he caught his whole life; rainbow, brook, and brown trout. To give the work a surreal feeling, I adhered them to the painting and the frame that I painted like a view from underwater. At various points on the frame, I stuck some of the flies he actually tied and a stringer of fish.

He Never Looked at My Aunt That Way, *2008. Egg tempera on panel with cast fish and tied flies.*

LIFE AFTER UNCLE JOE

After Uncle Joe's death, Florence, Joe's brother, Bob, and I continued the family tradition and worked at the Bungalow. Like Grandma, Florence was busy doing physical labor well into her late seventies. She liked the outdoors, and her house and yard always looked immaculate. She cleaned the lodge, mowed the lawn at the estate as well as her own, weeded her gardens, raked leaves, and was active with social clubs. She was even elected Senior Citizen of the Year.

Many times during the year, my family and I visited her on the weekends just to chat, or to help her with a project. Of course we were always expected to stay for supper. After spending a day working at the estate, I had a standing invitation to stop at her house on the way home to have a cup of tea with her. Inevitably, she had some of her homemade pie left over from the day before or some Italian cookies. We would spend time talking about family or the work we did that day. She liked the simple pleasures in life, and if I saw some unusual wildflowers growing around the estate, we would take a walk to see them. Occasionally, the Canada lilies would bloom along the stream or in the woods, and that would be a real treat. Unfortunately, cancer has ravaged my family, and Aunt Florence did not escape it. I remember the day she told me that she had felt sick for weeks and was finally going to see her doctor. After a barrage of tests, my aunt received the dreaded news: she had colon cancer. Within a year she was dead.

CHAPTER 16

Aunt Marian Lenore (Mae) O'Geen

Born: January 29, 1917, LeRoy, New York
Died: January 28, 1998, Buffalo, New York

Aunt Marian was the second child of my grandparents. She was about five feet two inches tall. My aunt was very shy, possibly because her eyes were crossed, supposedly from a fall she took in the barn when she was still a child. When she turned eighteen, she had corrective eye surgery. Marian was Grandpa's favorite child because of her accident, and he exempted her from doing any of the chores around the farm. Her sisters resented his decision, but because of Marian's gentle nature, she was well liked by all of them. She was extremely close to her sister, Concetta (Connie), and they remained inseparable all of their lives. They even married brothers and had a double wedding ceremony. Since their father, Frank O'Geen (Gugino) (Chapter 12), had died earlier in the year, on March 13, 1941, their mother, Carrie, forbade them to wear white, so Marian wore a rust dress with a matching hat and Connie wore a burgundy dress and hat. Needless to say, they hated what they wore, but they respected their mother's wishes and got married in this very strange wedding apparel. These dresses must have been hideous since my cousins cannot find any wedding pictures.

I remember my aunt as a very sweet and friendly person who was one of the nicest individuals one would ever want to meet. Whenever Marian visited Grandma, she was always so happy to see each and every one of us that she made us feel special. Many people could not tell my mother and Aunt Marian apart, as they they looked so much alike that they could have been mistaken for twins. In fact, all of the O'Geen sisters had an uncanny resemblance to each other, and were unmistakable as sisters.

Before my aunt was married, she made money as a babysitter and nanny. She worked for a couple on their farm taking care of their children, and liked that position a lot. Marian was a nanny for Great-Aunt Rose and Great-Uncle Joe Barone's (Chapter 5) twins, Gerald and Geraldine, but she didn't like that as much. It seems that her aunt and uncle treated her like an indentured servant rather than a niece. For example, they always made her eat with the children and not with them, making her feel inferior. Things were different on the farm, where she felt more like an adult member of the family.

Uncle Raymond Leonard Schrader

Born: August 31, 1912, Lancaster, New York
Died: December 21, 1973, Buffalo, New York

Uncle Ray was very short, five feet two inches, with a slight build. He was a tough little guy of German descent, and from a very young age I was scared of him. My uncle was not mean to me, but he had a look that said, "Don't mess with me." As I got older and was able to see through his facade, I found him to be friendly. He was a native of Lancaster, New York, which was about 40 miles west of LeRoy, near Buffalo, so it was a strange twist of fate that he met my aunt and started courting her. Ray's grandmother lived in LeRoy near the farm where my aunt grew up, so while visiting his grandma, my Aunt Marian caught his eye. Since Ray visited often, a romance ensued. He had a brother named Franklin who met my Aunt Connie the same way. The four of them were married on December 27, 1941. Then the four of them moved to Lancaster and lived just blocks apart from one another. Ray and Marian had three children, Nancy, Judith, and Richard. They grew up near Franklin and Connie's two children, Bob and Paul, and the two eldest remained close throughout their lives.

Uncle Ray was drafted into the army in 1944 toward the end of World War II at the age of thirty-two. The army was getting desperate and started taking men with children. He was in the Corp of Engineers and was sent to Pacific Theater, where he was stationed in Guam. He made the rank of Technician Fourth Grade. Before being drafted, he worked for a company called Buffalo Arms that made M2 Browning machine guns. There, he was a tinsmith, primarily doing sheet metal work. After joining the army, he did the same type of work, refitting machines. He was lucky, since he did support work in Guam and saw no action.

Uncle Ray and Aunt Marian, 1941.

My uncle graduated from St. Bonaventure College (he went there on a full scholarship) and acquired all the credentials to teach math. At the time, however, there were no teaching jobs. This is when he took a position working at Buffalo Arms. After the war, my uncle would have had to go back to school if he wanted to teach, so he worked at DuPont in Tonawanda until they moved to Delaware. He was offered a transfer but didn't take it. Uncle Ray worked in several places, and when there was no work, he helped his father, who was a plumber. Then there were no sheet metal jobs, so his father retired and Uncle Ray took over the business. The country was in a recession, and people had jobs to be done, but they could not pay. Uncle Ray struggled along for quite a while, until Buffalo Forge had an opening for a sheet metal worker and he went there for the last nine years of his life. At Buffalo Forge, he was probably over-qualified for the work he was doing, but he seemed to really like it since he didn't have to worry about collecting unpaid bills from his plumbing customers.

Franklin, Ray's brother and fellow Red Man, marching in a parade, 1970s.

LIFE IN THE SCHRADER HOUSEHOLD

Uncle Ray didn't like much Italian food except spaghetti and meatballs, which he loved. My aunt made her own sauce and always put a pork chop in it to give it the indescribable flavor of the sauce our family made. She let it simmer on the stove all day, sending the sweet smells of Sicily all over the house. Occasionally, she made stuffed rigatoni, but essentially that was it. She only made what her husband liked. She loved to go to Grandma's house, where she got her two favorite foods, stuffed artichokes and homemade ravioli. One summer, there was a large family reunion planned to take place at their house. Grandma was making *cardunis* and other Italian delicacies that were going to be consumed at the picnic. When we got there, Uncle Ray and Uncle Franklin were heading out the door on their way to their fraternal organization, the Improved Order of Red Men, to have a steak dinner. They didn't want any part of what the Italians called food.

The Red Men are a "non-profit organization devoted to inspiring a greater love for the United States and the principles of liberty." This patriotic organization is chartered by Congress, and traces its origins back to the secret patriot societies in pre-Revolutionary War times. The organization appropriated Native American (Iroquois) customs, rituals, and terminology. Each charter is referred to as a tribe or council.[1]

For certain important occasions like parades, the members dress up in full Native American costume. This is a reference to the Boston Tea Party when colonists dressed up as Mo-

----

[1] "Who Are the Red Men?," *The Improved Order of Red Men*, 2015 1998, http://redmen.org/redmen/info/.

hawk Indians. In the twenty-first century such fraternal organizations seem politically incorrect. To glorify parts of a culture and a group of people viewed as savages that Americans tried to wipe off the face of the earth is in poor taste. My uncles were attracted to the organization because of its patriotic and its charitable programs. In the late 1940's in the aftermath of World War II and the advent of the Cold War, Americans like my uncles were very patriotic and showed their love of country by joining organizations like the Red Men.

My uncle was the absolute head of the household, and my aunt did what pleased him. She rarely objected to anything he did. As a result, she never pushed her Italian heritage on her children. My cousin Nancy Hough told me that she regrets that her family was not more enthusiastic about being Italian the way other families were. Aunt Marian didn't really intentionally try to hide her heritage, but she didn't really want to talk about it either. Maybe it was because she had her sister Connie living just a few blocks away. Since they had each other, they didn't feel the need to tell "outsiders" about the family. As my cousin Nancy observed:

They were always very close and talked on the phone several times a day. We would go in one car to LeRoy and they would talk all the way down and all the way back. As soon as they got in their houses, they would be on the phone talking to each other. I think they were both happy to have moved away from LeRoy and out from under Grandma's scrutiny. I think they had great sympathy for Lena and Franny (her sisters) because they seemed to be constantly given advice by Grandma. Florence, Helen, and Dorothy (Marian's other sisters) didn't seem as affected by living so close to Grandma.

My aunt did give my cousin an interesting word of advice: "Don't marry an Italian." She felt that they were too domineering and didn't treat women right. In Sicilian culture, "the father can punish children severely" and he is "consciously feared."[2] Aunt Marian's mother, Carrie O'Geen, in a conversation to me in 1990, said that she felt that her husband Frank took her for granted and never gave her a compliment. The general consensus between Marian and some of her sisters about their father was that they were afraid of him. This was in contrast to Great-Uncle Tony Argana, whose children looked at him as a loving husband to my great-aunt, as well as a caring parent.

Uncle Ray did have a fondness for his Sicilian relatives because his own family life was very different. His mother rarely cooked and was not much of a housecleaner. She was the exact opposite of his mother-in-law, Carrie O'Geen. Even though he used to kid my aunt about the big family gatherings, I think he really enjoyed them. He socialized with the other men there. Sometimes, however, he used to get exasperated with the women's trivial bickering and would make a quick getaway to the Red Men's club.

In Italian families, the emphasis is on a strong family and community culture. If a family member needs help and someone has a skill to get them out of trouble, then that person steps up and volunteers. Ray and Franklin were regularly dragged into that. Whenever Carrie had any sort of plumbing or electrical problems, on a day off Ray and his brother Franklin would make the forty-five minute drive to LeRoy from Lancaster and fix whatever was wrong for free. Grandma would give them beer, but it was clear that they didn't like having to be there. When I got my first car from my godmother, Aunt Franny (Chapter 20), my uncles were enlisted by Grandma to get the car on the road. It was a 1960 Ford Fairlane with fins and bad

---

2   Paul J. Campisi, "The Italian Family in the United States," *The American Journal of Sociology* 53, no. 6 (1948), 445.

paint job that had been sitting in the garage for a year, so it needed a lot of help getting on the road. After a trip to Western Auto with my uncles to get a new fuel pump and a set of points and plugs for a good tune up, the car ran like new. This was the first time I bonded with them and saw them in a different light. It was then I realized what good family members they were. Because Ray and Franklin were brothers as well as brothers-in-law, I think they felt as though it was their family to a certain extent, regardless of the cultural differences. Since they were men, Carrie never challenged my uncles or tried to push them around like she did her daughters. She knew she couldn't get away with it.

My Aunt Mae and Uncle Ray got along well. Sometimes she thought he drank too much, but he never seemed to get into any trouble and always worked. One Christmas in the mid-1960s, Uncle Ray and the rest of his brothers-in-law were playing cards and drinking beer in the kitchen. Aunt Marian was worried that her husband was drinking too much and went into to the kitchen and told him to stop. Uncle Ray had already had a little too much to drink and so told her to mind her own business. Since my aunt was a sensitive soul, she started crying and went into the dining room where Grandma and her sisters were congregating. In a matter of seconds, Grandma appeared in the kitchen and demanded Ray to stop drinking. Ray didn't like being shown up in front of the other men, and told his mother-in–law to get back into the other room with the rest of the women. Grandma made a hasty retreat and came back with reinforcements, her two daughters Florence and Franny. She sat down across the table from Ray and read him the riot act in broken English with Florence and Franny glaring at him as well. All of the men stopped drinking. There were no hard feelings between mother-in-law and son-in law after that. Grandma expected him to act that way since he was a man and he was a good husband to her daughter, and besides, Uncle Ray had done enough work on her house to get a pass. She didn't want that perk to end.

Tragically, Uncle Ray had a massive heart attack at the age sixty-one while driving three men to work at Buffalo Forge in a car pool. Miraculously, he made it to the parking lot of the company before he succumbed. The nurse at Buffalo Forge tried to revive him, but to no avail.

After the death of my uncle in 1973, my aunt's life changed dramatically. Up to this point in her life, she took care of the house and was very dependent on her husband to take care of the outside world's business. Aunt Marian was nervous and tentative of new situations, and suddenly she was thrust into a role where she had to confront her fears. At the age of fifty-three, she had to get a job to make ends meet. In order to work, she had to get a driver's license, and when she passed the driver's test, everyone was amazed. There are certain incidents where driving requires a quick response, and Aunt Mae did not seem to be the kind of person who could respond quickly. But she overcame her fears, and in the process became more self-sufficient. I was impressed. Of course, it helped to have her trusty sister Connie at her side to be another set of eyes. My family always looked out for one another, so when Aunt Marian drove Uncle Ray's car into the ground, my Aunt Florence, who had been driving for some time, bought a new car and gave her old one to her sister Marian. She was one of only three aunts who learned to drive late in life, and none of the rest, my mother included, ever learned to drive. In fact, to think of them driving at all was a scary proposition. The O'Geen sisters, except Florence and Dorothy, were not comfortable around any sort of machinery and became hysterical when things went awry.

Aunt Marian sometimes seemed scattered, and did things that made me scratch my head. One day, with her newfound freedom with the car, she went to the grocery store and parked her car at the far end of the parking lot. She was always very aware of safety and wanted to be sure she parked where no one would scratch her car or make it difficult for her to maneuver or lie in wait to accost her. When she was through shopping, she came out and realized that she had not only left the car unlocked, but that she had left the car door wide open with the motor running. No respectable car thief would have even thought about stealing her car since it sure looked like it was part of a sting operation. Many a laugh was had reliving that escapade.

Aunt Marian's house was probably a hundred years old and located in one of the older parts of Lancaster. It had uneven floors and doors that creaked and didn't shut properly—all the characteristics that make an old house interesting and unique. However, this also caused problems on occasion. One winter in the late 1970s was colder than usual. My aunt called my mother, Lena, on one of these cold mornings, crying hysterically. My mother thought something bad had happened and asked her sister what was wrong. It turned out that her panic was brought on by some frost on one of the walls in her closet. Aunt Marian felt threatened by the cold that was invading her house and cried, "It's just like Siberia! It's the end of the world!" My mother was used to Aunt Marian's hyperboles, and explained that it was probably because the house was old and that the closet was on the outside wall of the house and probably had no insulation. That seemed to calm Aunt Marian down and lay to rest her fears that the end of the world was nigh.

Aunt Marian died of cancer in 1995. One lasting memory I have of her goes back to when I was three. My mother and I were visiting her for a few days at her home in Lancaster. It was early morning, and I was still in bed. I heard my mother and aunt talking in the kitchen, and the smell of perking coffee was in the air. It smelled delicious. When I got up, my aunt bought me cinnamon fry cakes for breakfast. To this day, whenever I smell coffee perking and eat cinnamon donuts, I think of her with fondness. To an Italian woman, this is a good way to be remembered.

CHAPTER 17

Aunt Concetta (Connie) Patricia O'Geen

Born: January 31, 1918, LeRoy, New York
Died: January 19, 2003, Buffalo, New York

Aunt Connie as a young woman, early 1940s.

Aunt Connie was the third child of Frank and Carrie O'Geen. She hated her birth name, Concetta, so she went by Connie. I think the name caused her unwanted attention in school and sounded so un-American that she was embarrassed by it. Connie was one of the tallest of her sisters, reaching five feet five inches. She was more outspoken than her other sisters and had an independent streak. All of the O'Geen sisters kept very clean houses but Connie's house was the cleanest. She was a cleaning freak. Her house was so clean we could literally eat off the floors.

When it was spring cleaning time at Grandma and my mother's house, Connie would come and spend a few days to help with the cleaning. First, Franny and Connie and my mother would clean Grandma's apartment, and then they would turn their attention to my mother's side of the house. Mind you, these apartments were very clean anyway, but Connie would go to extremes, like take the hardware off of the kitchen drawers and clean behind them in order to make sure everything was immaculate when she was through. She hated clutter and would also go through closets and drawers and throw out all of the things she thought were unnecessary. At times, however, important family heirlooms like Grandma's second favorite *carduni* knife disappeared after one of her marathon cleaning visits. She was a cleaning dervish. Connie was also a very devout Catholic attending mass every morning. She even worked for her parish in the rectory, cleaning and making meals for the priests.

THE BREAKDOWN OF OLD WORLD VALUES

Because of her independent and outspoken nature, Connie clashed with her Old World Sicilian father on many occasions. She grew up in the world where women were second-class citizens, and in Sicilian culture men were superior to women and the father was the absolute head of the household. In Paul Campisi's article "The Italian Family in the United States" he observes,

> There are two phases in the breakdown of the Old World foundation, the Conflict Stage and Accommodation Stage. The Conflict Stage is chiefly characterized by the conflict between two ways of life, the one American and the other Italian, and by the incompatibility of parents and children. This phase begins roughly during when the children unhesitatingly express their acquired American expectations and attempt to transmit them to the family situation, and when parents in turn attempt to reinforce the pattern of the Old World peasant family. This is the period of great frustration and of misunderstanding between parents and children. In this undeclared war between two ways of life it is the parents who have the most to lose, for the complete acceptance of the American way of life means the destruction of the Old World ideals.[1]

Left to right: Aunt Connie, Uncle Franklin, and Aunt Marian, 1941.

One day in 1985, when Aunt Connie was visiting my mother, I asked them about Grandpa and what kind of man he was. My aunt told me that she frequently clashed with him. It got so bad that when Connie had just graduated from high school she informed her father that she was going to move out of the house and leave the farm. She had plans of moving into LeRoy to live by herself in an apartment. A heated argument ensued.

From my grandpa's point of view, a move of this sort would bring tremendous shame onto the family. My aunt explained to me that in those days, if a woman lived alone it was because she was either a widow or a prostitute. It just wasn't done. Since Connie was neither, my aunt remained at home but her relationship with her father was never the same. Grandpa expected everyone to pull their weight and work together to help the family survive, and conflict was counter-productive. I believe my grandfather reacted in a way that from the point of view of his culture was perfectly accept-

---

1   Paul J. Campisi, "The Italian Family in the United States," *The American Journal of Sociology* 53, no. 6 (1948), 448.

able. He was only reacting to "the force of external pressures coming from outside the Italian colony."[2]

As I stated in the chapter on my grandfather, Chapter 12, Frank O'Geen tried to assimilate into American society, but it wasn't possible for him to totally assimilate, especially when it came to relinquishing his authority as head of the household. In Sicilian culture, the father's word is law, so Grandpa acted on the belief that he was within his rights as a father. The clash of generations is a timeless conflict. Sometimes the differences are reconciled and other times they go unresolved.

The sad thing about this episode between Connie and him is that my grandfather died before the Accommodation Stage, at which point the conflict is reconciled, was able to take effect:

This period begins with the realization by parents and children that the continuation of hostility, misunderstanding, and contraventive behavior could result only in complete destruction of the family. The ambivalent attitude of the children towards the parents, of great affection, on the one hand, and hostility, on the other hand, now tends to be replaced by a more tolerant disposition. This stage begins when the offspring reach adulthood and marry and establish households of their own, for by this time the control by the parents is greatly lessoned.[3]

All of my Grandfather's children married after his death, and whatever issues any of them had with him were never resolved. In fact, Connie got married only nine months after the death of her father. I am not trying to suggest that every daughter of Frank O'Geen had this kind of stormy relationship with him. To some, he was their loving father, and they had fond memories of him and empathized with his daily trials and tribulations. They had sympathy for him and the extreme hardships he endured during the Great Depression and great respect for what he was able to achieve under extreme duress. Life for an immigrant father caught between two worlds in harsh economic times could not have been easy for anyone.

My aunt, by her own admission, was a free spirit, and that probably contributed heavily to the stormy relationship she had with her father. Her son, Bob, told me that his mother mentioned on a number of occasions her friendship with an African-American classmate in high school. She enjoyed his friendship and didn't care what people thought. As Connie reminisced in later years, she lamented the fact that she didn't keep in touch with him. On the farm, Connie was exposed to people with different ethnic backgrounds. One of the hired men was an African-American. He helped Frank work the farm, so she saw how her parents, particularly her father, treated him. In effect, her father was a role model to her by teaching through example to be tolerant of others. She was exposed to the fact that people are the same no matter what their race is and should be treated with respect. Ironically, her father, Frank, the person with whom she constantly quarreled, was in affect her role model. I'm sure my aunt who endured her high school years with insults of her own was defiant when it came to standing up to people when she knew she was right.

---

2 Campisi, "The Italian Family," 448.
3 Campisi, "The Italian Family," 448.

THE LIGHTER SIDE OF CONNIE

There was another side to my Aunt that surprised us now and again. On most occasions she was straight laced, but there were other times when she came out with a story that would knock our socks off and send us into hysterics.

In 1987 I visited my Aunt Marcie MacPherson, the wife of my father's brother, Donald MacPherson (Chapter 27). There, I found out that Aunt Connie was not the straight arrow I had imagined. Aunt Marcie told me that while she was dating Uncle Donald, she heard that he was hanging out with Connie and driving around town with her. She was getting too close to Donald for Marcie's taste. Finding Aunt Connie, Marcie read her the riot act. Aunt Marcie told me, "She was getting too close to my man so I put a stop to it." The next time I saw Aunt Connie, I asked her about it. She started to laugh and said, "I was a real ball buster when I was young. I loved to tease the boys. I really did like your Uncle Donald but I wouldn't have stolen him from Marcie."

This was the first time I saw her in a different light. First of all, to use the term "ball buster" in a sentence was beyond anything I could imagine. Second of all, to think that she was popular with boys in high school was another circumstance that I could have never conceived happening. I never considered that my aunt had such a fun side to her, since I thought she spent all of her waking hours cleaning and going to mass.

One day, Connie told my wife and I a story that I couldn't believe since she had previously seemed so responsible. She had just gotten married to Franklin Schrader and they were going out to meet friends for a few drinks. When the group broke up, Franklin realized that he had drank too much and couldn't drive. Since my aunt didn't drive, they had a dilemma. They decided that my uncle would control the brakes and gas and my aunt would steer the car and be his "eyes" by giving him verbal instructions on when to apply the brakes and how much to press on the accelerator. Connie said they made it home without incident. She admonished me not to tell Bob and Paul, her full-grown sons, since she didn't want to give them any bad ideas.

Connie, like the rest of her sisters, integrated into American culture very quickly. But as much as my aunt considered herself to be a typical American woman, she wasn't totally immune to the Southern Italian belief that sometimes events and potentially tragic circumstances could only be avoided by the use of a *strega* to overcome a spell. When my cousin Bob was a baby, he had colic really bad, and like my mother, my aunt resorted to extraordinary means. On a visit to Grandma's, she took Bob to a *strega* who lived on Bacon Street, the heart of the Italian section of LeRoy. The *strega* rubbed olive oil on his stomach and said some prayers. When I heard this story from my cousin, I could not believe my aunt would resort to such means, since she seemed so American. She had moved out of the Italian community, and I thought this influence of Grandma was not part of her life anymore.

Uncle Franklin John Schrader

Born: March 3, 1921, Lancaster, New York
Died: April 2, 1986, Buffalo, New York

My Aunt Connie married Franklin Schrader on December 27, 1941. As I wrote in the previous chapter on my Aunt Marian, two sisters married two brothers in a double marriage ceremony. My aunt and uncle had a long and happy marriage, and had two sons, Bob and Paul. My uncle considered himself the head of the household, but he was not overbearing. Their marriage was a partnership; a very different relationship than the one Connie witnessed with her parents where her father was the absolute head of the household. On a vacation to LeRoy in 1984 when I still lived in South Carolina, I got a glimpse into the dynamics of my aunt and uncle's marriage.

My sister had a terrier named Willy that Connie absolutely adored. Connie told me that if I ever found a dog like Willy to get it for her. This came as a real surprise, since my aunt was a clean freak, and she never had a dog when her boys were home. As it turned out, a stray animal, that was the spitting image of Willy, turned up at our house in South Carolina. Since we already had three dogs that we had taken in, it was out of the question to keep a fourth. Our other dogs were medium- to large-sized dogs, so the terrier became known as Shorty. Shorty turned out to be a terror, chewing everything in sight and being a constant nuisance. I called my aunt to tell her of the good news that I had found a match for Willy, and she was excited. I was worried, however, that when my aunt got the dog home, she would be calling us to take it back since Shorty was such a demon. My aunt and uncle met us at Grandma's house on the day of our arrival. I should have sensed something was up when my aunt met us as soon as we walked in the door. It was love at first sight. She swooped up the dog and brought it into the living room and told Uncle Franklin, "See our new dog. Her name is Shorty!" Franklin was not amused and said, "over my dead body." Connie replied, "That can be arranged."

I couldn't believe that she hadn't told him, and I was worried that I would be stuck taking care of that mangy mongrel for the rest of its life. Connie assured

Franklin and Shorty watching TV, 1983.

me that Franklin would get used to the idea of having a dog. Connie told her husband that they had to take the dog, since she told me to bring it up north for her. She wanted the dog, and that was the end of it. Thankfully, they left with the dog, but not before Uncle Franklin gave me the evil eye on the way out the door. We held our breath, and the next day my aunt called me to thank me so much for the well-mannered dog. She didn't expect us to train it for her. I guess Shorty just wanted to be an only dog.

I had remarked to my wife that Shorty behaved so well on the trip to LeRoy, which was very unlike her. As I was packing the car to leave for home I found the reason why she was the model-traveling companion. While Shorty was in the back of the hatchback, she chewed up my jumper cables. I guess that was her parting gift to me.

Shorty became so spoiled that she became queen of St. Mary's Place. She became a constant companion to my aunt on walks around town and took naps with Uncle Franklin in the afternoon. After my uncle died, Shorty and Connie were inseparable. I was worried when I saw my uncle's first reaction to the unexpected new member of the family. The general perception of their marriage was that Uncle Franklin was the head of the household and made all of the decisions. I was wrong, since Connie let him make all of the inconsequential ones on his own, but when there was an important decision to be made, she weighed in loud and clear. Her strong independent nature allowed her to stand up to Franklin, and that made her very different from her other sisters.

Shorty met her end in a very unfortunate way. As I discussed in the last chapter, Marian and Connie were extremely close sisters and visited with one another several times a day. One day, Marian drove over to see her sister and parked her car in the driveway. Shorty by this time was old and on her last legs. She had complete freedom and my aunt would let her loose in the yard, since she would never run away. When Marian was through with her visit, she got in her car and started out the driveway. As she backed up she hit something. When my aunt got out, she saw that she hit Shorty. There were no obvious injuries however. The general consensus was that Shorty went under the car and died and when Marian backed up not knowing the dog was under the car hit her. Aunt Marian was beside herself with grief and guilt. There was such a close bond between the two sisters that Connie told Marian that she believed that the dog died before her sister even got in the car and that Marian wasn't the cause of this tragic set of circumstances. Connie never held anything against her sister and their friendship remained the same as it always was.

LIFE WITH FRANKLIN

Connie was an excellent cook. She made her own spaghetti sauce that her son Bob called the best he ever had and the one he compares all others to. She canned her own tomatoes, a process that she undoubtedly learned from Grandma. As a concession to her German husband, she really didn't make any other real Italian dishes. She subordinated her culture and only made food my uncle favored, like Swiss steak, and made no special ethnic dishes. Like Grandma, Connie was also a great pie maker. I especially liked her chocolate pie and cheesecake topped with cherries that she made specifically for me at family gatherings.

Uncle Franklin was much friendlier than his brother, Uncle Ray. At any family gathering, he had a standup comedy routine that contained a series of jokes that he heard either at the Red Man's club or at work. Some of them were hysterical but others were just plain corny, but at any rate we couldn't help but laugh. At my wedding reception in 1973, Uncle Franklin and my wife's brother, Bill, who just graduated from high school, really bonded. Over many beers, Bill spent the whole reception listening to Uncle Franklin's jokes one after the other. He was a funny and good-hearted man.

One of Uncle Franklin's arms had something wrong with it, and he couldn't lift it more than shoulder height. As a result he was classified 4F, which meant that he was medically ineligible to serve in the military. So instead of fighting overseas during World War II, he did his part to fight the war against fascism by working at Buffalo Arms with his brother Ray. After the war, he continued to be a sheet metal worker and did layout work marking patterns on the sheets of steel, and later he moved to an office job, setting up the job routing through the plant. Later he moved to Buffalo Forge, which is where he worked for most of his life.

Uncle Franklin also took a correspondence course in electronics, and was very good at fixing radios and small appliances. He was a very handy man for sure. Whenever Grandma needed an appliance fixed, she sent it to Uncle Franklin. During Christmas 1974, my wife and I were visiting my mother in LeRoy. Whenever we made a trip home, my mother had a list of people for us to visit that included Aunt Connie and Uncle Franklin. On a Sunday during our vacation, we made plans to visit them. When Grandma heard we were going to visit my aunt and uncle, she asked me to do her a favor and bring a broken radio to Uncle Franklin for him to fix. She loved listening to the radio, especially on Saturday at noon to a program from Batavia that featured Italian music. She had missed it the day before and wanted it fixed before the next weekend. Grandma still had that Depression mentality that if something could be fixed, then it should be fixed: "don't waste your money on buying something new!" she would say, especially if Uncle Franklin could repair it for free.

I took the radio that was in a cardboard box and went to my car. We had armloads of stuff to bring to Connie, so my wife and I were really loaded down. The driveway where I parked the car bordered the parking lot of St. Joseph's Church, and mass was just getting out with the churchgoers getting into their cars. I put everything that I had in my arms down on the driveway, opened up the trunk, and loaded it.

I got in the car, started it, and put it in reverse. My wife noticed that there were people in the parking lot waving their arms and yelling at us. I was in a hurry and ignored them until I heard the crunch. I had run over the radio. I jumped out of the car, and to my horror the radio was crushed into a million pieces. My wife said, "Now what?" The only thing I could think of was, 'let's pick it up and get out of here quick, and I'll figure out something later.'

When we got to my aunt and uncle's house, we visited for a while, and later my uncle asked to see the radio. I met him in his shop and gave him the box with broken radio crushed to smithereens and knowing how he liked a good joke asked him, "Do you think you can fix it?" He looked at it for a few moments speechless. Then he picked up the tiny glass and plastic pieces and inspected them very carefully. Putting them back in the box, he said, "I don't think I can." Then we all started laughing. He promised to tell Grandma that it was beyond repair, which it obviously was. When we got back to LeRoy, Grandma kept asking us if we were sure Franklin couldn't fix it. Months later, I heard through my mother that Grandma was still asking Franklin for her radio. That old woman must have been telepathic.

MY GOODHEARTED AUNT AND UNCLE

My aunt and uncle were very generous people and never hesitated to help others. Connie was especially loyal to her sisters and would have done anything for them. As a group, they remembered all of the slights from when they were little and knew each other's business, but when it came to helping one another out, they all bonded together. In 1984, one of the last years of my mother's life, Aunt Connie and Uncle Franklin acted like a personal Make-a-Wish Foundation for my mom. At this time, I was married and still living in South Carolina. I had two small children, a son Jesse who was three, and a daughter Caitlin, who was an infant. My mother had only seen her grandchildren a few times. We made yearly visits to New York to see both of our families, but to an Italian grandma at the end of her life, the urge to see her only grandchildren was very strong, and that was not enough. My mother thought that she might not see them before we made our next trip, so my aunt and uncle volunteered to drive her down to the house she had never seen and the grandchildren who hardly knew her.

My mother very seldom went on trips, so when she called out of the blue and told us that she was coming the next day to visit us, I knew that her cancer was out of remission, and this time might be the end. She never learned to drive and really had no money for such frivolous things as a vacation. As was typical of her, she never let on how sick she actually was, so she made it seem like the trip was nothing special.

After the initial shock of my mother's visit was over, the reality hit that Aunt Connie, the cleanest person in the world, was coming with her to visit a house that had two kids, three dogs, and five cats, so we started cleaning immediately. The next day came and I made a trip to the grocery store to buy my uncle's favorite beer, Pabst Blue Ribbon, and his favorite snack, pretzels. The visit went fine and my aunt squelched the urge to clean. I was so touched by their kindness. I tried to express my gratitude to them and tell them how much it meant to me, but they were just happy that they could be of some service.

The odd thing about the trip was that they were leaving the next day. They broke up an eighteen-hour trip into two days, stayed an afternoon with us, and then left bright and early the next morning. I tried to get them to stay a while, but my mother felt like she had imposed enough on my aunt and uncle's generosity, so she used the excuse that she wasn't feeling very well and had to get back to New York. Whenever anyone in my family made a decision, nothing would change their minds.

The trip gave my mother a dose of adrenalin, and she got the strength to fight her cancer again. Time and time again, my aunts stepped forward to boost her spirits, and that seemed to allow my mother to beat the odds and make a miraculous recovery. She lasted a few more years and finally died on March 17, 1986. Uncle Franklin died of cardiomyopathy, a form of heart disease, on April 2, almost four weeks later. At least he died the day after April Fool's Day so that he had one last laugh.

When Marian died in 1998, Connie missed her very much, as one can imagine. Her beloved sister, who she was so close to and spent her whole life with was gone. By this time, there were only two sisters left, Connie and Dorothy, out of the seven. To try to fill the void, Connie called her youngest sister Dorothy every day; they were fourteen years apart. It wasn't nearly the same, since Connie would call her to talk with her about her neighbors in Lancaster whom Dorothy didn't know. When Connie became sick with colon cancer, Dorothy would drive to her house and spend a few days or a week with her after Connie had her chemotherapy treatments. Finally on January 19, 2003, the day after my birthday, Connie succumbed to the dreaded disease that devastated both sides of my family.

CHAPTER 18

Aunt Helen O'Geen

Born: July 28, 1919, LeRoy, New York
Died: April 29, 1994, Buffalo, New York

Helen O'Geen was Carrie and Frank O'Geen's fourth daughter. She was short, about four feet eleven inches tall. In pictures of her when she was five or six, she can be seen sticking her tongue at the photographer or making faces. I'm sure Grandma thought that she ruined family pictures and that her daughter was "a little devil." During her early twenties, she worked part time for George Shelby, the local jeweler in town, and came into contact with the local version of the jet setters. Apparently she was quite a party girl, but that had to be done carefully so Grandma wouldn't hear about any bad stories about her that might circulate around town. If she did stay out late and Grandma heard about it, the next day she would hear about it from Grandma.

Helen, like the rest of my aunts, was a closet Italian. When they were working or socializing with non-Italians, they acted much differently than when they were at home. In public they acted like Americans, but when they visited one another or Grandma, the hand gestures took over and the noise was deafening with everyone talking at once. They were bicultural.

My aunt considered herself to be a person of exquisite taste. She dressed in fine clothes and her house was immaculate. She was very fussy about her fingernails and had white acrylic ones. She liked her jewelry and had a fondness for strappy sandals. Helen always wore stylish clothes, and when I was young she used to paint my toenails red, which really upset my mother, an obvious extension of her childhood. Other times she would dress me and other male cousins up in her high heels, necklaces, flowered hats, and her mink stole, and tell us that we looked like movie stars. Around the age of four, I remember sitting on her lap in Grandma's kitchen drinking a cup of tea with her after supper. Helen made the best tea that was essentially sugar and milk, and my sister and I eagerly drank it. My aunt had hot lips—by that, I mean that she loved hot peppers and when you gave her a kiss your lips would burn. Helen was one of my aunts that liked to go out and have a good time. She would, without much prodding, head out the door with Great-Uncle Pete on one of his infamous bar excursions (Oh, I mean visits to his "friends"). For this reason, I don't think she was one of Grandma's favorite daughters. She did have a sense of family history and told me many stories of relatives long since departed. She kept family history alive and passed it on to me.

Helen was vivacious. Of all of my aunts, Helen was the most fun and had a tremendous sense of humor. At least when she was single and after she became a widow she seemed always happy and in good spirits. Her laugh was like a cackle rather than like a laugh. Helen worked for the phone company for her whole life. In the 1950s before there were automated phone systems, telephone operators placed calls. I remember visiting her when she was working one day. When I walked into the room, there was a wall where several women were plugging in wires and asking people who they wanted to talk to. There were hundreds of wires that looked so confusing to me that I thought my aunt must have the most difficult and confusing job in the world. Ironically my Grandma MacPherson was her supervisor.

My aunt was always trying to do things to make us laugh. Whenever I wanted to call someone, I would pick up the phone and if my aunt was working she made sure that she picked up our line and say in her funniest telephone operator voice, "Number pleaze," pretending that she didn't know who we were. (When I first heard Lillian Tomlin's comedy routine on telephone operators I thought of Aunt Helen.) Taking the bait I would say, "Helen, it's Tommy." Sometimes she would answer, "Tommy who?" That would send me over the edge. Of course, there was no privacy when she was working. I can remember my mother talking to one of her friends and then shouting, "Helen, quit listening!" There would be click on the other end so you knew she was gone. Phone conversations in those days were not necessarily confidential—especially when Helen was on duty.

Like my other aunts, Helen became American at the expense of her heritage. By attending public school and working for the telephone company, her social circle expanded to include many non-Italian friends. In addition, she knew everyone in town and they knew her. This exposure gave her access to an alternate way of life and a blueprint for respectability.

Uncle Joseph D'Angelo

Born: May 21, 1921, Warsaw, New York
Died: December 8, 1979, Batavia, New York

Aunt Helen married an Italian widower, Joe D'Angelo, in the summer of 1960 at the age of forty-one. Joe lived in Oakfield, New York and had three children from his first marriage. Their names were Carl, Mary Jo and Jeanne. I don't know why it took her so long to marry, since she had a very active social life and went out with her girlfriends on the weekends when she didn't work. They were an odd couple. Joe was a totally blue-collar type of guy, and Helen was more sophisticated, liking the latest fashions and dining out. We think that she married Joe because this was her last chance to escape Grandma. She was the only aunt to marry an Italian. At first I didn't like Uncle Joe. I asked Grandma for her opinion. I asked her, "What do you think of Joe?" She replied, "He's a social climber." Even Grandma could see that they were an odd couple. He was loud and very outgoing, and so totally different than any of my other non-Sicilian uncles. They were quiet, and banded together by themselves in another room to play cards and drink beer, I'm sure as an excuse to get away from the cacophony of noise made by all of the Sicilian women that masqueraded as conversation. When Joe came on the scene, the whole dynamic changed. He was loud, and his very large personality took over the room. It took a while for the other uncles to warm up to him and some never did. Grandma sure warmed up to him and made him spaghetti and meatballs every Sunday. Unlike Father Zupa, he gave Grandma the best compliment one could give an Italian grandma by telling her it was the best meal he ever had. Every Sunday.

Uncle Joe led a life that would have scarred most of us, but he ended up a kind and happy man who loved life. Joe's troubles started at his birth. His mother died while giving birth to him, and his father blamed him for her death. His father was so distraught that he put his infant son into a wastepaper basket and left him. Joe was put in an orphanage but was eventually rescued by an aunt who raised him as if he was one of her own children. Throughout the years, Joe never had any contact with his father; years later when he found out that his father was in a nursing home and not doing well, he started visiting him. Joe was very forgiving and didn't seem to hold anything against his father, and visited him until the old man died. His actions demonstrated the kind of man he was, and explains why he bonded so well with our family.

He was a little taller than Helen, about five feet six inches, with dark olive skin. He seemed to think he was a ladies man since he was always flirting and dancing with women. When Aunt Helen threw a bridal shower for my fiancé Linda, Uncle Joe made a beeline to my future mother-in-law, Lucy, and told her that he would be honored if she would dance with him at the wedding. Lucy didn't know what to think and asked me to protect her from him. I tried to explain to her that it is just his way of welcoming her into the family, but she was not amused by his aggressive behavior. For Italians, weddings are a time of great celebration, and there was nothing Joe liked better than a good wedding. It was one

Sunday afternoon at Grandma's house, mid-1960s. Left to right: Uncle Joe, Great-Uncle Jimmy, and Helen. Aunt Franny is in the background straightening up the house and Uncle Joe is dominating the room.

of the few times he didn't get yelled at for smoking, drinking or dancing. The dance never happened at the wedding, and Lucy kept her distance from him. Years after we were married, Joe asked Linda how her mother was and we told him she had named him the "Dancing Uncle." He was very amused.

Uncle Joe looked Italian and was proud of who he was. He was unashamed and didn't care who knew he was Italian. He was outgoing, bossy, confident, and knew everything. He fit into the family, and a family member's fight was his fight. He was loyal could be counted on for anything. If he was asked to do a favor for someone, he did it without complaint. When Grandma renovated her house so that we could come and live with her, it was Uncle Joe D'Angelo who accepted the job and did all of the remodeling. Since Grandma was family,

Uncle Joe did all of the work at a discounted rate. He wanted to do it for free, but she wouldn't let him. It was through him that I learned that blood is thicker than water and family comes first. Whenever Grandma needed something repaired and Joe couldn't do it, he sent someone who could. He drove my aunt nuts as well as his three children with his stubbornness, but he meant well and was good-hearted. His son, Carl, who looked just like him, worked on and off with him in the family business, but not for any length of time since Uncle Joe was always riding him and Carl either quit or was fired.

One evening, my wife and I went out to supper at the country club with my aunt and uncle. Joe insisted on taking us there since he knew I loved clam sauce and linguine, and the chef made the best he ever had. After I tasted it I told him it was good, so in typical Uncle Joe fashion, he called over the cook so that he could tell me what his secret was. The chef replied,

Uncle Joe and Aunt Helen making the rounds in LeRoy on a Sunday afternoon, 1968.

"Progresso." Uncle Joe was unfazed by that response and thought the man was just being humble. The conversation then changed to child rearing. Uncle Joe used to say that he never meddled in his children's lives and never told them what to do. My aunt nearly choked on her food. "Joe!" she said. "Why is it that Carl quits all of the time when he works with you? The two of you are always fighting like cats and dogs!" Joe, without flinching, replied, "Well, I only say something when I know I'm right." Everyone but my aunt started roaring with laughter. Such was life with Joe D'Angelo.

Uncle Joe was tough as nails and was a sergeant in the Marine Corps during World War II. He was very patriotic, was an ultra-conservative, and loved Richard Nixon. He was in the Battle of Guadalcanal and told us stories of his military service. He was a very good storyteller and his stories mostly centered on humorous events. Since he was a carpenter by trade, he had the unenviable job of making crosses for his dead comrades' graves. After the war, he went into business as a contractor and always had more than enough work because of his reputation as an honest man and because the work he did was of the highest quality.

In one of his stories, he said he was making some crosses when the air raid siren went off. He ran for cover and jumped in the nearest foxhole. He dove in headfirst and to his horror he realized that he had jumped into an open latrine. The air raid went on for a couple of hours with machine gun fire and bombs exploding all around him, and by the time it was over he was sick to his stomach. In fact he was sick for days. As he was telling the story, he was laughing as hard as we were. I'm sure he saw unimaginable carnage, but he never talked about it nor did he seem to be affected by it. When he died he had a military funeral.

My great-uncles liked him, and I remember the animated conversations they had at Grandma's kitchen table. Great-Uncle Pete naturally gravitated to him and they became quite good friends smoking their cigars, with Uncle Joe ushering Great-Uncle Pete from drinking establishment to drinking establishment. Even the straight-laced Great-Uncle Jimmy respected Joe because of his work ethic and devotion to the family. It also didn't hurt that Uncle Joe was a devout Catholic and went to church every Sunday and all of the Holy Days. Aunt Helen did, however, try to limit the amount of time he spent with Great-Uncle Tony for fear that he would be corrupted by my great-uncle's lifestyle. In fact, all of my aunts did the same with their husbands.

A typical day for him was to be out of the house by 7:00 a.m. He drove to the Sterling Diner on Main Street where he would buy breakfast for people he knew, and then he was off to work. In the middle of the day, he would go have lunch at the Casino (if he was in town), an Italian restaurant owned by my cousins, and then go back to work and then back to the Casino again after work for cocktails. At the Casino he would buy rounds of drinks for the house. When someone went out with Joe, he/she never bought a drink or a meal. He was a generous man, and it was not hard to imagine why he had a hard time saving money. Aunt Helen had to step in try to restrict his generosity, but that only worked for a while and he was back to his reckless spending ways.

He was a stickler for one thing, however: he wanted a clean house. One day when he came home from work and found the vacuum cleaner at the top of the stairs, he pushed it down the stairs because it was in the way. Helen got in his face and said, "I don't do that with your tools!" It was funny to think that my aunt looked at her vacuum cleaner the same way Uncle Joe thought of his saws and hammers.

MARRIED LIFE

Helen and Joe's wedding was a small affair, and not every cousin and friend was invited. They were married in St. Joseph's Church, across the street from our house, and Grandma had the reception in her backyard. It was a really scaled down reception with no music or dancing, and in no way could it be confused with an Italian wedding. It resembled more of a family reunion or a picnic. Helen wore a simple, short white dress and Uncle Joe wore navy blue suit. She was forty-one and he was thirty-nine. All of her sisters and their husbands were there, and some of Uncle Joe's relatives were in attendance. A few of the Grandma's brothers and their families were there, and of course Great-Aunt Mary and Great-Uncle Tony. The one thing that was Italian was the food, and the large metal tubs filled with block ice loaded with beer and soda from the local bottling works. My cousins and I had a great time eating and drinking as much as we liked. I remember being very sad when I saw Helen and Joe leave for their honeymoon. I knew that the next time I visited Grandma, Helen wouldn't be there anymore. This was just before we moved in to live with Grandma, and our Sunday visits to Lake Street had been a lot of fun when Helen was there. I really enjoyed all of the attention she showered on me.

After the honeymoon they took in Boston, they bought their first house in a lower-middle class section of LeRoy. Helen had Joe remodel it, and he spent long hours removing walls to suit my Aunt's fancy. Then after four years (and I'm sure that it was because of my Aunt's insistence on saving some money) they bought my aunt's dream house.

She had a wonderful new home and achieved social status through it. Her house became one of the most beautiful houses in LeRoy. We had a family joke that the only reason Helen married Joe was to get away from Grandma and have her own house so she could decorate it. Whenever she shopped on Main Street, people would stop her and tell her how beautiful her house was and that delighted her to no end. The house was built in 1875 in a fairly upper-middle class section of LeRoy. She moved into the house on July 16, 1964 and sold it on October 25, 1993. She had an obsession with early American décor, and decals of eagles and other American symbols graced her home. Her neighbors were a doctor on one side of her house and a truck driver on the other side—a real American melting pot of a neighborhood. The house had hardwood floors throughout it, and my aunt had my uncle renovate it along strict guidelines so that the historical essence of the house was enhanced; hence, the early American decor. Helen had exquisite taste, and her house became the centerpiece of the major family holidays like Christmas and Easter, supplanting everyone going to Grandma's house. Helen liked to show her house off and my mother would bring her friends to visit Helen so that they could see firsthand that magnificent domicile.

On the side of the house, right next to the driveway was a redbud tree. I had never seen one before, and when it bloomed in the spring before the leaves emerged, thousands of little pink blossoms lined the branches. This tree just added to the elegance of her house. When I moved back to Western New York in 1985, I transplanted some of the little seedlings from this tree to both houses I have owned as a way of remembering her.

After Helen married, she wasn't as much fun. Her life changed dramatically. She had three stepchildren to take care of, Carl, Mary Jo, and Jeanne, and four if you count Uncle Joe. Joe lost his first wife, his children were young, with Carl, the oldest, about eight years old when she died. There was friction between them with Helen getting along the best with Carl. Helen tried to be a good step-parent and never tried to replace their mother, but she was critical of them and they resented her for that, and of course they missed their mother. I remember Helen was always throwing my sister and I up in their faces as examples of proper behavior. Luckily, they didn't seem to hold it against us. The situation was not easy for anyone. For the most part, Helen stepped aside and let Joe handle the discipline.

Helen and Joe on their wedding day, 1960.

Aunt Helen did not like animals, so I don't know what possessed Uncle Joe to bring home a dog for her. Joe's cousin Tyna had the dog originally, and for some reason couldn't keep it any longer so Uncle Joe got it for Helen. It was a well-behaved dog, and Uncle Joe was good-hearted and wanted to make sure it had a good home. It wasn't just any dog, but a toy poodle named Cocoa Monique. It was an apricot colored purebred that came with papers. It was the first purebred dog that anyone in our family owned. In fact, Cocoa became the rage of the family, with my cousin Nancy making a turquoise sweater with Cocoa knitted on the sweater with the same color of her fur. At any rate, I guess Joe thought that she needed a companion, or it was the ultimate status symbol, in his eyes, that movie stars and the rich flaunted. It must have been one of those times when Joe knew he was right so he adopted the dog.

Helen loved the dog and it became the child she never had. The dog went everywhere with her with Helen always carrying it. It was hysterical to watch them drive up to Grandma's house. Since Joe was a carpenter, he always owned a Chevy pickup truck with a cap for his tools. When they got to Grandma's, the truck doors would open and out stepped Uncle Joe, cigar in hand and in his work clothes, and Helen dressed fashionably and holding little Cocoa. It was a surreal image of contrasts. On Sundays when Joe went to church, he always dressed in a black suit that I'm sure was at the insistence of my aunt. Since Cocoa was a favorite with Aunt Franny, Grandma withheld her objections about bringing animals to her house. When Cocoa died, Helen stayed home from work in mourning for several days.

A few years later Uncle Joe tried to get us a Boston terrier that someone he knew had to give up. It was a well-trained animal and he tried his best to talk Grandma, Franny, and my Mother into letting us have it. He tried his best for hours, but nothing worked. I guess his charm worked on Helen but he had no chance with them.

Uncle Joe's middle child, Mary Jo, married and had two little girls. Mary Jo was short petite and pretty with black hair and dark brown eyes. She was said to look just like her mother. Helen and Mary Jo got along the worst of any of the other of Joe's children. With the birth of Mary Jo's daughter Wendy in 1974, however, their relationship improved. Wendy had a severe neurological disease that doctors thought was a result of Mary Jo's husband's tour of duty in Vietnam because he had been exposed to defoliating chemicals like Agent Orange. He was always sick and couldn't keep a job. Helen loved Wendy and showered her with attention. She thought that the poor girl was malnourished, so she made sure that there was plenty of food around when she visited. Wendy couldn't walk or talk, but Helen thought that she understood what she said, so Helen read her stories and spoke to her about everything. My aunt tried to stimulate her senses by touching her and having her taste different foods just to keep her mentally engaged. Wendy eventually died in 1979 at the age of five, and Helen was heartbroken. Helen decided to bury Wendy at a site close to the plot she had bought for Joe and her so that Wendy's grave would be facing hers.

Joe died of cancer on December 8, 1979. He was in much pain the last year of his life, and when I visited that summer I could hardly recognize him. He was gaunt, and the happy, outgoing man I knew was gone. Joe was always the life of the party, and holidays like Christmas were not the same ever again.

LIFE AFTER UNCLE JOE

After Uncle Joe died in 1979, Helen relaxed quite a bit. She had her dream house paid for and her step kids were out of the house and on their own, but then her health started to fail. She had a heart attack and then developed diabetes and had to give herself injections. Despite this setback, she became the fun loving Aunt Helen I knew when I was a kid. By 1985, Linda and I had two children, Jesse and Caitlin, and I accepted a teaching position at SUNY Geneseo. Helen was very impressed that I was hired at Geneseo. We visited her regularly, and that really lifted her spirits. When my mother died in 1986, Helen essentially became my kids' Grandma. We either visited her weekly or called her on the phone, and consequently, she became very close to both of my children. Both Jesse and Caitlin were exposed to Helen's delightful way of making tea and still remember fondly the tea parties they had. Unlike my

My daughter, Caitlin, and Aunt "Helly," 1988.

mother and Aunt Franny, Helen actually liked Linda. When we visited her, we took her out grocery shopping or to the used bookstore where she bought Harlequin romances by the armload. A visit usually included a trip to McDonald's for coffee just so her friends would have to pay attention to her great-niece and great-nephew as payback for all of the times she had to pay attention to other people's kids.

Caitlin and Helen hit it off from the beginning. Cait was outgoing and never failed to make Helen cackle uncontrollably. Helen had a willing participant to dress up and paint her fingernails. My daughter called her "Helly," and that tickled Helen to no end. My son, Jesse, on the other hand, was very quiet and never spoke two words to anyone when we visited the Italian relatives. I think he was overwhelmed by all of the noise and attention. They thought he was anti-social, but Helen defended him saying he just enjoyed his own company. She understood him and he liked her. My son was content to bring a book and read or play computer chess during the whole visit. Some of my aunts thought this was very odd behavior and he was a peculiar boy, but Helen would seek him out and ask him questions in a quiet way. As a result, they bonded.

When I was in graduate school, I took a watercolor course and brought home some of these paintings for my relatives to see, and Helen fell in love with them. Throughout the years, I gave her the ones she liked and she had them framed. She liked them so much that she hung them in her living room in a place of honor. At various times, Helen would give me a lecture on "good" art. She had an interest in art, when she was young and she collected art books that included some of the Impressionists and Modern masters. After seeing some of my landscapes, she really insisted that I start painting red barns and nice floral still lifes since they would go really well with her decor. She was disappointed when I declined. I know she would have liked the Italian identity series and the family portraits.

The painting *Aunt Helen of LeRoy* is a painting that is filled with symbolism that reflects the different stages of my Aunt's life. Her portrait is based on a photograph of her taken in the late 1940s, when she was in her late twenties and a social butterfly. She is dressed in the latest fashions that reflect her acceptance in the American community. The house in the background symbolizes her marriage and the social status she achieved in her middle age. I included a redbud tree since in my mind the tree stands as a memorial to her. I have three redbuds in my yard that she gave me before she died, and I always think of her when I look at them. Around my aunt's house there were families of mourning doves that nested in her mailbox and the bushes that surrounded the front of her house. There is a nest with two eggs to the right of her in the bushes. Aunt Helen never liked them because she thought they were bad parents. The nests of mourning doves are not a thing of beauty, and they seem to be just thrown together, and sometimes the nests and eggs actually fall out of bushes and onto the ground. She used to patrol the perimeter of her house looking for nests that had fallen out of there hiding places and then put them back securely where they belonged. The semi-nude figure on the left side of her is from a Renaissance painting entitled *Vulcan* by Piero Di Cosimo. The female figure is carrying a toy poodle that represents all of those annoying little lap dogs Helen had over the years. The oleander bushes behind her are from the Palatine Hill in Rome, which represents her Italian heritage. The frame refers to the doorways and the interior of her house that she spent so much time decorating to her exacting standards.

The last year of her life was difficult for her. As her health deteriorated, she required more and more close supervision, and many times she had to be rushed to the hospital by ambulance. By this time, her youngest sister Dorothy was retired and was the caretaker of Helen and her older sister Florence. It was impossible for Dorothy to take care of both of them at different houses,

Aunt Helen of LeRoy, *2009. Egg tempera on panel.*

so Helen was persuaded to sell her house and move back to Lake Street. On October 25, 1993, her magnificent house was sold to a young couple Helen had handpicked. She wanted to make sure that they would keep the house in as good condition as she did. My aunt became so depressed and withdrawn that she never accepted any invitations to visit them. The pain was too much to bear.

In late April 1994, Helen was rushed to Buffalo General Hospital where she had an operation on her carotid artery. On the 29th I drove to Buffalo to visit her, but by the time I got there she had already passed away earlier that morning.

CHAPTER 19

Antonina (Lena) Joan O'Geen (Gugino)

Born: March 13, 1921, LeRoy, New York
Died: March 17, 1986, Batavia, New York

Lena, my mother, was the fifth child of Carrie and Frank O'Geen. She was born with the name Antonina but never used it. Her name was just a reminder of a culture that she tried to hide from the non-Italian world. She was short, standing five feet two inches, but that was relative considering the height of her parents (at four feet nine inches and five feet two inches). She had the dark olive skin associated with Sicilians, and hair black as night. Even though my mother had good looks, she was very self-conscious about her appearance and tried to hide her dark olive complexion behind a pink foundation that my sister and I found unnecessary. We tried to make her more comfortable with her Mediterranean looks by talking about what beautiful skin color she had, but she wouldn't hear of it. She was in total denial and told us she didn't know about what we were talking.

Lena's high school graduation photo, 1940.

During my mother's childhood, her family and the other Sicilian families in LeRoy were the butt of racially insensitive slurs. They were called names by their classmates and were generally made to feel inferior to the "real Americans." They were called "spaghetti eaters," "dagos," "guinies," and "wops," and had to withstand insults that linked their parents to the mafia. She was unlucky and lived a hard life growing up poor in the Depression on a farm, and later endured a failed marriage.

CHILDHOOD

My mother, like her sisters, had a difficult childhood. Since her parents were mentally and physically exhausted struggling to work a farm and feed an ever-increasing family, there was not time for displays of affection so she felt ignored by her parents. Mom told me one time that she knew she was not one of Grandma's favorites.

She was very close to her two sisters, Helen, who was just a little older, and Franny, who was four years younger. Rita Cinquino, our cousin who spent vacations on the farm visiting my mother and Helen, told me that when she visited, "Aunt Carrie (Grandma) would pay a lot of attention to me and make Helen and Lena play with me. I think that made Helen and Lena jealous because their mother didn't pay them as much attention."

Lena struggled in high school and graduated in 1940, after being held back a year due to academic difficulties. Right after graduating, she met my father, Neil MacPherson, working at the Vitel Hosiery Company that was situated in LeRoy. He was a foreman and she worked on an assembly line making the stockings. This job proved to be critical in my mother's assimilation process, since she came into contact with non-Italians in a different context than what she experienced when she was in high school. In the process, she achieved a certain amount of independence from her parents. As the children of immigrants joined the workforce, non-Italians perceived them differently, and these children embraced the customs of the new culture at the expense of the old one. Second generation children like my mother were caught between both cultures, and she was forced to move between each one, either trying to fit in or become invisible when she was with non-Italians. She became a chameleon.

BECOMING A DENTAL HYGIENIST

During high school, Lena worked as a babysitter for Dr. Murray, a dentist on Main Street in LeRoy. He encouraged her to go to the Eastman Dental Dispensary School in Rochester, New York to become a dental hygienist. Grandma worked and scraped together whatever money she could to help my mother pay for the tuition, and my mother worked at Vitel Hosiery for the rest of it. She graduated in 1942 and became a professional, gaining respect from the outside world that was so elusive to her first generation parents. When my mom graduated, Dr. Murray hired her.

My mother looked at the Murrays as the ideal family. They were, in her eyes, what an "American" family was supposed to be. The Murray family was well-respected and lived in a very tasteful house on Lake Street in LeRoy. They had four well-behaved children that were always dressed in the finest clothes. The Murrays treated my mother like she was part of the family and she felt welcome in their home. I remember as a small child visiting them at their magnificent home one afternoon. The interior design of the house was very formal and elegant. Compared to our small, run-down apartment, I thought I was in a mansion.

With them, she was able to leave the behind the stigma of be-

Left to right: Grandma, Nancy (the first grandchild in the family), and Lena, circa 1944.

ing Sicilian and gain some acceptance from outside the Italian community. She wanted to be part of the upward mobility that made America the place of hope that prompted her grandparents, Cologero and Maria Barone, to leave Sicily and immigrate to the "Land of Opportunity." But deep down inside she realized that this level of wealth and respectability would be something that she would never be able to achieve. When Dr. Murray moved his practice to Rochester and started an oral surgery practice, she became very depressed. He wanted her to work for him in his new office in the Sibley Tower but she had to say no. She had neither a car nor a driver's license, and to take the bus to Rochester meant that we would be with a babysitter all day and into the evening. In her eyes this was not worth it since she was brought up to believe her most important role in life was being a mother. Lena always put her children first, a lesson she passed on to me. She did try to work for the dentist who took over Dr. Murray's practice, but found him too sarcastic and eventually quit.

I remember her mulling over and over in her mind how could she keep working for Dr. Murray, but it all came back to the fact that she had two young children. My mother was so proud of what she accomplished, and now she gave it all up to be a mother full time. She left on such good terms with him that he told her if she ever changed her mind to give him a call. Lena never seemed to regret her decision to be a stay-at-home mom, and I never saw any signs of resentment in her. I always thought we, her children, were the center of her life and loved us more than anything in world.

Lena (center) with her sisters, Florence (left) and Helen (right), 1944.

THE MIXED MARRIAGE

My parents became romantically involved while working at Vitel Hosiery Company, the same place where Lena's sister Florence worked. One of the ways immigrant children assimilate into society is to join the workforce and to form relationships outside of the culture of their parents. This was an opportunity my mother would not have had if her family had remained in Sicily where women stayed home and raised children. When my father announced his engagement to Lena to his family, everyone was surprised, since no one even knew he had a girlfriend.

My mother married Neil Lewis (Mickey) MacPherson when he returned home from World War II. They were married on June 15, 1946. My mother was raised as a devout Roman Catholic and my father was a Methodist. Since my father was not Catholic and did not want to convert to Catholicism, the marriage was not allowed to take place in St. Joseph's Roman Catholic Church. The ceremony took place in the rectory where all "mixed marriages" were held.

When my mother married my father, it symbolized a very important departure away from the Old World way of courtship. Their wedding was not arranged, and Lena married someone who was not Italian, like her sisters Marian and Connie, but one major difference was that her husband was not even Catholic. For Italians, marrying a non-Catholic was drastic change from tradition.[1] I am not sure what Grandma, Carrie O'Geen, thought about my mother marrying a non-Catholic, but my father and Grandma had a civil relationship with my father affectionately calling her "Ma." They actually seemed to like one another. After they were married, they lived in Grandma's house until they were able to find their own place.

The Mixed Marriage, 2009. *Egg tempera.*

On the other hand, my grandmother on my father's side, Marguerite MacPherson, disliked my mother from the beginning. MacPherson family members recall that Marguerite had issues with my mother because of her ethnic background and her religion. She treated my sister and me like her other grandchildren, but I felt the tension between my mother and grandmother. On the other hand, Grandpa MacPherson really liked my mother and he welcomed her into the family, but his death on August 5, 1957 left her with only Marguerite to contend with.

This matrimonial bond also symbolized to my mother that she had attained respectability and unanimity at the same time. She married into a family that emigrated from Scotland

---

1 Paul J. Campisi, "The Italian Family in the United States," *The American Journal of Sociology* 53, no. 6 (1948), 443–49.

in 1801 and was one of the founders of LeRoy, New York. The MacPhersons were instrumental in starting the first schools and they were involved in the early local politics. The MacPherson family in LeRoy was well respected, so when this daughter of Sicilian parents married into an old established family, my mother believed that the days of ridicule and insults were soon to become a distant memory, since now her last name was MacPherson not O'Geen, a made up Irish-sounding name associated with Sicilians who lived in LeRoy.

As can be seen in the painting, *The Mixed Marriage*, my father was much taller than my mother standing nearly six feet tall with blond hair and blue eyes and a fair complexion, while my mother was five feet two inches with olive skin, black hair, and brown eyes. Like their appearance, culturally they were complete opposites. My father was close to his brothers and a very few cousins, but not to the degree of a typical Sicilian family, where any close friend was considered an aunt or an uncle.

Since second generation children encounter discrimination for being different, they try to assimilate into the dominant culture by distancing themselves from the values and beliefs of the first generation. One way to gain acceptance is to marry someone outside of your culture and become more American through marriage. If the resulting union produces children, then the goal of assimilation becomes obtainable. We were encouraged by my mother to not admit to our Sicilian heritage when we were at school or playing with non-Italian playmates. By marrying into a family that were the among the first settlers to the area, my mother was assured that my sister and I would not have to go through the ridicule that she experienced growing up in a hostile environment. Since my father was of northern European ancestry and very fair, I received many of his recessive genes, so my mother's goal to have children that were lighter than she was became a reality. We were also able to hide

My mother in happier times, circa 1947.

behind my father's name while growing up in the 1950s. It also came in handy when I moved to Columbia, South Carolina and had Klansmen for neighbors.

In *The Mixed Marriage*, I depicted my father as the psychologically damaged war veteran he was. From his war experiences he suffered from post-traumatic stress syndrome that left him barely functional in life back in the States. Behind him, I placed his 1939 Chrysler Imperial as a symbol of his innocent life as a teenager before he enlisted in the army. Over my father's left shoulder, looming in the background are the ruins from the Battle of Monte Cassino. It was in this battle in which he was wounded and received his medals for bravery.

He left a happy go lucky young man that everyone liked and came back a brutally damaged war hero who shut himself off from the outside world. He was a shell of his former self.

I deepened the orbital cavities to make his face look like a death mask, since he psychologically died in that conflict. For my mother, I chose a rose garden I saw while I was in Florence, Italy. Since she grew up in poverty, lived through the Great Depression, and persevered in the face of discrimination, she figured marriage to a blond haired, blue-eyed Scotsman was going to be like living in a "rose garden." How could life be worse? She was soon to find out.

My mother had a devastating event happen a couple of years after her marriage to my father. She became pregnant in 1948 but lost the child, a boy, due to the fact that the umbilical cord was wrapped around her unborn baby's neck. My father blamed our family doctor for his death. Neil thought the doctor should have known from the prenatal checkups that there was going to be a complicated delivery and that a Caesarian section should have been performed. My mother, on the other hand, fully exonerated the doctor from any wrongdoing and he continued to be our family doctor against my father's wishes. Lena could not summon the courage to blame her doctor, much less find a new one since she was just a daughter of immigrant parents and was grateful that her doctor treated her with respect. In her eyes, she could not bear the prospect of running across him or any of his family members across town if she changed practices. She just wasn't strong enough to stand up for herself. I also believe that this tragic event made her very protective of my sister and me to the point that we were allowed very little freedom, even as we grew older. Like her mother, she watched us like a hawk and suspected that we were always planning to do some horrible thing that would bring shame onto the family. As we grew up, Lena still tried to treat us like little children, and any time we wanted to go out with friends and she said no, and an ugly altercation ensued.

MARRIED LIFE

My earliest recollections of my parents were around the age of three. I remember living in a tiny four-room apartment that had a small convenience store in the front of the building. The house was located just on the outskirts of LeRoy on Lake Road, just down the street from Grandma. My father made a living driving a truck for a beer and soft drink distributor. He drove a very large green truck around LeRoy and the surrounding towns, and his route consisted of various mom and pop neighborhood grocery stores. Since my mother didn't drive, we didn't go to many places, and if we did, we walked. We walked the half-mile to Grandma's house and even to Main Street, which was farther up Lake Street. I remember being exhausted when we finally got back from our mile-plus shopping trips for groceries and other essentials.

Our house was a happy place even if we were poor. My parents got along and I was happiest when Dad was home. Sometimes he would be late getting back from his day on the road and he would come directly home in his giant old green truck and Mom would have supper ready. After supper, the big treat would be to drive the truck back to the garage. I remember Dad picking me up and I would put my face in the soft fur collar of his aviator coat. It seemed to me that I was a mile in the air and wondered if I would ever be as tall as him when I was grown up. I can still remember him carrying me out through the back porch to the truck and then the three of us would get in it. I would sit in Mom's lap in those pre-seatbelt days, and watch in awe as my father shifted the truck as we drove to the garage with the truck whining and shaking the whole way. It was so difficult to make ends meet that I remember days when the insurance man made his rounds to collect the payments for the car premiums. We didn't have any money so my mother and I would hide behind the couch or under the bed until he left. Besides the uncertain financial situation, I think my mother was the happiest at this time in her married life.

After my sister was born on December 30, 1954, we had to move to an apartment since we had barely enough room for the three of us. The apartment was on 14 Church Street across the Oatka Creek, which went through the middle of town and was the dividing line between the Italian community and the American community. The richest people in the village lived in this section of town, and I had non-Italian playmates who resided there. The neighborhood was a mix of northern European working middle class families with a very few Italian households scattered here and there. This was the neighborhood where young Italian or mixed couples moved to start a new life away from customs of the old country and to begin the process of assimilation.

As I got older, I realized that my father didn't spend much time at home, and there were times I wouldn't see him for weeks since he got home from his drinking binges after I was in bed and he was gone very early in the morning before I got up. When he did come home he was usually drunk and passed out shortly after he sat in his chair. Sometimes my mother would wake up in the morning and find that he never came to bed. She would find him passed out half in the car and half out of the car with his head on the ground. How he drove home and went to work driving his truck all day was beyond me.

My mother tried to make the best of the situation and devoted all of her time to taking care of my sister and me. If it wasn't for her, I don't know what would have happened to us. Like all good mothers, she saw to our every need. She made sure that we did well in school and took us to the library every week in the summer, and made us devote a certain amount of time each day for reading for "pleasure." She made sure we had manners and knew how to greet people, and above all we respected our elders no matter what their cultural background. She essentially passed on to us the ideals that she learned from her parents. My mother constantly reinforced concepts like hard work and the idea that family bonds are the most important thing in life. Lena was a good Italian mother. By that I mean that she made sure that we got to

Mom and me, 1951. I'm in there somewhere.

know our aunts and uncles, and of course, Grandma. We went to St. Joseph's Church every Sunday at 11:00 a.m., and then we walked across the street to have lunch with Grandma. Usually Grandma made a vegetable bone soup that was out of this world. Since I didn't like vegetables in those days, Grandma would strain them out for me before she put the bowl in front of me. Then I would sprinkle Romano cheese on top. Even Grandma spoiled us, although she groused about wasting good vegetables and gave us a lecture about the Depression.

During these years, my mother had a somewhat close relationship with my father's family. Before I was born, my parents would go out and see a movie with my father's oldest brother Donald and his wife Marcella, who was an Irish-German Catholic. I also remember my father's youngest brother, Bill, visiting the house. My father was a great outdoor cook, so my uncle would bring porterhouse steaks for everyone, and over a few beers they sat around outside and cooked them. When we visited Grandma (Marguerite) and Grandpa (Donald) MacPherson, I remember that Grandpa and Uncle Bill would talk to my mother, and they seemed very friendly to one another, while Grandma MacPherson was cold to her. Grandma would, however, shower me with all sorts of attention and bake a batch of her scrumptious, homemade molasses cookies that I could eat as many as I wanted of. I liked visiting them, but it was a different household. Being much quieter than my Italian grandmother's house on the other side of town, I had to sit in my chair and I didn't say much unless I was spoken to.

After the death of Grandpa MacPherson, my mother did not look forward to visiting her mother-in-law. Since I was only six years old at this time, I don't remember Grandma MacPherson saying anything that was over-the-top to my mother, but I do remember Grandma not being as friendly to her. Aunt Marcella who got along really well with Grandma, was also Catholic and never received the same sense of hostility because of her religion, so this reaction must have been because of Lena's Sicilian ethnicity. My mother picked up on the fact that her mother-in-law was less than thrilled of the marriage and withdrew. At times, I remember the two of them having tense moments that seemed to last forever.

Marguerite (Grandma MacPherson,) was very passive aggressive and would make her feelings known by sending home food to our house that was just for our father. She would exclude us from family gatherings and then tell us all about how much fun everyone had the next time we saw her. My father was too intimidated by Marguerite to say anything, which only infuriated my mother even more. There were many awkward moments of silence when we were the only ones visiting her. Since Lena had just as strong of a personality as her mother-in-law, neither one of them would ever think of making a concession to the other one. Now that my mother was an adult, she was not going to accept the same slights and insults, imagined or real, that she did when she was growing up. So she fought back with no holds barred.

One incident that was a flashback to the vicious bigotry she endured throughout her high school years and contributed to the low self-image she carried with her throughout her whole life, began as a well-intentioned family outing with the MacPhersons. My father's youngest brother invited us to spend an afternoon swimming at a private club where he had a membership, called Godfrey's Pond. There was only one catch: this club had an exclusive membership, and African-Americans, Jews, Hispanics, and Italians were not allowed to become members, or even allowed to visit the place as a guest. When my father asked us if we wanted to go, my sister and I enthusiastically said yes, not knowing about the racial restrictions, but my mother said, "No way." My sister and I did not understand her objections so she explained it to us. It never occurred to me that we were different and why did it matter? But the lure of swimming was too much for us so we worked on her until she relented.

On the day of the big trip, my father gave us special instructions that almost blew the whole excursion. He told us that when we drove up to the gate of the private club there would a man guarding the entrance. When he came up to the car he expected my mother, my sister, and I to look in the opposite direction so that the man wouldn't know that we were Italian. This made me uneasy, and for the first time I felt inferior and thought maybe our own father was ashamed of us. Lena exploded. All of the years of being ridiculed by classmates who thought they were better than her came to the surface. Now that Lena was an adult, she didn't have to take the ridicule, so she stood her ground. Mom yelled back at Dad that there was no way she was going to turn her head just to get in Godfrey's Pond. After Dad assured us that he would make sure nothing would happen to us, we got into the car with my mother fuming and my father trying to ease the tension.

When we got to the gate sure enough there was the guard. My aunt and uncle went first and explained that we were their guests. The man came up to our car and peered in the front window and asked my father a few questions. My mother defiantly looked at him and then he scanned the back seat and saw my sister and me. Either the man was blind, or the look on my mother's face must have given him pause, because he let us in without any incident. There were two ponds for swimming at the Godfrey's Pond recreation area: Back Pond, which was muddy and undeveloped and Godfrey Pond, which was clean with a diving board and other amenities. After we parked the car and set up at a picnic table near Back Pond, we all got into the water. My uncle's children were used to swimming in Godfrey Pond and jumping off the diving board and they didn't like Back Pond with all of the mud and dirty water, so my uncle took them to swim in the adjacent clean pond. I thought that would be great, but then I found out that only members were allowed in the Godfrey Pond area and we would have to stay at Back Pond. Off everyone went, including my father, to have fun at the pond. My mother's eyes nearly popped out of her head, and grabbed my father's arm, ordering him to either stay with us or take us home. Dad assured us that he would return in a few minutes and left us. The minutes turned into hours, and when they finally came back my mother wouldn't talk to anyone. It got very awkward, so my father finally took us home. On the ride home my parents screamed at one another. My mother tried to explain to him how humiliated she was and how could he abandon us. My father thought that Lena was being overly sensitive about everything and that she was rude for not talking to anyone. My father's insensitivity hurt my mother the most. As usual, my sister and I just looked out the window and wished we were home.

After that day, we didn't associate with my uncle's family, and Bill rarely spoke to my mother ever again. My mother was mad for days, and it wasn't long before she was on the phone calling her sisters one by one explaining all of the gory details. My father left the house and went to a bar. My sister and I were left with the ugly feeling that another family outing had been a disaster.

With that said, not all of the time on Church Street was full of conflict. There were some happy times. On Halloween, Mom would take us trick or treating to East Main Street, just around the corner from our apartment, where the rich people lived. Her idea was to sneak a peek into the houses of these wealthy people to see how they lived and how the rooms were decorated. If she couldn't peek inside then we were supposed to be her spies and fill her in on what we saw. Inevitably, my sister and I were too young to share her interest in spying on these people, so the information we relayed to her was not very detailed. Other times when I came home from school, I would find her watching American Bandstand on TV. Even though she was born in 1921, she was a fan of early rock and roll. If the TV wasn't on then she was listening to rock and roll on the radio. When Elvis made his first appearance on the Ed Sullivan Show in the late 1950s, we were watching it at Grandma MacPherson's house. Uncle Bill, Grandma, and my father thought his performance was scandalous, but Mom thought he was really exciting. She had a real interest in popular music that also included Dean Martin, who was her absolute favorite performer. The fact that he was handsome, funny, Italian, and a ladies' man didn't hurt. In the 1960s when he had his variety show, she would watch it every week with her sister Franny and Grandma.

Since we lived on Church Street, Main Street was just a short walk away, so trips "uptown" were not the ordeal when we lived on Lake Road. On shopping days we walked and did the shopping at a grocery store owned by our cousin, Agostino Rubino. This was an old Italian grocery store, where one could get all sorts of delicacies like snails, octopus, fennel, and anise. Old Mr. Dimick was be one of the butchers, and he would give us a raw hot dog to eat or a piece of ham. But the real treat was when we completed the grocery shopping, because then we would stroll across the street to the drug store where Aunt Franny worked. The store had a soda fountain in those days, and Aunt Franny always bought us an ice cream sundae or a root beer float. High times were had by all of us.

Some of the fondest memories I have of living on 14 Church Street was when we went with Mom to pay the rent. The owner of our apartment house was a *paesani* named Cosmo Baglio who owned the LeRoy Bottling Works. When the rent was due we would walk down Church Street, take the footbridge across the Oatka Creek, and make the short walk to the bottling works on Mill St. The LeRoy Bottling works produced Mil-kay brand soft drinks in two flavors: orange and grape, which were made from natural flavors. The production room was in the front of the factory so when you walked in the front door you saw the whole assembly line of bottles making their journey on the maze of conveyer belts to be filled with sweet, carbonated soda. This automated assembly line never ceased to amaze me. The stairway that led to Cosmo's office was just inside the main door. What I remember most about Cosmo's office was the gigantic Atlantic blue marlin that he had caught on a trip to Florida, which was hanging directly behind his desk. It had an array of sparking deep and sky blue colors on its fin and when you moved around the room, they turned iridescent violet. I was truly fascinated. Cosmo would be situated behind his desk usually puffing on a cigar. I don't know what held my attention more: the marlin or the assembly line. While Mom was paying the rent and busy talking to Cosmo, I usually asked permission to go back to the stairway so I could watch the parade of bottles go down the conveyer belts. Many times when Mom was through conducting business, Cosmo would follow her down the stairs and give Mary and me bottles of whatever kind of soda we wanted. I usually picked orange. It was the best orange soda ever. As you can see, many of my early memories revolve around food or the old Sicilian people with whom I came into contact.

One day in 1960, my mother took me aside to have a talk with me. She told me that Dad had made a drastic change in his life. This is when I first found out that my father became a Jehovah's Witness. My mother explained to me what that meant, and that she was very concerned because my father wanted to start taking the three of us to bible study with him.

By 1961, he quit his job driving a truck and was trying to make a living selling vacuum cleaners door to door. His thinking was he would have plenty of time to do Jehovah's work. Whatever was left of my parents' marriage quickly deteriorated, and my mother grew to hate him with a passion. Now he was never around, not because he was drinking, but because he was trying to sell vacuum cleaners during the day and studying the bible every night with his newfound friends.

To make matters worse, Neil was not bringing home a regular paycheck because he wasn't a successful salesman at all. The financial situation became so dire that we had to move out of the American section of LeRoy back into the Italian part of town to live with Grandma and Aunt Franny. Aunt Helen was getting married, so now there would be room for us in the old house, and Helen's new husband, Joe D'Angelo, was a carpenter by trade and was going to remodel Grandma's house to make an apartment for us in the old house on Lake Street. Mom told me that she was going to try to get a job from her old boss, Dr. Murray, as soon as possible, and that the new situation would be ideal because now Grandma and Aunt Franny would be around most of the time to babysit us. That hit me hard. The last thing I wanted to do was leave my friends and the Little League field next to our apartment to go live with a house full of old ladies in a neighborhood that really was old school Italian, but we had no choice.

Another factor has to be considered as to the reason why my mother so worried about my father's newfound obsession. My mother was a devout Catholic who obeyed all of the laws of the church to the letter. In the early 1960s, Catholics were forbidden to step foot into a church of another denomination, much less go to a bible study class of another faith. She believed all of the teachings of the church without question. The egg tempera painting, *Madonna with Angels*, depicts her devout religious beliefs. The portrait of her is based on a photograph that was taken when she graduated from the Eastman Dental Dispensary School, when she was full of hope for the future. The composition is based on the Cimabue egg tempera on panel, *Maesta of Santa Trinita*, painted sometime between 1280 and 1290. The subject of the painting is an enthroned Madonna, surrounded by angels. Since my mother believed her most important job in life was to raise her children, the theme of the Madonna most represented who

Madonna with Angels, *2011. Egg Tempera.*
Middle panel of the triptych, The Holy Family.

she was. The third angel from the top on the left hand side of the painting represents me. When I was young, we used to sit together on the couch and watch TV. I used to twirl my fingers in her hair so much that they would get tangled in it and, when I finally did get my fingers loose, my poor mother's hair would be in knots. Her hair was so soft, black, and beautiful, that I could not resist touching it. The violent thunderstorm above her represents the impending catastrophic events that were soon to overwhelm her life: the marriage to Neil and her impending fight with breast cancer. Her dental hygienist uniform is a symbol of her assimilation and how she saved us from perpetual poverty when my father couldn't handle life anymore and had to withdraw from the real world.

RETURN TO SICILIAN CULTURE

In the early days of her marriage to Neil, she did her best to make only the food he liked. She made roasts, scalloped potatoes, and chipped beef on toast, but never cooked lasagna or even spaghetti and meatballs. She never even learned how to make Grandma's spaghetti sauce. My father did like pizza, so we had that once in a while, but usually we went to a pizzeria for that. Lena subordinated who she was and where she came from. She seemed almost embarrassed to admit to her heritage in the early years. When Mom moved back with Grandma she didn't have to hide any more and I think that made her more comfortable. When Lena lived on Church Street, she had non-Italian friends; when we moved back to Lake Street, she had her Italian relatives and neighbors for her social structure.

The move to Grandma's house became our safety net and allowed us to live a lower-middle class existence. Grandma was such a kind hearted person that she would never turn down any of her family when we were in need. However, by moving back in with her, my mother was giving up the independence she desperately sought. She was admitting that life was too tough for her. She was too fragile and scared to fight adversity alone and moving to Lake Street was like living in a cocoon. This decision was a crucial point in my mother's life. "The majority of second-generation children leave the Italian community but retain strong ties to it,"[2] as my mother did when she moved across town out of the Italian neighborhood. The move out of the Italian neighborhood resulted in further attempts to become Americanized. It was through direct contact with the MacPhersons that our family was shaped in the model of contemporary American families. After my father failed as a provider, she returned to her roots and moved back into the Italian neighborhood and the culture of her parents. My mother's contact with the non-Italian world was reduced to a minimum, which was very atypical of second-generation families, where very few returned to the old neighborhoods once they left them.[3]

The move was somewhat confusing to me, since when I started kindergarten, the words of advice she gave me were not to admit to anyone that I was part Italian. Her goal as a mother was to give my sister and I a different experience than the one she received at the hands of cruel classmates. Mom would counsel me that if anyone asked what nationality I was, no matter if it was a teacher or a student, I was Scottish. In fact, my mother had a kilt made in Scotland in the MacPherson plaid for my sister. Eventually she acquired a tam-o-shanter

---

2   Campisi, "The Italian Family," 446.
3   Campisi, "The Italian Family," 447.

with our tartan, so that when my sister went to school, no one could ever mistake her for being anything other than Scottish.

Eventually the religious differences were too much for my parents' unstable relationship, and they separated. My mother never dated again and spent the rest of her life at 36 Lake Street with Grandma and Franny. I remember one time a friend asked her why she didn't go out to meet someone and have fun. She replied, "I had my chance at fun and it didn't work out. I'm prepared to spend the rest of my life alone." Since the Church was very clear on its stance on divorce and remarrying, Mom was not going to risk being excommunicated over a relationship with another man. She followed the teachings of the Church to the letter, so she remained single. However, I know of at least one man who showed an interest in her. He was a jeweler who she knew in Rochester. His name was Izzy, and he worked in the same building that she worked in. When a string of pearls that Great-Aunt Kitty MacPherson gave Mom needed repairing, she took it to him to fix. Lena told my sister that he wanted to do something special for her but would never let him. We never could get her to tell us what this special favor was. It is sad to think that she might have had a happier life if she was willing to socialize and go out and meet people outside of the Italian community in LeRoy.

After my mother moved back to her Sicilian family, Franny and Lena became inseparable. Left to right: a family friend, Lena, and Franny at a church function, 1978.

Eventually, my father asked for a divorce. He met a woman after he moved to South Carolina and wanted a second chance at life. When Mom picked up the pen to sign the papers, she started crying. My sister and Aunt Franny, who were sitting at the table with her, were moved by this outward display of emotion. I guess the nagging feelings of what might have been haunted her all of those years and it was too much for her to confront. Here he was moving on, and Mom knew that she never would. In a fit of vindictiveness, my mother said she would never sign the papers so that he would be as miserable as she was for the rest of his life. Franny told her sister that if she stayed married to Neil, if he defaulted on any loans, she could be responsible for his bills, realized that this was the final chapter of their life together.

Neil was moving on with his life and wasn't looking back; he was looking toward the future with a new family. In comparison, Mom's life with Grandma was stifling and her future was bleak. To Lena, it didn't seem fair that she was the one to end up alone, because through her incredible inner strength, she was the one who held the family together in the tumultuous years they were together as a couple. After a few days, Lena signed the papers and put them in the mail.

LIFE WITH LENA

My mother was a very difficult person to live with since she always had to know our business and then tell us the right way to do things. She was never wrong. After my sister Mary married and moved out of the house, the newlyweds built a house in the country to (hopefully) be far enough away from Lena so that her meddling could be kept to a minimum. Since my mother couldn't drive, my sister and her husband felt safe. My mother was so proud of the fact that her daughter was living in a house they built that she had to show all of her friends how beautiful it was. In my mother's eyes, my sister was living the American Dream that my mother was never able to achieve.

My poor sister could not decorate her house without parental interference. Mom tried to dictate the style and color of the curtains, how they should be hung, and how the furniture should be arranged. They had many fights over this topic with my sister finally doing it her own way. One day, Mary went to work and came home only to find that the furniture in the rooms had been rearranged, and the curtains were pinned exactly the way my mother wanted them. My sister was livid and called Mom to ask why she had entered their house when they weren't home and rearranged everything. Mary especially stressed the fact that Mom had no business in her house if no one was home. Lena calmly told her that she had some friends that she wanted to show the house to, and the house couldn't be shown in the state that it was. So Lena had her sister Franny drive her to the house so that Mom could redecorate the house before her friends arrived so that she wouldn't be embarrassed, since obviously Mary had no taste. Mary was so upset that she just went to bed without rearranging the furniture. My brother-in-law John worked the second shift in a factory and got home around midnight and went right to his favorite chair without turning the lights on. To his surprise, the chair wasn't there and he fell on the floor.

A few weeks after this family blow up, my wife and I were visiting LeRoy for Christmas and were staying with my sister and brother-in-law. My mother had not been over to the house since her indiscretion and showed up unexpectedly. She walked in the house and was not pleased with the fact that Mary had moved all of the furniture back to where it was originally, and while my mother was on the subject she wanted to know why my sister hung paintings so high ("Everyone knows that paintings should hang at eye level!"). John, who had had a few beers, said, "Ma! If we hung artwork at your eye level then everyone else wouldn't be able to look at them since they would be at their belly buttons." We all started laughing hysterically except for my sister and mother. These incidents are so funny now, but when they happened, they caused great aggravation for those who were involved. Lena's control issues were so consuming that she never took the time to know who we were and missed out on so much in life.

CANCER

The most catastrophic event in my mother's life was being diagnosed with breast cancer in 1973. She was fifty-two years old. I was a senior at SUNY Oswego and got a phone message from Aunt Franny to call home. Mom told me that she was going to have an operation the next day. It was very difficult for her to talk about it with me. I, of course, wanted to leave and be with her, but she told me to stay in school. She had my sister and Aunt Franny to take care of her, so there was no need for me to miss any classes. So I stayed in Oswego. The tragedy was the lump that she had on her breast went undiagnosed for years and she was too afraid to do anything about it. When she finally went to see her doctor, he immediately got her into surgery to have the lump removed.

Lena had a mastectomy then endured agonizing treatments of chemotherapy and radiation on and off for the next thirteen years. She lost her hair and was sick and tired most of the time. Throughout her whole life she suffered from migraines, and now she had them on top of everything else. Luckily, she was living with Grandma and Franny and she had the whole support group of her sisters and cousins who were there to give her rides to the doctor's office or to Strong Memorial Hospital in Rochester for treatments; and of course they were there just for moral support as well. As I mentioned in Chapter 9, Great Uncle Rosalino, Grandma's brother, owned a pharmacy in Rochester and supplied Mom with the expensive drugs she needed. Tests taken after the mastectomy showed that the cancer had spread into her organs, and she spent the next thirteen years fighting it with every ounce of strength in her body. It went into remission several times and then they would find it spreading again. Mom never gave up and I suppose that is why she lasted so long. If she cried about her situation, she never did it in front of us and above all never gave us any information about her situation. That was Aunt Franny's job. There was very little communication between us about anything important even up to the day she died, so I guess she still thought we were little children and had to be shielded from the tragedies of life.

By this time, her beloved Dr. Murray had retired. She went to work for Dr. David, a dentist who had a practice also in the Sibley Tower. Mom was a very good dental hygienist, and through the years gained more experience as a dental assistant to Dr. Murray when he performed oral surgery. As a result, she became even more marketable. Dr. David had been trying to get her to work for him for years but she remained loyal to Dr. Murray. She came home one night after a meeting with Dr. David about her salary and benefits and was in a foul mood. It seemed that Dr. Murray had taken advantage of her loyalty and had been paying her a pittance of her new salary. All of those years we could have used the extra money to pay bills, but instead we had to scrimp and save while he lived the high life in Rochester. She felt betrayed by the person who she held in the highest regard because she expected him to take care of her. On the other hand, my mother never asked her employer for a raise, so half of the blame rested with her outlook on life. She learned early in life from Grandma not to make waves, to become invisible. As a Sicilian growing up in LeRoy, the first and second generation did not call attention to themselves because those with power might retaliate against them or inflict measures detrimental to their families, over which they had no control. In her opinion, if a person had a job, he/she was lucky and shouldn't want to get on the wrong side of the boss by being greedy or seeming ungrateful.

Lena had the most potential to do well, but because of her character and personality, she didn't make it. She had personality flaws and feelings of low self-esteem that did her in. My mother had a serious professional medical degree with skills that she could have exploited and given her greater financial stability. She fully accepted the immigrant belief that 'I am the intruder and not worth it.' Her feeling was, 'Because of whom I am, I get to suffer and I should be grateful for what I have,' so my mother would never ask for what she really deserved. Possibly it was because of her gender that added to her insecurities by growing up in a time when women were considered second-class citizens.

Mom still worked full time but wasn't happy working with her new employer. In her early sixties, it became too much for her try to keep her job with Dr. David and undergo treatments, so she retired. Mom thought that he didn't understand enough about how she felt

Mom and Cait, 1986.

after her treatments and he wouldn't let her off on days after chemotherapy. One day during the summer when I was home visiting her, Dr. David came to the house. Mom told me she didn't want to see him and wanted me to get rid of him. I wanted no part of it, but she insisted. I told Mom to talk to him for just a little while because it was the right thing to do since he drove all the way from Rochester just to see her. When I answered the door, this nice man introduced himself and said he wanted to see how Lena was since he hadn't heard anything from her. He had tried calling her but she was never home and was afraid that something had happened to her.

I tried to explain to him that she was really sick and didn't want him to see her in such bad shape. Dr. David insisted that he would only stay a short while and that she had been such a wonderful employee. All he wanted to do was pay his respects. I tried to get Mom to let him in but she refused and got really angry with me. Then I knew if I had let him in there would have been an ugly scene and that she would never forgive me. Once you got on Mom's bad side she seldom forgave anyone. I went back to him and said, "I'm really sorry but she is in no shape to see anybody." He left but I could tell he didn't buy my excuse. I guess my mother wanted to keep the outside world at bay because her house was her sanctuary especially when she was sick. Even though she was still disappointed with the circumstances of her employment with Dr. Murray, in her eyes, Dr. David never was able to measure up to him.

Several times her health deteriorated to the point that we thought she was going to die, but her grandchildren kept her going, and she literally rose from her deathbed. On one such occasion just before Easter in 1985, I received word from Aunt Franny that Mom had been transported to the hospital and the doctors thought that this was the end. If I wanted to see her before she died I better bring up the family because Lena was on her last legs. I was told by Aunt Franny to bring my navy blue suit just in case she died so that I would have something to wear to the funeral. I had two children, a son and a daughter, whom she rarely saw. Mom adored my son Jesse and my daughter Cait, who had been born the previous year. She had only seen Cait twice. We kept our trip a secret so just by chance if she didn't make it before we got there, she wouldn't die with that on her mind. We drove into LeRoy the next day from South Carolina and immediately picked up Aunt Helen, and we all made the trip to the hospital in Batavia. When we got to her room, Helen wanted to let Caitlin walk into the room by herself to surprise Mom. Cait walked in and we heard Lena say, "Who is this little girl?" Before Cait could walk to the bed Helen hurried into the room and said, "Don't you recognize your own granddaughter?" Then the rest of us walked into the room and the first thing that came to Mom's mind was, "What are you doing here? You should be at work." I told her I was on Spring Break so we thought we would surprise her and make the trip so that she could see her grandchildren.

Mom looked terrible. She was very thin and extremely weak looking, much older than her sixty-four years. It was then I told her that there was a job opening at SUNY Geneseo and I was applying for it. She got so happy said she would start saying the rosary and have Grandma light some candles. In her mind I was going to get the job and that was that.

Shortly after we returned home to South Carolina, I got a phone call from Aunt Franny. She couldn't believe it, but right after we left, Mom's whole attitude changed and before long she was up and out of bed walking around the hospital so the doctors let her come home. They were amazed that she had made such a miraculous recovery. As it turned out, I got the position at SUNY Geneseo a month later and for the last year of her life she saw her grandchildren every Sunday and got to know them before she died. Of course, Grandma got all of the credit for my new job because of her pull with the authorities in heaven.

Very early in the morning on St. Patrick's Day 1986, the phone rang and woke me up out of a dead sleep with the news we were dreading to hear; Mom was in the hospital and this time there would not be a miraculous recovery. We had been to see her the previous Sunday she was weaker than ever. I called Mary who lived in Pittsburgh to come home. Linda and I got to the hospital at 8:00 a.m. and the room was filled with her sisters, Franny, Florence, and Helen. She was lying in bed with her eyes closed, receiving Last Rites from the priest. We sat in the room all morning with me holding her hand and trying to talk to her, but she never acknowledged that she heard me. At noon my sister arrived and we got her a private room so that she could die in peace.

Around 3:00 p.m., John, my sister's ex-husband, and his girlfriend came to pay their respects. Since the divorce, Mom got particularly close to them. Lena was not fond of John before they were married but after the fact she grew to love him very much. I think the stigma of having a divorced daughter brought too much shame on the family and she had to confront the fact that her children weren't perfect. Mom would have John and his girlfriend over for supper and she would even do his wash for him. As soon as we greeted them, Lena woke up like they had just come over for coffee and donuts. All of my aunt's eyes bulged out of their heads and my sister's mouth dropped open. John leaned over to give Mom a kiss and Lena put her arms around his neck, but she was so weak that her arms dropped to the bed in exhaustion. Her sister Franny burst out sobbing and the rest of her sisters gasped. The intensity of this dramatic scene prompted Aunt Florence to usher my sister and I out of the room for the duration of John's visit. After fifteen minutes, they left and Mom laid back down and closed her eyes.

We were all so incredulous that we couldn't speak. We just looked at one another. Finally, at 7:00 p.m. Aunt Franny pulled Mary and me out of the room and into the hall and told us that Lena was waiting for us to leave because she didn't want to die with her children in the room. After I convinced Mary that this was the proper thing to do, we said our final goodbye and gave her a kiss telling her we would be back tomorrow morning. We left the hospital and made the ten minute drive to Grandma's house, and by the time I got there, the doctor called and told me that she had passed away. He added that he had never seen such a proud and tough woman in his life, and that medically speaking she should have died years ago, but the strength she got from her family and grandchildren allowed her to cheat death all of these years. On her visits to his office she told him over and over how proud she was of her son, the college professor.

I was still trying to make sense of the day's events that it was hard to believe what he told me. When my aunts arrived at Grandma's house, they told us that as soon as we left the room, Mom's breathing changed and she died in a matter minutes. I thought to myself that if that is all she wanted, I would have left hours earlier just so that the end would have come sooner and Mary would had been spared the episode with her ex-husband. I still don't know what to make of that day. My wife tells me it was all to get back at Mary for divorcing her husband, but whatever was the reason, she went out on her own terms. On March 17, 1986, St. Patrick's Day, my mother entered into her eternal reward.

For the wake, my sister was searching for the set of rosary that Dr. Murray had bought my mother on one of his trips to Ireland. It contained green stones that had quickly become her favorite pair, but they were nowhere to be found. The only pair she found were the ones that Dad got her when he was in Italy during World War II that appeared to be made of pearls. These were the pair she wore prior to getting the pair from Dr. Murray. Mary was conflicted because of the rocky relationship she had with Neil, and told Aunt Franny about her dilemma. Franny told Mary to go ahead and use the ones that her husband had given her, because at one time there was love between them.

For all of my mother's sacrificing her own wants so that my sister and I could enjoy a better life, it only made her even more dependent on her family members and more isolated from influences outside the Italian community. My mother had the most potential to do well, but because of her personality and character, she did not exploit the possibilities that could have given her greater financial security. In the dental community in Rochester, she could have had her choice of jobs but she embraced the attitude of being an immigrant and not worth it. Her feelings were, 'I get to suffer and I should be grateful for what I have,' so she would never ask for what she deserved. Her Uncle Cosmo and Uncle Tony saw that the possibilities in the world were there for the taking, but she shied away from asserting herself. Some of this attitude was based on her gender. The 1960s were a time when the Women's Movement gained momentum, but it left Mom behind since she would not make waves. Even her sisters who were homemakers became more successful in life since they all married successful husbands and owned their own houses. By moving back home with her family, Lena had the perfect setup and support group that would have given her the opportunity to find a better job and financial security. Ultimately, my mother was more fragile than the other sisters, and was not resilient enough to get to plan B. The circumstances were too hard to overcome, so she gave up.

Whether it was complacency or whether she was afraid of new situations, Mom relied on other people instead of herself. Of all the sisters, she was the one that retreated away from assimilation and went in the other direction. The whole scenario of working for Dr. Murray, because of some misguided notion that she owed him for the rest of her life for helping her get started, only went so far as an excuse. Thinking that she wasn't good enough to expect to get a higher paying job or that we weren't good enough to have the best doctors reveals what a low self-esteem she had. My mother accepted what life threw her way.

Every day when my mother looked in the mirror, she was reminded that she was different. Her olive complexion and physical features made her extremely self-conscious, so she believed that she would never fit in because of her looks and lived in fear of reprisals from the non-Italian community. By the time I was old enough to know her as a person, she had become bitter and disillusioned. It is hard to imagine her when she was young and hopeful. Old photos of her, when she was a young woman, reveal that she had friends and was even affectionate with Dad.

Lena also suffered from the rescue fantasy – "a man will save me." When he didn't, she was not prepared to bounce back from life's troubles. When my parents' marriage failed and she lived to see my father remarry and have a new life, her bitterness increased more than ever. He got another chance in life, but her self-imposed existence of seclusion and isolation only exacerbated the loneliness and rancor she carried with her for the rest of her life. Lena was haunted by the thought of what could have been, which only added to her emotional baggage. If she had remarried and allowed herself a second try at a relationship, perhaps her life would have had a different and happier ending. Instead, she took her resentment out on her loved ones, which only pushed them further away from her. My sister and I did not care what people thought, and we were willing to make life-altering changes even if it went against church teachings. My mother might have held it against Mary and I that we rejected her outlook on life and adopted one where we were more willing to stand up for what we wanted and be more like the MacPhersons. I guess we learned the lesson on how to become Americans too well.

CHAPTER 20

Aunt Frances (Franny) Ann O'Geen (Gugino)

Born: March 25, 1926, LeRoy, New York
Died: January 6, 1992, Batavia, New York

Aunt Franny, 1949–50. She was very stylish and wore the latest fashions, and had an especial fetish for Italian shoes.

Aunt Franny was the sixth child of Frank and Carrie O'Geen. She was the tallest of all of the O'Geen sisters, reaching a height of five feet six inches. Her hairstyle, from my perspective, looked like a variation of a beehive hairdo that made her look even taller. Franny's hair fascinated my sister and me because it felt like cotton candy and it never moved when we touched it. She was pretty and looked very Sicilian, having a beautiful olive complexion like my mother. Franny was an odd mixture of Old World and American values. Occasionally, she would let her guard down and I could see that she believed in a lot of the superstitions that were handed down from her parents. One day I asked her about the *malocchio*, or evil eye, and she got very upset with me. She remarked that this topic is something no one ever talks about because if we did, we would be in big trouble. Franny hated braggarts, and felt that if someone tooted their own horn, bad things would happen to them. She honestly believed that God or some spirit would hear it and find him/her, and then that person would be living the life of Job. There were unexplainable forces that we just didn't taunt with arrogance.

When Aunt Franny was young, her hair was very dark, and as it got gray she colored it with a very subtle shade of light brown mixed in with gray. She looked very stylish and acted very proper. Franny always dressed perfectly with everything matching. Even when she wore a housecoat she looked dressed up. During the early 1960s, my aunt bought an outlandish dress hat every Easter that usually had flowers of some sort on it. Although one year, she actually bought a subdued Jackie Kennedy-style hat, which was a drastic change from the colorful ones she preferred. They ranged from bright red and dark green to violet. After she died and my aunts were cleaning out her closets, I made a request that seemed strange to them. I asked them if I could have her beautiful Easter hats. They looked at me as if I had lost my mind, because no one wore them anymore; they couldn't be for my wife, and besides, what would a man want with women's hats anyway? To my mind, they really represented her better than anything else, and I could use them as props in still life for watercolor classes and now for my installations. They were in mint condition and still in their original boxes. So after my aunts gave each other some perplexed stares, I became the proud owner of Franny's Easter hats.

In addition to hats, she bought a pair of new shoes every year that were made in Italy. On one of her trips to the Old Country, she bought some shoes that she thought were the most comfortable in the world. So every year she ordered a pair and waited impatiently for them to arrive. Because she had to have shoes that matched her dresses, there were so many shoes of different styles and colors in her closets that she could have opened a shoe store. At one time there were as many as fifty pairs of shoes. Sadly, I never got to her shoe collection before they were unceremoniously thrown away.

Left to right: Cousin Mary Micelli, Aunt Franny, Alfredo the restaurant owner, and Camille Barone on one of my aunt's trips to Rome.

Aunt Franny never married, and lived all of her sixty-five years with her mother. She became the designated caretaker for Grandma at an early age, and took the brunt of Grandma's hard Old World ways. She told me one time that "someone had to do it. Young people today are so lousy that when their parents get old they ship them out to an old folks' home. They show no respect for their elders. Momma will die at home. I may not be so lucky. Who is going to take care of me when I get old?" Franny had very little freedom to do what she wanted because Grandma objected to everything that would make her more independent. Either my aunt was intimidated by Grandma and was afraid to stand up to her, or she didn't want to make waves. I think Franny felt that life was easier if she just did what Grandma wanted her to do; consequently, she carried a heavy burden throughout her life. The toll of her compliance was high blood pressure, and my aunt looked unhappy most of the time.

Franny was even more religious than my mother. One day, she told me that it would the greatest thing in the world if Mary, my sister, became a nun and I became a priest. She even had our names chosen. When I told Lena, thankfully she didn't have the same enthusiasm for the idea. Mom made a beeline to Franny and told not to push this topic ever again.

Since Franny lived with Grandma all her life, she never learned how to cook even the simplest of meals. The joke around the house was that she couldn't even boil water for tea.

Grandma made all of the meals; in fact, Grandma wouldn't have had it any other way. Since Franny never married, she had a few close girlfriends that she went out with to dinner and a movie or on trips. Surprisingly, even though she lived home all of her life, she made trips to Italy and Las Vegas. Her life was a real dichotomy. On the one hand, she was super religious and lived a very mundane life; on the other, she loved to gamble. Her favorite place to travel in the United States was to Las Vegas. She hated Atlantic City and thought it was sleazy so she stayed away. Vegas had class. On trips to Vegas, she took in some shows and played the slot machines; nothing high stakes, but just for fun. Her favorite performer was Wayne Newton. Her trips were the only escape she had from a mundane and dreary life.

Sin City and the Holy City (see below) is a portrait of my aunt that I painted in 2006. She is seen holding my daughter seated on a variation of a Carlo Crivelli throne complete with fruit and vegetables. When I took the photograph of her that I used in the painting one Sunday afternoon, she yelled at me because I took it while she was wearing her bathrobe. She actually hated to have her photograph taken, and many times all we got was an image of her running away from the camera with her hands covering her face. I assured her that I would never show it to anybody, and that it would be for my daughter when she got older to remember her by. So when I painted the picture, I tried to make the housecoat look more like a dress. On the left is Valledolmo, Sicily, the birthplace of her parents, and to the right is the Vatican with St. Peter's Cathedral. While in Rome, she bought the latest fashions and really enjoyed the nightlife. In the painting, I drastically changed the Renaissance throne into a giant slot machine that always comes up cherries. Now my aunt can spend eternity reading her prayer book and having a little fun on the side. I glued glass beads to her sleeve, headpiece, and shawl, to suggest her love of fashion and the glitz of Vegas that she enjoyed.

Franny was my mother's best friend. When we left Church Street and moved to Lake Street to live with her and Grandma, they became inseparable. Many evenings, Franny and my mother would wait until Grandma went to bed and then they would go over to our apartment and smoke and gossip all night. Then the next day Grandma would yell at them for smoking in the house.

Franny was also my godmother and took a special interest in me. When Christmas came around and I wanted to get Mom what she always wanted and asked for every year, a "brassiere" and a slip, Franny always came to my rescue. I could never bring myself to walk into the local dress shop and ask for these undergarments for my mother. Franny never

Sin City and the Holy City, *2007. Egg tempera on panel.*

took any money from me and always told me to save it for college. On birthdays or if I got a particularly good report card, Franny would give me five or ten dollars as a reward for working hard. While I was in college without fail, she sent me ten dollars a week for spending money. She was a very special person who spoiled my sister and me. During the rough financial times that my mother faced, Franny slipped her some money to tide her over until payday. She was very generous and loyal to her family. Franny always said, "Family comes first. Don't ever forget that."

One of my earliest recollections of Aunt Franny was when I was around four years old and she gave me my first introduction to Italian food. My mother, my sister, and I were visiting Grandma around suppertime. They were just finishing up when we walked into the kitchen. I remember sitting on her lap. I was very curious about the bowl of rigatoni and sauce on the table. I had never seen this kind of food before. Grandma called them "stovepipes" and so I had to try them. I sat on Franny's lap and she fed me, and of course fell in love with this "exotic" dish.

Franny and me in front of the house on Lake Street, 1951.

Franny was my sister's favorite aunt, probably because my aunt paid more attention to her than the rest of them. Mary really admired the way Franny looked with all of her matching outfits and gloves. My aunt was always letting my sister try on her jewelry, hats, and shoes. She spoiled my sister and me with ice cream treats that she kept in her freezer. There was always a Nutty Buddy or ice cream sandwich that she would give us if we were particularly good. Of course, she also had to have one with us. She loved pieces of sweets and was such a picky eater that for many meals, all she ate was celery and maybe a raw fennel, followed by a dish of her favorite French Vanilla or pistachio ice cream. She hated meat except for that occasional hot dog she liked burnt to a crisp that I cooked for her outside on the grill.

Grandma told me one time that she tried to get Franny to go to college, but she didn't want to go. She also had an opportunity to work for Kodak but again turned it down. My aunt ended up working two jobs instead. She was secretary for St. Joseph's Roman Catholic Church, which was right across the street from her house, and for a drugstore on Main Street owned by the Sirusa family. Franny was a highly regarded secretary, and Monsignor Healy, the pastor at St. Peter's Church, tried unsuccessfully for years to have her quit her job at St. Joseph's and work for him at St. Peter's. Whenever he would see me, he would tell me to put in a good word for him with Franny. I tried to tell him she was very loyal to her parish and that would never happen, but the Monsignor was an imposing figure, in his hat with the red ball on top and his cassock trimmed with red, so I made sure I told my aunt. If I saw him coming I would duck down an ally to avoid him, but he had a sixth sense and always found me. Then the inevitable question would follow: "Did you put in a good word for me?" I dreaded having to tell him that she was happy at St Joe's. Then he would ask questions about world history, and if I got them right, which I always did, he would remark that I was one of the few young people today who had a sense of history and understood the threat of Communism. Monsignor was a Chaplain in the National Guard and took the threat of Communism very seriously. His parting shot was for me to remember to keep working on Franny. If she ever switched parishes, however, Grandma and many other church members in the Italian community would have stopped speaking to her. Even a higher salary and Monsignor's imposing figure couldn't convince her to change her affiliation. Franny could not be bought because to her, loyalty was a trait that was greater than anything else in the world.

My aunt got a job at the Cut Rate Drug Store when she got out of high school and had that same job for her whole life to the year she died. The owners of the store were three highly respected pharmacists who were of Sicilian descent. They were role models for many Italians, and they helped change the perceptions of the non-Italians who thought that Italians were subhuman. She never made very much money and I guess the combination of fearing the world outside of LeRoy and being comfortable with her life kept her where she felt safe. But what a price she paid. On her rare day off, she cleaned the house for Grandma or went to the hairdresser. The rest of the time she worked. She lived a very mundane life. Franny never made much money at either job.

As late as 1955, the drugstore had a soda fountain where the high school kids went to hang out after school. Around the age of five, I remember at the end of an exhausting shopping trip we stopped to get an ice cream sundae. The place was packed. I remember my aunt making ice cream sodas and socializing with all of the kids of parents she knew, and they liked her. Most of the kids in public school knew her and had good things to say about her. Many times when they found out she was my aunt they were impressed. There was a lot of noise and commotion and I loved it. I wanted to go there every afternoon.

By the time the late fifties rolled around, the soda fountain was gone and the store expanded and sold more cosmetics. Franny usually worked the front register, and from this vantage point she could see the whole world of LeRoy pass before her eyes. She observed who was going where and who was doing what and with whom, but more importantly she could see what my sister and I were up to. If I walked home with a girl, my mother knew about it before I walked in the door. There were other ways to go home but I had to cross the Oatka Creek to go to and from school. There were only three bridges in the village and they were spaced far apart. My only hope was to duck down Mill Street, which was across the street from the Cut Rate, but Franny had an eye like a hawk and never missed anything.

When I was a sophomore in high school, I had a girlfriend and we were walking up town to a local hangout to get some Cokes. I made the mistake of holding her hand when I passed by Franny's outpost. Franny thought it was scandalous for high school kids to hold hands in public and expressed her opinions many times to my sister and me. My aunt thought holding hands lead to more dangerous forms of physical contact between teenagers and would probably lead to unwanted pregnancies. That evening, after Mom got home from work and Franny had a chance to inform her of what she saw, I got a lecture about holding hands in public, and more importantly, "who was this girl?" My Italian friend Alec Spinello, who lived most of his life in Italy, told me that it was the same for him in his small town. There were relatives and friends—or a better word for them were spies—all around his hometown, who reported to his mother what he was up to. This really kept me on my toes, so I paid very close attention to when Franny was working at the rectory so I could have some fun with my friends on Main Street. But then again, there were other relatives and friends who were working in other shops on Main Street to pick up the slack when Franny was not working at the drugstore. There was a network of spies all over town that kept parents informed of the whereabouts of their children. Main Street was a no man's land for a kid.

Sometimes I took advantage of Franny's working at the drugstore by stopping in to see her. It always paid off because she would always buy me an ice cream treat or a candy bar. One of the pharmacists had a daughter who was interested in art, so they carried basic drawing supplies. Franny would make sure that I was always well stocked with pencils and drawing pads because she liked to see the drawings I could do. One year, she even bought me a box of soft pastels that kept me busy many lonely nights.

Franny and her friend Aggie worked at the Cut Rate all of their lives. They were loyal and devoted employees. There was not a retirement plan for either of them, so one of the owners told them that in lieu of a retirement plan, he was going to leave them a substantial amount of money in his will. I think it was around $100,000, which was big money 25 years ago. Franny was ecstatic. Her loyalty had paid off just like she used to preach to us. My aunt repeated over and over again, "if you are a good and don't cause trouble, you will be rewarded." She made plans with her sister Dorothy and my mother to do some traveling when she retired. Franny, like my mother, was not very lucky. When her benefactor was on his deathbed, his wife made him change his will so that Franny and Aggie were totally left out of it. When the lawyer for the family informed my aunt that she had been taken out of the will, she was devastated. She loved traveling more than anything, and she had been waiting for her retirement to start enjoying life. It was one of the few indulgences she allowed herself. So the trip to Vegas the three of them were planning was in jeopardy. Sadly, none of the other owners stepped up. They all made a fortune in that store because all of the Italians in town did their business with them, but in the end they were greedy and were only looking out for themselves.

Everyone in town liked Franny. My aunt knew everyone because she had the opportunity to come into contact with people from all walks of life and all ethnic groups who lived in the town. Franny was well liked by many of the people she came into contact with at the drugstore and from church, and on her birthday she got mountains of birthday cards. She especially became friendly with teachers since she respected them so much and she could get an informal report on my sister and me and then pass on the information to Mom. There was nothing like a surprise teacher evaluation to keep you straight.

As I mentioned earlier in the chapter, Franny did have a social life and had several girl-friends with whom she went out to dinner, to see a movie, or travel with her on trips to Las Vegas or Italy. They were all woman of Italian descent or cousins. One exception was Eleanor Townsend, a rich woman, who lived in a mansion on West Main Street. This woman was also an artist who had an apartment Italy and wrote and illustrated a book on Sicily. I was invited to her house one time to show her my artwork, and I found her to be a very knowledgeable and worldly person. Eleanor repeatedly invited Franny to go to Italy with her, but she went for months and Franny couldn't take off work for that long or leave Grandma for that length of time, so she missed out on the trips of a lifetime. Eleanor was very generous and always brought back expensive gifts for Franny. One time, she took my aunt to New York to see Beverly Sills. Despite her friend's generosity, on many occasions Franny would make excuses not to go out with her. It was as if my aunt felt uncomfortable with her generosity since Franny could not reciprocate to the same degree. Eleanor had everything, so what could my aunt get her? Franny did not like to take advantage of people. She might have thought that the relationship was too one-sided, so she withdrew.

Franny surrounded by desserts, 1990.

Occasionally Franny had a date, but they were few and far between because she never had a real interest in getting married. One time I asked her why she never married. She replied that after seeing the marriages of her sisters she was not impressed with marriage or men in general. I think if she would have met someone who was religious and sophisticated, she might have found happiness. When Franny was in her early forties, she finally decided it was time to learn how to drive, so she asked the driver education teacher from the high school to give her lessons. Franny was tall for our family and this man barely came up to her shoulders. He was short, Catholic, and of Lebanese descent. They went out on one date, and when she got back home she said she hated it so much that she never wanted to do it again. He made a drastic mistake by trying to get my sister and me to tell her what a good guy he was. He would call me into his classroom and tell me how much he liked my aunt. I wanted to tell him he was wasting his time with her but it was not any of my affair. Desperate actions like this only turned off my aunt. She kept declining his dates and he finally got the message. He was devastated. Eventually he moved away and took another job in another school district.

To Franny's credit, she wasn't going to settle for just anybody in order to leave home and get away from Grandma. However, Grandma did drive Franny nuts every time she had a date, giving her a curfew or telling Franny she couldn't even go out. My aunt never really had a chance to find a husband living under these circumstances. At times, Franny did what she wanted to do, but it was under extreme duress. Other times Grandma accused my aunt of sneaking in her boyfriends after she went to bed. My mother would tell Grandma to leave Franny alone, but that only made Grandma mad at my mother. The next day after a date, Grandma would interrogate Franny on what she did and why she came home so late. I knew just how Franny felt, since it sounded like the third degree I got whenever I went out. Grandma was also worried that Franny would find someone and leave home, so she did her best to break up any relationship, real or imagined. After a while, Franny stopped dating and Grandma got her wish.

Franny even had less of a sense of humor than Mom, but when she did laugh it was the strangest sound imaginable. It sounded very similar to the noise of a laughing hyena. When we heard it, we all smiled. She liked her nieces and nephews better when they were young and innocent. Inevitably, each of us disappointed her in some way as we became adults, when our flaws became more obvious to her. I put too much pressure on myself to try to have her be proud of me all of the time. It was impossible to live up to that kind of unrealistic code of ethics. She had high standards for everyone and expected them to meet these unrealistic standards all of the time. We were human after all, and not perfect. When I was little, my aunt had a favorite Italian word she used whenever she was pleasantly surprised about a report card or if we got an award. She would say, "Minchia!" As we got older it was shortened to just one long, "Miiiiiiiiiii!" or "Mischa!" I always wondered what it meant, so I asked my friend Alec, who is from a little town near Venice, the meaning of this word. When he told me I almost died. It seems that when my aunt was thinking she was expressing enthusiasm, but she was really saying "dick," a slang term for "penis." So here was this very pious woman who never swore, and who, to my knowledge, was never intimate with a man, was enthusiastically yelling out the name of male genitalia. This revelation puts a whole new context on our conversations and the conversations she had with my children. She sensed it was a word of excitement and she was right. It was a word of high excitement.

When my mother died, Franny became really lonely. They had been inseparable for years and were allies against Grandma. Now she had to live with Grandma by herself. Her other sisters certainly jumped to her defense when Grandma crossed the line, but it wasn't the same. Aunt Franny missed the camaraderie of her older sister. They were confidants and shared each other's fears and secrets. They knew things about each other that no one else knew.

When my mother knew the end was near, she asked her two sisters, Franny and Helen, to take her place to be grandmothers to my children, Jesse and Caitlin, which they eagerly did. Franny absolutely adored my daughter Caitlin, and the portrait of my aunt in *Sin City and the Holy City* is based on a photograph taken shortly after Mom's death in 1986. The family tradition of bringing out the charm bracelet to let the nieces play with it started all over again. Caitlin held court and made Franny laugh until tears came to my aunt's eyes. Franny really doted on Caitlin, and especially liked her blonde hair and blue eyes, the symbols that our Sicilian family had finally been assimilated to the point that now the fourth generation actually looked "American."

A few years after the death of my mother, I stopped taking my children to mass in LeRoy. Linda thought that they needed some sort of religious upbringing, and they even expressed an interest in going to Sunday school because their friends were. So she started taking them to a Protestant church in the town where we were living. My aunts Franny and Helen were not amused and stopped talking to us. Aunt Helen eventually came around but Franny never did. Religion was such a touchy subject with me that after what I endured with my parents, I made sure I would never force my religion on anyone. Religion was not going to break up my marriage.

Whenever we visited Grandma, who was still alive, Franny would walk out of the room and act like we weren't there. She even ignored her great niece and nephew. I asked her one time why she was mad at me. She responded in the coldest voice I ever heard that she wasn't. I told her that it is one thing to be mad at me but not the kids. They were innocent, but she angrily walked away and never spoke to any of us again. I tried to visit her in the hospital when she had cancer but I was told that she didn't want to see anybody.

I wasn't surprised at the reaction of my aunt. Living with her all those years, I knew her very well and I understood the depths of her devout Catholicism. I grew up in a very chaotic household and I didn't want the same fate for my family. So I made a choice and hoped that Franny would be able to understand my position, but sadly she never did. I was her godson and favorite nephew, so her disappointment concerning my actions was too great for her to overcome, because loyalty to the family was the most important core value a person could have. What I did to her was beyond disappointment; I brought shame onto the family. To this day I regret that we parted on such terms.

Franny died on January 6, 1992. As you can imagine, the whole town showed up and there were plenty of priests and nuns in attendance. Father Zupa gave one of his best eulogies and he even shed a tear toward the end of it. There wasn't a dry eye in the church. As the family was putting her passing into perspective, we all couldn't help but think that Franny lived a tragic life and that she missed out on so much. Her reaction to the pressures of life was to avoid all conflict and keep a low profile even when she had the high road. I think she feared the outside world so much that she used Grandma as an excuse to avoid trying new experiences and standing up for herself. I vowed I wouldn't make the same mistake.

CHAPTER 21

Aunt Dorothy Onalee O'Geen (Gugino)

Born: February 29, 1932

When I asked my aunt for an interview for a chapter about her, she replied, "All you need to know about me for your book is that I was born, I worked, and I'm gonna die. Put that in my chapter." In respect for her, I will keep this chapter short. Aunt Dorothy was the last child of my grandparents, Frank and Carrie O'Geen. She was nine years old when her father died. She said that Grandma had the wake in the parlor of the house on Lake Street, and for years she had a hard time even walking through the room without conjuring up the image of his corpse.

As a result of being the youngest, she benefited the most since her parents and sisters paved the way to assimilation. They received the brunt of harsh treatment from non-Italians while she was able to become an "American girl" and leave the Old World customs behind. It seems that during her youth in the 1930s to the 1950s, she received some of the same type of harassment at the hands of her classmates that her sisters encountered, but after World War II, society eased up on the Italians. Since many Italians served their country with distinction, society as a whole looked on them in a different way than before the war. Many Americans had

Dorothy (left) with Great-Aunt Rose (right), her godmother.

to serve side-by-side with Italian-Americans, and in the process they found out that they were all just people. Another factor that contributed to assimilation was her personality. Dorothy was strong willed and was able to stand up to much of the prejudice and even give it back when necessary.

Aunt Dorothy is a mere five feet two inches tall, with brown eyes and black hair. She is the only daughter who went to college (my mother went to professional school), earning a bachelor's degree in chemistry from D'Youville College in Buffalo, New York. Her first job was working in a research laboratory at the University of Rochester and then she landed a job with Jell-O and later with General Foods in Dover, Delaware.

Dorothy was different from the rest of her sisters. From an early age, she had a very strong independent streak and pretty much did what she wanted to do. Grandma was powerless to stop her; she finally met her match. My aunt did not put with up Grandma's meddling and gave her a piece of her mind when she needed it. One day after Dorothy had retired and returned home, Grandma and my aunt had a lively discussion about where Dorothy had been earlier in the day. After Aunt Dorothy told Grandma it was none of her business what she was doing, Grandma remarked that, "I wish you would have stayed in Dover." Grandma spent a lot of time being mad at Dorothy, since she couldn't push her around like she could Aunt Franny.

Since Dorothy had a prestigious job, her older sisters deferred to her and looked up to her. If Dorothy had an opinion, then she was probably right. Aunt Dorothy was the only person who could change my mother's mind once she made a decision. One day when my sister Mary was a teen, she and Mom were having an argument. Mary wanted to go out with her friends, and Mom was totally against the idea and wanted her to stay home where she could keep an eye on her. Dorothy heard them arguing and came over to our side of the house and asked them what was wrong. Mom told my aunt. Dorothy said, "Well, let her go!" Incredulously, Mom changed her mind and told Mary to be home by 11. It was impressive the clout she had over her older siblings. Of all of Grandma's children, Dorothy was the one who became a successful career woman who lived life on her own terms, something the rest of her sisters could only realize in their dreams. My aunt traveled around the world and bought new cars. She successfully assimilated into American culture and lived the American Dream.

When Aunt Dorothy went to public school, she still encountered the same ethnic prej-udice that her sisters had endured. Even as late as 1950 when she graduated from high school, there still was a significant segment of LeRoy that perceived and treated Italians as inferior intellectually and culturally. In New York State today, we take the contributions of Italian-Americans for granted since this nationality has since become the largest ethnic group. The fears of non-Italians have come true in that we moved into their towns and decided to stay, and in the process transformed society. Life in these little towns changed and made our state and country different, adding rich cultural traditions to the predominantly white Anglo-Saxon society that was prevalent in the late nineteenth and early twentieth centuries. As the decade of the 1950s moved on, the stigma of belonging to this ethnic group was finally starting to ease up, and now Italians were hired for high paying factory and white-collar jobs, provid-ed that their names didn't sound Italian.

Dorothy with her great-nephew Jesse and great-niece Caitlin, 2009.

LeRoy's claim to fame is that it is known as the "Home of Jell-O," and naturally the company employed a lot people who lived in the area. My aunt got a job as a chemist that tested the quality of the products despite Jell-O's practice of not hiring people who had Italian names. I guess she was lucky that Gugino had been changed to O'Geen at Ellis Island. The all-important apostrophe in a name was a highly sought after component to employment in small towns like LeRoy in Western New York. I recently met a Canadian couple at a restaurant in Geneseo, and I struck up a conversation with them. The wife was of Armenian descent, and she told me that her father encountered the same type of prejudice in Canada because of his nationality and dark complexion. He ended up changing his name that included an "O" with an apostrophe, and miraculously he was bestowed with the "luck of the Irish." Somehow, because of the name change, a person was instantaneously transformed into a more desirable employee.

After General Foods of Dover, Delaware bought Jell-O in the early 1960s, Aunt Dorothy received an offer to relocate. She accepted and worked for them for the next twenty-five years until she retired. My aunt told me the story of a man whose name ended in a vowel who was supposed to get a promotion, but the word was that he was too swarthy, so he was passed by. My aunt kept a low profile and did very well at General Foods, but she still had to deal with the stigma of being Italian. Today, she is defiant and gets angry when she relives those times. It is not a pretty sight to see Aunt Dorothy when she gets mad.

To my surprise, after Aunt Dorothy retired from General Foods, she moved back home with Grandma. She loved living in Delaware with her friends, and I couldn't imagine why she would want to relocate back to LeRoy, New York. Aunt Dorothy told me that she couldn't let Franny shoulder the burden of taking care of both my mother, who had cancer, and Grandma, so out of a sense of duty she came back home. Grandma was ecstatic that her baby was coming back home.

At one point while she was still in Delaware, Dorothy made plans to take a trip with my mother and Aunt Franny to Las Vegas. This was Dorothy's way of doing something nice for her two sisters who were less fortunate than she was. Since my mother had never gone anywhere in her life and never had a real vacation, and Franny had been stuck home dealing with Grandma and her constant scrutiny for all those years, they were all looking forward to a little fun. But before Dorothy retired and was able to move back home, my mother died of cancer in 1986. With the trip postponed indefinitely, time ran out

She Played Like an Angel, 2009. *Egg tempera on panel.*

for Aunt Franny as well when she died in 1992, with Grandma following a few weeks later. Now Dorothy was stuck living in LeRoy, because upon her retirement she chose New York State as the place where her medical benefits were going to be administered. Apparently this decision was irrevocable, and the red tape would have been staggering if she had decided to move to a different state.

Dorothy never married. She was very generous and bought an incredible amount of Christmas gifts for Grandma, her sisters, and all of her nieces and nephews, as well as great-nieces and great-nephews. My aunt loves shopping so much that she starts to buy gifts the day after Christmas looking for bargains for the next year's gifts. All she asks in return is a phone call or a visit from us once in a while just to talk. In some ways, she is like Great-Uncle Jimmy (Chapter 4) because if we neglect to thank her or call her, she unceremoniously cuts us off.

Since Aunt Dorothy was the youngest of her surviving sisters, she became the main caretaker of them when they reached old age. At one time, she had her sisters Florence and Helen living with her because of their health problems. Aunt Florence had cancer and died at the family home on Lake Street, and Aunt Helen had diabetes and a heart condition. Aunt Helen sold her dream house and moved in with Dorothy. When they died she had two remaining sisters, Connie and Marian, who lived near Buffalo. They also got cancer. My aunt took care of them by either bringing them to her house in LeRoy or routinely spending a few days at their house in Lancaster, New York. Dorothy was a very loyal person, and wouldn't even think about shipping off a family member to an extended care facility. To Dorothy, family is the most important bond in life even if they drive her nuts.

Dorothy is alone now and laments the fact that she moved back home, since all the relatives she loved are dead and she is far from the friends and location where she enjoyed life. My aunt regrets having put off the trips she planned to take with Lena and Aunt Franny, but she has managed to travel to Alaska and even went to Hong Kong while it was still a British protectorate. She still enjoys going to New York City during Christmas and staying in an expensive hotel in Manhattan and seeing a Broadway Show with her friend from Delaware. Of course, she thinks that Frank Sinatra was the best entertainer of all time.

The panel painting, *She Played Like an Angel*, depicts Dorothy around the age of ten playing her violin on the front steps of the house at 36 Lake Street. The violin was given to my aunt by her Uncle Jimmy and Aunt Pauline (Chapter 4), and was one of the instruments that belonged to Hy Lammers, Aunt Pauline's brother, who played in John Philip Sousa's orchestra. Dorothy is the featured musician serenading the viewer with an accompaniment of an angelic orchestra. The heavenly orchestra is a fragment from the painting, *The Lady of the Assumption gives St. Thomas Her Belt*, by Bartolomeo Della Gatta. Dorothy was the only daughter of Grandma's to take music lessons, which further demonstrates that she became the most American of her family.

The old LeRoy neighborhood has changed, and the Sicilian neighborhoods of her youth are long gone, as well as St. Joseph's Church. Now she has to go to mass at St. Peter's Church (renamed the Church of the Holy Family) with the rest of the parishioners from the old Sicilian congregation.She lives in one of the few single residence houses left on the street since most of the old middle class houses that were kept in immaculate shape are now apartments that have seen better days. This Old World section of LeRoy is a changed place. Her house sits in the middle of a non-descript neighborhood that has lost its charm. You can't smell Aunt Ida's breaded veal cutlets cooking on a late afternoon for Uncle Ross, or as you walk around the neighborhood, the sweet smell of tomato sauce bubbling on the stove for lunch after Sunday mass is gone. None of it exists anymore. Everyone has died or has moved on to better houses in affluent neighborhoods or relocated to other parts of the state or country. All that is left of that long lost world are the memories.

CHAPTER 22

The MacPherson Clan: The First Through Third Generations

SCOTTISH ORIGINS

Both the Sicilians and the Scots have similar roots based on ancient, tribal peoples who held onto old ways, distrusted outsiders, and tried to maintain their parallel social structures of clan and family. For the Sicilians, the village was the center of life and religion (see Chapter 1). For the Scots, the clan was the dominant social structure. Persistent stereotypes had a relatively positive impact on the Scottish side and a profoundly negative impact for generations of Sicilians. The history and stories of my ancestors exist on parallel but opposite planes; the one side with recorded histories and documented genealogies, the other with oral traditions of family narratives and anecdotes.

Another similarity between the Sicilians and the Highland clans was that both groups of people had different customs, and their ways of life seemed almost foreign to the mainstream cultures found in southern Scotland and England, as well as on mainland Italy. In Scotland, the Highland clans spoke Gaelic, and in Sicily each paese (village) had their own dialect that was sufficiently different from mainland Italian that the rest of Italy did not understand. This language barrier was a major factor that put the Highland Scots and Sicilians on the fringe of their respective cultures. With southern Scotland becoming more oriented to life in England, the Highlanders seemed more out of step, and relations between the two groups became more strained: "Highlanders dressed differently, had different customs, and their wild mountain land sometimes seemed almost foreign to people living in the lowlands."[1] Anti-Highland feelings were persistent. Southern Scots viewed themselves as Anglo-Saxon and superior in every way to the Highlanders.[2] My Sicilian relatives also lived in the remote mountains and were poor and out of touch with mainland culture. Sicily has the unique distinction of having Italian, Spanish, Greek, and North African influences in their culture, which sets them apart from their Italian relatives on the mainland. Because of these differences, my ancestors from both Scotland and Sicily were considered the most undesirable of elements who emigrated from their respective countries.

The power structure of Scotland, and in particular the Highlands, was based on a feudal system, where a king ruled all, then under him were the stewards (earls, lords, etc.) of the great provinces, and next were the chiefs of the clans.[3] According to Alexander MacBain, "The clans were very powerful and their chiefs ruled the Highlands of Scotland with little

---

1 Ann Lindsay Mitchell, *The Macphersons* (Glasgow, Scotland: Lang Syne Publishing, 2007), 8.
2 Based on a conversation with Dr. Eric Richards, Flinders University, Adelaide Australia, on 3/19/2011.
3 Alexander Macbain, "The Lordship of Badenoch," *Clan Macpherson Association*, n.d., http://www.clan-macpherson.org/museum/documents/The_Lordship_of_Badenoch.pdf, 3.

hindrance"[4] until the Jacobite uprising in 1745 and the massive emigrations that took place in the eighteenth and nineteenth centuries weakened their influence. John Erskine, Earl of Mar explained in 1726, "Those of the same name and clan look on themselves all as gentlemen and bretheren, and the chief as the comon father or parent from whom they all come and count their linnial descent so that they fight ... as children of the same family joined in regiaments togither ..."[5] The Scottish clans were territorially based, and mostly lived a very pastoral way of life.[6] At other times, feuds fueled unrest and lawlessness. The clans stole and waged war against one another over territorial disputes when peaceful and legal means had been exhausted. For protection against larcenous forays into clan territory, there was a vigilante group that protected the Macphersons of Badenoch from raiders of neighboring clans.

The genealogical trail begins in 1215 with a man named Gillicattan More MacGillespick, or Gillespick, a member of the old Clan Chattan. His fifth son, Muirrach, was the father of Ewan ban Mhuirich, the father of the founders of the Macpherson lineages. The name Macpherson originated from the offspring of Ewan, the parson, who was living in Kinguisse in the 1380s. He had three sons, Kenneth, John, and Gillis, who acquired the surname Macpherson, which literally means "Son of the Parson." From these three lineages, all of the Macphersons of Badenoch are descended. My branch of the clan is descended from Kenneth (Slighk Kynich vic Ewin), the oldest of the three brothers,[7] making me the twenty-first generation of the Macpherson family.

My Sicilian family, on the other hand, can only be researched through church records in Sicily and documentation found at Ellis Island to 1790. The name "MacPherson," "Macpherson," and "McPherson" are all forms of spelling preferred by individual families in Scotland and Western New York. In Gaelic our last name is Mçpherson with a diacritical mark (comma) under the "c" that makes the pronunciation "mock" not "mic."[8]

Despite its pious sounding the name, the clan evolved into a fighting clan and had many noted military heroes due to its strategic location in Badenoch in the Central Highlands. "This clan can bring a regiment of well armed men to the field. In time of peace, they are said to be as corteous and industrious as the lowlanders, and in time of war, can endure the fatigue of the rudest highlanders."[9] I saw this side of the clan in my father, Neil (Chapter 28), and his brother Bill, (Chapter 29). They were both very physically imposing men, and in my eyes, they knew no fear. My uncle told me stories of my father, a highly decorated veteran of World War II, standing up to antagonistic drunks who bragged about their war experienc-

---

4   Alistair Moffat, *The Highland Clans* (New York: Thames and Hudson, 2010), 7.

5   Hon. Stuart Erskine, ed., "Lord Mar's Legacies, 1722–27," *Scottish History Society* 26 (1896), 219.

6   Alan Gibson Macpherson, *An Old Highland Genealogy and the Evolution of a Scottish Clan* (London: Oliver and Boyd Limited, 1966), http://www.clan-macpherson.org/museum/documents/alang01.pdf, 1.

7   Alan Gibson Macpherson, "The Clan Chattan Historians," *Journal of the Clan Chattan Association* 7, no. 5 (1981), 3.

8   Whenever the Gaelic spelling of MçPherson is used I am referring to the generation who was born in Scotland. In fact, Black Alex and other first generation relatives used the spelling MçPherson whenever they signed their names. When McPherson is used as a last name, I am referring to the preferred spelling of generations of relatives who succeeded the first generation. When MacPherson is found, I am referring to my branch of the family who changed their name to the proper English spelling in the 1920s. Even though the spelling is different we are all relatives.

9   Shelagh Macpherson-Noble, ed., *The Invereshie Book* (Clan Macpherson Association, 2009), http://www.clan-macpherson.org/museum/documents/InvereshieBook.pdf, 7.

es, and who questioned Neil's pacifism with the end result of my father giving them a good thrashing.

The history of Clan Chattan, our ancient clan, is very obscure. Many theories have surfaced over the years as to its origins. In Germany, there was a warlike people called the Chatti.[10] They resisted Roman power for years until they were finally forced to leave Europe and made their way to northern Scotland in the year 76 A.D.[11] In Gaelic they were known as Cataobh, or cats. So it has been suggested the pre-Christian Chattan worshiped the cat and were referred to as the "Cat men." The favored theory connects the clan to a name originating from a church-derived name, in this case to a religious figure, St. Catan of the early Celtic Church.[12]

Clan Chattan was an ancient loose association of sixteen clans that evolved into a very powerful force in the history of the Highlands. It had its principal seat in Badenoch, one of the most interior districts of Scotland and home of the Macphersons. The Mackintoshes and Macphersons comprised the two main divisions, even though they were bitter rivals.[13] The rest of the alliance was made up with smaller family groups joining for protection. The Battle of Invernahavon that took place in 1370 (or by other accounts, 1386) illustrates the rivalry between the members of Clan Chattan in this precarious alliance. Around four hundred men of Clan Cameron were returning from a raid on Badenoch and were overtaken at Invernahavon by an alliance of Clan Chattan comprised of members from Clan Mackintosh, Clan Macpherson, and Clan Davidson. As Clan Chattan was making plans to attack their enemies, a disagreement arose as to whether the Davidsons or the Macphersons would occupy the right wing, the position of honor. With Clan Mackintosh universally accepted as head of this alliance, their chief chose the Davidsons for this honor despite the fact that the MacPhersons had been members of Clan Chattan from its beginnings. The Macphersons left in disgust. With the loss of the Macpherson contingent, the rest of Clan Chattan forces resulted in inferior numbers to their enemy.

The battle resulted in the total defeat of the remaining Clan Chattan members. At this point or possibly the next morning, the Macphersons had a change of heart and decided to rejoin their allies and returned to battle. They attacked the Camerons with such ferocity that they changed defeat into victory. The Mackintoshes later claimed that the Macphersons were forced into battle by a man from Clan Mackintosh who went to the Macpherson camp pretending to be a member of Clan Cameron, calling the Macphersons cowards.[14]

Several years later at the Battle of the Inch (also known as the Battle of the Clans), one of the most grisly and utterly strange blood baths was fought in late September 1396. Several versions of whom were the combatants in the battle exist, with the favored modern account—also supported by clan history—indicating that the Macphersons fought the Davidsons over the slight they received in the Battle of Invernahavon. Other historians suggest that Clan Chattan were fighting Clan Kay, a clan that they feuded with for over 300 years

10 Macbain, "The Lordship of Badenoch," 9.
11 Macpherson-Noble, ed., *The Invereshie Book*, 53.
12 MacBain, "The Lordship of Badenoch," 9.
13 Mitchell, *The Macphersons*, 14.
14 Macpherson-Noble, ed., *The Invereshie Book*, 282.

over territorial disputes.[15] Either way, Macphersons, as part of Clan Chattan, were involved in this horrifying event. The dispute got so out of hand that the King (Robert III) sent two of his noblemen to secure a compromise, but they failed. The two chiefs suggested that they settle their differences with a trial by combat. Thirty men from each side were chosen, with the monarch awarding honors to the victors and a pardon for the defeated. The men were armed with only broadswords.

The North Inch of Perth, along the River Tay, was chosen for the battle. The area was walled in on three sides to keep spectators at bay (or maybe the combatants from running away) and a grandstand was set up for the royalty to view the spectacle like they were viewing a jousting match. When the combatants arrived with great pageantry, it was discovered that the Macphersons were one man short. Either the missing man lost his nerve and ran away, or by some accounts turned up sick and was unable to participate. The Macphersons did not want to fight short-handed and no member of the Davidsons wanted to step down from the fight, so the Macphersons asked for a volunteer. A smith named Henry Wynd, also commonly known as the Gobh Crom or Crooked Smith, emerged from the crowd and volunteered to fight for the missing man for the price of three half crowns to be paid for the rest of his life. Henry was small in stature but a fierce fighter and his offer was accepted.

With both sides at full strength, the pipers blew their respective battle songs and both clans charged toward one another and fought with incredible fury and commenced to hack one another to bits. The shouts of courage immediately turned to screams of agony as lost arms caused the wounded to bleed to death from the hand-to-hand combat. After about fifteen minutes, as if on cue, the men retreated to regroup and rest. There were about twenty men from each side that were either dead or mortally wounded lying on the field. The carnage resumed when the pipers sounded the battle charge. Again they met head-to-head in the middle of the field, and after a short time there were ten Macphersons and the Gobh Crom to only one of their foes. The lone survivor was severely wounded and fled the scene by swimming across the river Tay. The victors were seriously wounded and did not have the strength to chase down the escaping man, so he lived to see another day.[16]

This barbaric display of carnage exemplified a set of attitudes. Alistair Moffat, in his book The Highland Clans, explains, "Lowland Scotland thought of the clansmen on the North of Inch as little more than sub-human savages whose lives were cheap and whose death made suitable sport."[17] The ferociousness of the battle and sense of duty of the clansmen on both sides was both remarkable and shocking. One has to wonder if there is such a thing as a hereditary soldier gene that can be passed down through the generations. Was this the source of valor that made my great-grandfather volunteer to fight in the Civil War, my great-aunt to serve in World War I as an army nurse, and my uncle and father to enlist in World War II? It is easy for me to imagine that my father could have been one of the eleven survivors. From his distinguished war record and what I saw of him, he could turn on a switch and become a man of courage who knew no fear.

The uneasy alliance between the Macphersons and the Mackintoshes in Clan Chattan continued for centuries. In 1688, a series of brutal tribal disputes broke out among the clans

15   Macpherson-Noble, ed., *The Invereshie Book*, 283.
16   Macpherson-Noble, *The Invereshie Book*, 283.
17   Moffat, *The Highland Clans*, 42.

in the north and west.[18] The chief of the Mackintosh was intent on punishing the MacDonalds for an old score. He considered himself superior to the Macphersons because he was acknowledged as head of Clan Chattan. On this occasion, the Macphersons and Grant of Grant refused to assist him.

Mackintosh was furious. He wrote to the Earl of Perth, bringing to his attention the lack of subservience and asked the Earl to do what he wished to the two chiefs.

That next day the MacDonalds lay in wait for the approaching Mackintoshes who were routed and captured. Macpherson of Cluny heard about it and rushed upon the MacDonalds who were too battle weary to fight and who made their peace with the Macphersons. The MacDonalds saw that they were vastly outnumbered, and when the Macphersons insisted that Mackintosh be surrendered to them, they relinquished their prisoner. Needless to say, that Mackintosh was humiliated and mortified at being saved by someone to whom he felt superior. Mackintosh was, however, taken by Macpherson of Cluny to his house and "treated with great courtesy and charm."[19] Such was the peculiar way of life in the Highlands that isolated the Highlanders from the rest of Scotland and England.

The Macpherson clan was involved with some of the most stirring events in Scottish history. When Robert the Bruce fought to free his country from the English in 1314, it was the Macphersons who were his staunchest supporters, exterminating his enemies who had settled in Badenoch.[20] William Macpherson of Invershie was the first man in Scotland to join King Charles I at the outbreak of the Civil War of 1644, "defeating a crack regiment of Covenant cavalry in Glen Cova and capturing Blair Castle." In another example that alludes to the warring prowess of the Clan is the legend of the historic Black Chanter. (A chanter is a pipe on a bagpipe that has finger holes to play a melody.) "According to popular legend, it fell from heaven during a skirmish between the clans (The Battle of the Inch) that took place in the presence of the King and his nobles in 1396."[21] The legend was graphically described by Sir Walter Scott in his "Fair Maid of Perth." After that day, if the Chanter was with the Clan in battle, the Macphersons were never defeated. The Black Watch, the oldest highland regiment in the British army, was formed from predominantly Macphersons and other loyal clansmen in 1739.[22]

HISTORY BEHIND THE SCOTTISH IMMIGRATION TO BIG SPRINGS

Like other Scots of his day, my great-great-great-grandfather, Alexander "Black Alex" McPherson, left Scotland because of deteriorating economic conditions as a result of a series of rebellions from 1700–1750. According to historian James Mackay, "Four-times in less than half a century, the peace in Scotland was disrupted by rebellion which had begun in the Highlands and was largely made possible by the chiefs who were able to mobilise their clansmen under a feudal system that had not altered for centuries."[23] The English saw the

18   Mitchell, *The Macphersons*, 15.

19   Mitchell, *The Macphersons*, 15–16.

20   Donald Francis McPherson, *McPhersons of Genesee County* (D.F. McPherson, 1983), 218.

21   McPherson, *McPherson of Genesee County*, 8.

22   McPherson, *McPherson of Genesee County*, 8–9.

23   James Mackay, ed., *Pocket Scottish History* (Scotland: Lomond Books, 2009), 262–263.

clan system as the root of all the problems in the Highlands and now the government moved to destroy it forever.[24]

The Highland chief derived his power from the ties of blood and family. He held the clan land as virtual head of an extended family, where the land was "held in trust by the chief for his people and their descendants."[25] With the destruction of the clan system, he became owner of the land and his clansmen became tenants. "For a generation, the age-old concepts of chief and clan continued, but the ancient traditions of loyalty and kinship was gradually eroded."[26] In due course, the destruction of the clan system marked the beginning of a drastic change in the economic character of the Highlands. The end result was a series of Clearances that began around 1780 to 1850, with the explicit purpose to move the surplus population off the land to "facilitate its efficient economic exploitation."[27]

The Highland economy relied on a feudal system whereby tenant farmers rented land from landowners or clan leaders year to year.[28] In the process of the clearance, the landowners took back the small farms that the tenants had been working for generations.[29] The Highland Clearances were particularly brutal affairs, with many Scots dying of exposure and starvation after their homes and crops were burned to the ground. Some of the displaced Highlanders were relocated to unproductive parts of Scotland and others forcibly emigrated from Scotland.[30] This meant that the farms were converted to sheep grazing grounds and required fewer men. Many Scotsman were left without any means of support, so they gathered up their families and whatever possessions they had and immigrated to America. Like other Scots of his day,[31] Black Alex left Scotland as a direct result of the bleak economic conditions caused by the Highland Clearances. Lowland Scots, in collaboration with Highland chieftains and landowners, took over Highland farms when prices for wool skyrocketed, effectively putting the tenant farmers out of business. In addition to the economic assaults on Highlanders, attempts were made in the early nineteenth century to eradicate Gaelic. For many Highland Scots, this latest belittling attack on their culture was the last straw that pushed them to emigrate.[32]

In 1798, a party of displaced Scotsmen from Perthshire sailed to New York and traveled to Johnstown, located west of Albany in Fulton County, to find a place to settle down. Mr. Williamson, a Scotsman who had been in America for a long time, was now an agent for the Putney Tract. Upon hearing of the arrival of his countrymen, he made the trip to Johnstown to see them. He found them without much money but ready to confront the wilderness of the New World. Mr. Williamson became more than a friend; he became their benefactor. He offered them a very desirable location in the Big Springs area (now called Caledonia) of

24   Mackay, *Pocket Scottish History*, 262.
25   Andrew Lang, *A Short History of Scotland* (New York: Cosimo, Inc., 2005), 263–264.
26   Mackay, *Pocket Scottish History*, 262.
27   Lang, *A Short History of Scotland*, 65.
28   Based on a conversation with Dr. Joseph Farrell 3/18/11 at Flinders University, Adelaide, Australia. He is Professor Emeritus from the University of Strathclyde, Scotland.
29   McPherson, *McPherson of Genesee County*, 218.
30   Based on a conversation with Dr. Joseph Farrell, Flinders University, Adelaide, Australia, 3/18/2011.
31   McPherson, *McPherson of Genesee County*, 239.
32   Based on a conversion with Dr. Eric Richards, Professor of History, on 3/19/11 at Flinders University, Adelaide Australia.

Western New York. He offered them land at $3.00 an acre to be paid in wheat at a later date and enough provisions to tide them over until they grew their own food. Four of the members of the group made the trip from Johnstown to Big Springs to check out the parcels. They were pleased with the potential of the area and the deal was finalized.

In March 1799, while winter still had its grip on the land, these hearty pioneers moved to their new home in sledges. There were a few furnished log cabins already at Big Springs that provided temporary shelter. Shortly after, land surveyors arrived and each settler had a lot that bordered the stream. (The same stream that Uncle Joe Burkart (Chapter 15) worked and fished over 120 years later.) That fall, more Scotsman immigrated and settled at Big Springs and the following spring more followed.[33] Just two years later in 1801, my great-great-great-grandfather, Alexander MçPherson, also saw the potential of the Big Springs area and would join his countrymen.

The land they came to settle was a primeval forest that had never been logged or improved. It was a pristine, primitive wilderness with trees so impenetrable that the sun never directly hit the floor of the forest but filtered down and created a permanent twilight. The bank along Allen's (Oatka) Creek was a "wild dark forest of hemlock and oaks that extended back over the hills and along the scattered levels."[34] The only roads were marked trails used by Native Americans who meandered through the woods and along the creek.

Simon Pierson, an early pioneer to the area in 1806, gave an account of the mindset of these newcomers. After coming to grips with the "heavy timber and putrid atmosphere," he expresses the desire of the European immigrant to tame the land:

And then ten thousand wants rushed to our astonished vision. We wanted the trees cut down and burnt up, and fences made; we wanted log houses to shield us from the storms of winter and summer; we wanted boards, nails and glass; we wanted roads cut through the woods instead of marked trees; we wanted log bridges made to keep our horses and wagons from sinking, we wanted school-houses and meeting houses.[35]

---

33 McPherson, *McPherson of Genesee County*, 218.
34 McPherson, *McPherson of Genesee County*, 239.
35 McPherson, *McPherson of Genesee County*, 232.

THE FIRST GENERATION

Great-Great-Great-Grandfather Alexander (Black Alex) William MçPherson

Born: August 8, 1755, Crubenbeg, Inverness-shire, District of Badenoch, Scotland

Died: October 17, 1833, LeRoy, New York

Great-Great-Great-Grandmother Elizabeth "The Fair" MçPherson

Born: August 17, 1764, Invertromy, Inverness-shire, District of Badenoch, Scotland

Died: May 9, 1827, LeRoy, New York

Left: Black Alex, Anonymous, Charcoal. Early Nineteenth Century. Collection of David Frost.

Right: Elizabeth "The Fair" MçPherson, Anonymous, Charcoal. Early nineteenth century. Collection of David Frost.

My great-great-great-grandfather, Black Alex, was born in Crubenbeg, in the Badenoch district located in the central Highlands of Scotland. Badenoch is very rugged with little of the soil being tillable. It is only 110 miles from the North Sea and is cut up into hills and hollows with rocky peaks and deep glens. There is not much to keep the young in this inhospitable land when there are easier places in the world to make a living.[36]

My great-great-great-grandfather was called "Black Alex" because he had black hair. The Scots had a tradition of giving nicknames to distinguish the difference between them because so many had the same names.[37] In my family alone, every generation had several men named Alexander William, so these nicknames helped when trying to differentiate between them. Even up to the fifth generation, relatives were still named after him, with my father's youngest brother one of the most recent.

Black Alex married Elizabeth "The Fair" or Eliza McPherson, on February 15, 1781. Her maiden name was also McPherson[38] but they did not claim one another as relatives. She was from an unrelated part of the clan. "A basic characteristic of the Highland Clan was its agnatic structure (meaning relatives are descended from the same man), binding men and women related to each other by patrilineal descent (a system in which one traces descent through males) often bearing the same surname,"[39] as was the case of my great-great-great-grandparent's marriage. Their marriage was an endogamous marriage; that is, they married within the clan with both parties having the same surname. A marriage of this type was very characteristic among clan members. The tendency for this type of union was probably "an expression of a need to retain and circulate wealth within a clan"[40] and reinforced the agnatic structure and maintained continuity of a clan's territory.[41]

They had thirteen children in total, with three dying in infancy. They were:

Helen McPherson

> *Born: February 13, 1784, Crubenbeg, Scotland*
> *Died: June 15, 1861, LeRoy, New York*

John McPherson

> *Born: 1786, Crubenbeg, Scotland*
> *Died: May 25, 1853, LeRoy, New York*

---

36   McPherson, *McPherson of Genesee County*, 200.
37   McPherson, *McPherson of Genesee County*, 187.
38   Alan Gibson Macpherson, "Migration Fields in a Traditional Highland Community, 1350–1850," *Journal of Historical Geography* 10, no. 1 (1984), 1.
39   Macpherson, "Migration Fields," 1.
40   Macpherson, "Migration Fields," 3.
41   Macpherson, "Migration Fields," 1.

Angus MƈPherson

Born: April 8, 1788, Crubenbeg, Scotland
Died: died young buried in Kingussie, Scotland

Alexander MƈPherson

Born: April 17, 1790, Crubenbeg, Scotland
Died: died young buried in Kingussie, Scotland

James MƈPherson

Born: 1791, Crubenbeg, Scotland
Died: May 3, 1857, LeRoy, New York

Nancy MƈPherson

Born: 1793, Crubenbeg, Scotland
Died: ?, LeRoy, New York

Angus MƈPherson

Born: 1795, Crubenbeg, Scotland
Died: August 14, 1814, LeRoy, New York

Isabel MƈPherson

Born: 1797, Crubenbeg, Scotland
Died: May 10, 1840, LeRoy, New York

Donald MƈPherson

Born: Crubenbeg, Scotland
Died: Oswego, New York

Allen MçPherson

> Born: *March 1801, Crubenbeg, Scotland*
> Died: *November 22, 1883, Almena, Michigan*

Alexander "Boss Alex" MçPherson (my great-great-grandfather)

> Born: *August 1, 1803, LeRoy, New York*
> Died: *May 9, 1879, LeRoy, New York*

Mary Ellen MçPherson

> Born: *1805, LeRoy, New York*
> Died: *September 11, 1876, Bowen, Michigan*

Margaret MçPherson

> Born: *LeRoy, New York*
> Died: *Bowen, Michigan*

Black Alex made a living in Scotland as a tacksman and a shepard.[42] Tacksmen were highly educated, well respected within the Highlands, and "took central roles in clan society."[43] In the social structure, a tacksman was among the gentry of the clan between the chiefs and above the tenant farmers, with his tenure, in some cases, lasting for generations. The tacksman paid a yearly rent for the land from the landowner and in turn rented it out to the tenant farmers, but he often kept some land for himself. Tacksmen supervised the tenant farmers for the chiefs of the clan and were well paid. Tacksmen were relatives or near-relatives of the chief, or were descended from ancestors who bore the title before him. They were indispensable to the clan chiefs since the estates were expansive and many of the farms were located in remote areas. The chief, therefore, would have little authority over his tenants. The tacksman was the middleman and looked after the financial interests of his laird (lord), and in the process his own, directed the efforts of the tenant farmers. Tacksman were also responsible for recruiting the clan's army when the chief called for military actions.[44]

Since it took a generation for the Highland Clearances to destroy the clan system, Black Alex was able to hold onto his position as tacksman until the end of the eighteenth century before finally emigrating from Scotland in 1801. A person with his background and education was a sought-after commodity in the United States after the Revolutionary War, and

---

42 McPherson, *McPherson of Genesee County*, 243.
43 Moffat, *The Highland Clans*, 44.
44 Moffat, *The Highland Clans*, 44.

attempts were made to recruit educated Scots, like my relative, to immigrate to America.[45] They came to America with money to invest and a drive to help build the new country. Tacksmen were among the professions targeted because their expertise and experiences were very desirable for nation-building.[46]

In addition, other clan members had already settled in New York, so word could have gotten back to those left in Scotland that life in the New World had great opportunities for those willing to take the risk. Other McPhersons had already bought land around the area of LeRoy, New York, which might explain why Black Alex ended up in the same place.

They must have been very thrifty since he was able to save up enough money to book passage for his large family to start a new life in America.[47] Since Black Alex was a tacksman and owned land, he was probably paid for the land that was confiscated, and this would had been the source of income he had to invest once he arrived in America.[48] In July of 1801, he sailed from England with his wife and their eight children, with his brother-in-law, also named Alexander MᶜPherson, and his family. After reaching America, they stopped at Albany, New York to figure out where they were going to buy land and start their new life. Elizabeth's family decided that they wanted to keep their allegiance to England, so they left for Glengarry, Ontario, Canada, but Black Alex liked the look of the land and proceeded to Johnstown in Fulton County, where he found other Scotsmen. Alex, Eliza, and the children remained there one season, until no doubt lured by reports from those who had trekked west; they made a momentous decision.[49] "Black Alex left his family in Johnston while he went on to Canandaigua, New York, to the Phelp-Gorham Purchase Tract Office to inquire of a land grant. He obtained the last portion of a triangular section on Allen's (Oatka) Creek."[50] After returning to Johnstown, he gathered his family and traveled on to Big Springs, now called Caledonia, just 8 miles east of LeRoy.[51]

There are few tales handed down of their adventures traveling to Big Springs, although one about a stubborn ox has managed to make it through the years. When they reached the Genesee River near Avon, which was just six miles from their destination, they found a number of families waiting for the river to lower because it was too deep to ford. Black Alex did not want to wait, so he made a raft. When he tried to drive the oxen and the cart onto the raft, one of them balked and refused to step foot on it. Tired of trying to coax it onto the raft, Black Alex unyoked the ox and shouldered it himself, and with the help of others, pushed the cart onto the raft. When the stubborn ox saw his mate and cow moving quickly away from him, he went down the bank and into the cold water, and after he reached the other side he was none the worse for wear.[52] After I read this story for the first time, I realized that I travel down on the same road, Route 5, to Caledonia from Avon and cross the Genesee River at the same spot that my relatives did over two hundred years earlier.

---

45   Arthur Herman, *How the Scots Invented the Modern World* (New York: Three Rivers Press, 2001), 347.

46   Based on a conversation with Dr. Eric Richards on 3/19/11.

47   McPherson, *McPherson of Genesee County*, 180.

48   Based on a conversation with Dr. Eric Richards on 3/19/11.

49   McPherson, *McPherson of Genesee County*, 236.

50   McPherson, *McPherson of Genesee County*, 43.

51   McPherson, *McPherson of Genesee County*, 236.

52   McPherson, *McPherson of Genesee County*, 236.

After arriving at Big Springs, Black Alex found a place for his family to stay with some of his countrymen, and traveled west along Allen's (Oatka) Creek until he came to his parcel. Black Alex's property was located on the westernmost section of the creek. The land was rugged and hilly, which reminded him of his home in Scotland.[53] Since Crubenbeg is located just north of the River Truim, a tributary of the nearby River Spey, renown for its salmon population, the hills and trout-rich waters of Allen's Creek may have been the main factor that attracted Black Alex to settle in this area. When my Scottish ancestors arrived in Western New York, they arrived in circumstances that would be especially advantageous to them. The Seneca Indians had been cleared out of the area—although the land was wild, they weren't challenged in taking it over. Scottish immigrants to the U.S. frequently continued their Highland existence by becoming hunters, constantly moving and living on the margin. But, Black Alex arrived with a different idea—he was going to buy land and establish a dynasty. Black Alex easily bought as much land as he wanted, where he established the family on a series of farms. Black Alex had a vision of being a founder and he succeeded in that vision, possibly because his experience as a Highland tacksman, during a time when the economic structure of farming imploded, had taught him that to secure prosperity, he needed to own as much land as he could. As landowners in the new country, the McPhersons formed the core identity for the area they settled, and became the standard whereby other new groups would be measured and judged as they defined the process of assimilation. Defining his role in this dominant culture with ease, my great-great-great-grandfather bought 360 acres and lived next to his countrymen, other Scots, who, like him, opted for settled lives. Some ninety years later when the Sicilian branch of my family immigrated, they were treated as outcasts in their new country because they were not part of the established culture that had been forged by the McPhersons.[54]

My ancestors seemed so fearless and self-assured when they immigrated to America, and once they bought property they carved out a chunk of the wilderness to call their own. It took a resourceful people with an iron resolve to accomplish such a feat. Many generations later, the same traits were passed onto my father, Neil (Chapter 28). Besides his acts of heroism during World War II, I saw these same traits in him when he risked life and limb running into burning buildings to save lives and property, making him the bravest man I have ever known.

After Black Alex bought his land and moved his family into their log cabin next to Allen's (Oatka) Creek, he was $7.00 in debt. He was a hard worker, and eventually the accumulated holdings totaled 1,383 acres, much of which he improved. In 1830 and 1831, as his sons got older, married, and needed places of their own, he divided up the property and they became owners of various portions of his holdings, in effect becoming the head of the clan surrounded by his extended family. In the early days he hauled wheat to Rochester, New York, about twenty miles away, and sold it at twenty-five cents a bushel, taking in exchange barrels of salt worth $14.00.[55]

---

53   McPherson, *McPherson of Genesee County*, 236–240.

54   Based on a conversation with Dr. Charles Burroughs, Case Western Reserve University, Cleveland, Ohio on 3/9/2011.

55   McPherson, *McPherson of Genesee County*, 243.

While the log cabin was being built on the new home-site, it is probable that Eliza and the children stayed in the houses of generous friends in Big Springs. The log cabin had one room with a loft, and the family lived in this structure for eight years until a new house was constructed around 1811. In its day it was considered a mansion. All of the wood used to build the house was harvested from the property. The frame was put together with wooden pins and some of the old boards used in the construction were more than twenty inches wide. "The floorboards in the hall and the beams in the cellar give evidence of the hard and careful hand-labor."[56] Today the house is still in the family and is in mint condition.

In 1805, Black Alex and three neighbors felled some huge basswoods and built a very rough log cabin schoolhouse at the foot of Fort Hill a mile from his house. Fort Hill was an ancient Native American fortress, where pioneers to the area found earthworks, arrowheads, and parched corn. Education was highly valued in Scotland and public schools were widespread—even many poor people learned to read. By 1750, just five years before Black Alex's birth, "Scotland became Europe's first modern literate society."[57] It is no wonder that my ancestor and his Scottish neighbors placed such an importance on education for their children, even if they were farmers living in a wilderness. They took time out their busy day to build a schoolhouse close to their settlements so that their children could receive a basic education. Today, a stone marker that was commemorated on August 20, 1926, marks the site of the first schoolhouse in the area.[58]

Black Alex and Eliza, their children, and their children's children were a deeply religious family, and in times of trouble their religion comforted and supported them. They were loyal members of the Beulah (Presbyterian) Church in Mumford, traveling the eight miles on horseback every Sunday to attend services in all kinds of weather. "It is recorded that at one time twenty-seven McPherson families were in attendance at the Beulah church."[59]

Black Alex worked and suffered much to become successful in America. At times he could be hard-hearted and tough. In 1812, Duncan and Isabel MᶜPherson emigrated from Scotland, and their plan was to travel to Western New York where Isabel's Uncle, Black Alex, lived. Duncan was what was called in those days a "wee mon"—someone who is short of stature and slight of build. When Black Alex, who was a robust and dominant man, met his nephew for the first time, he was not "favorably impressed with him." Even though "Wee" Duncan was a tireless worker, all of his energy did not "fully establish him in the good graces of Uncle Black Alex." At a vendue (public auction), Duncan wanted to buy a yoke of young steers and asked his uncle to loan him the money. Alex laughed at the idea. "If Wee Duncan could not meet the note then I would have to pay it." A neighbor saw Duncan still looking at the oxen and asked the "wee mon" why he hadn't placed a bid on them. Duncan replied to him, "I have no money and no one to go a note for me."[60] The neighbor offered to lend him the money, and when the note was due he paid it off.

This kind of family interaction surprised me because of my strong Sicilian upbringing. I could not imagine my Sicilian grandmother treating a hard working nephew in need like

---

56   McPherson, *McPherson of Genesee County*, 240.

57   Herman, *How Scots Invented the Modern World*, 23.

58   McPherson, *McPherson of Genesee County*, 239.

59   McPherson, *McPherson of Genesee County*, 237.

60   McPherson, *McPherson of Genesee County*, 203–204.

that. The Scots were a different breed and looked at the extended family in much different ways, especially in this instance, where a relative was just starting out in a new country and needed assistance.

CULTURE SHOCK

Many amusing incidents happened to Black Alex and his family as they were making their way to Western New York, learning hard lessons as they became familiar with their new country. The accounts of my cousins, Duncan and Isabel MᶜPherson, are amusing misadventures that have been passed down from generation to generation. After they arrived in New York City in 1812, they had their first taste of American watermelon, which they relished. Passing through one of the settlements on their way to Western New York, they saw a field filled with what they supposed were watermelon. Since their first experience with this delectable fruit was such a positive experience, they wanted to taste it again. After taking one of the fruits from the field, they cut it open, eagerly popped a piece into their mouths, and to their disappointment, they became introduced to another American favorite, pumpkin, a fruit that is not so delicious raw.

One night along the journey, they stopped to camp. Isabel started foraging for firewood when two little black animals scampered toward her. She thought they were two little kittens, so she called to them, "Kitty! Kitty!" Picking them up, she petted them. My cousin thought about taking them with her, so she put them in her apron. The two cute little animals were actually skunks, and they really resented her hugging them so tightly and they ungratefully sprayed her, as these creatures are wont to do. She dropped them very quickly and wondered where all of the strange perfume came from. Skunks are not found in Scotland. It was a rude "welcome to America" moment.

After they had settled in their new log cabin, Isabel set out one morning before daybreak to fetch some water from the spring located nearby, when she met a bear that was quietly sitting on the path. In the dark of early morning, she thought it was a calf that had wandered from its mother; she patted it on the head and said, "Bossy! Poor Bossy!" It then turned and ambled away.[61] Everything was so new and strange to these pioneers.

FAMILY STORIES

Black Alex voted in many of the elections. One year there was a controversy over one election and many votes were challenged, including his, based on a claim that he was never naturalized. When asked about it, he admitted he never became a citizen. He was told if that was the case he couldn't vote to which Black Alex responded, "'But I will vote. I always have voted before and I will today.' When he was asked on what authority he could vote he raised his hand and said, 'I did not come to the United States, they came to me.[62] I and all men like me are the United States.' He voted."[63] This certainly must be a reference to the recruitment of Highland tacksmen like Black Alex.

---

61 McPherson, *McPherson of Genesee County*, 203.
62 According to Dr. Eric Richards of Flinders University, tacksmen were recruited to immigrate to the US, so this is could be what Black Alex was referring to.
63 McPherson, *McPherson of Genesee County*, 226.

In Black Alex's day, it was customary for the father to be matchmaker for his children. Once when he was in Canada visiting his friend Alexander McVean, they both thought it would be a splendid match if Black Alex's daughter Mary married Alexander McVean's son, Archie. So one day, Archie arrived in the United States and presented himself at the MçPherson farm. Mary was told she had to go upstairs and get dressed to make a good impression. She obeyed her father and went upstairs to change, but never returned to the parlor. Instead, she dressed, snuck out the back window onto the roof of the lean-to, and slid down a tree that was on the corner of the house, and then snuck through the fields until she reached her brother John's house. Here is where Duncan McDiarmid, the man she loved, worked. Mary told him the situation, so they borrowed a horse and they rode to Caledonia where they were married that afternoon.[64] Even in those days, love and romance sometimes triumphed over age-old traditions. Apparently, Alexander McVean held no grudge against Black Alex for this embarrassing episode since, Alex McVean's only daughter, Jane, married Black Alex's son, Alexander, a few years later (Jane and Alexander were my great-great-grandparents). Mary and Duncan moved to Michigan where they lived and died.[65]

If one compares the women on my Scottish side of the family with the ones on the Sicilian side, there is a tremendous difference in terms of how independent they were. One has to take into account that strong-willed women were in both families, but I couldn't imagine either my grandmother (Chapter 3), or her sister, Great-Aunt Mary Argana (Chapter 7), going against the wishes of their father and defying him in such a strong way. All three women were among the first generation of immigrants, so there was still a strong pull to follow the culture and customs of their parents. Possibly, Duncan and Mary moved to Michigan because of the backlash they received for going against the wishes of her domineering father, but this type of reaction would never have happened in the Barone family. The shame that an action like this would have brought onto the family would have been unthinkable to my Sicilian relatives, and would have been the biggest deterrent to doing something so defiant. Guilt and shame didn't seem to be very important tactical ploys amongst the MçPhersons as it was with the Barones as a means to keep their children in line and to adhere to Old World values.

Life in the frontier was difficult and dangerous. Black Alex and Eliza's fifth child, Angus, met a cruel death early in life. Angus was reaping grain with a scythe on a very steep hill. Reaping grain on a steep hill can only be accomplished by cutting the stalks and working up the slope. When he reached the top, he slung the scythe over shoulder and started down the hill to return to the bottom. Angus must have tripped and fallen on the scythe. When he was found some time later, he had lost a lot of blood and, subsequently, he died of his wounds.[66]

---

64   McPherson, *McPherson of Genesee County*, 236.

65   McPherson, *McPherson of Genesee County*, 178.

66   McPherson, *McPherson of Genesee County*, 49.

THE SECOND GENERATION

Great-Great-Grandfather Alexander (Boss Alex) MçPherson

Born: August 1, 1803, LeRoy, New York
Died: May 9, 1879, LeRoy, New York

I believe this photo is of my Great-Great Grandmother Jane MçVean MçPherson. Note the diacritical mark under the"ç."

My great-great-grandfather, "Boss Alex," was the seventh in the birth order and first child of "Black Alex" and Elizabeth "The Fair" to be born in the United States. He was called "Boss Alex" because he took charge at barn raisings and logging bees, organizing everyone into groups with different responsibilities so that the buildings and the work could be done in a timely fashion.[67] He had the homestead just next to Black Alex's farm where he raised his family and continued to farm. He was a Second Lieutenant in the local militia, and "held several responsible positions in his town," with his reputation being beyond reproach.[68]

Great-Great-Grandmother Jane MçVean MçPherson

Born: May 1, 1807, Feracht, Scotland
Died: April 22, 1893, LeRoy, New York

Jane came to the United States at the age of eleven in 1818 with her father, Alexander MçVean, and her four brothers. Her mother died on February 7, 1818.[69] Her father bought a home in Canada near York (Toronto), where she received her education. Since Boss Alex's mother had a brother who lived in Canada, the family traveled from LeRoy to visit them and other friends who lived there. It is not hard to imagine why so many of the MçPhersons mar-

---

67   McPherson, *McPherson of Genesee County*, 205.
68   McPherson, *McPherson of Genesee County*, 243.
69   McPherson, *McPherson of Genesee County*, 177.

ried Canadian Scots through arranged marriages or from courtship. On December 12, 1826, Jane married Boss Alex and she moved to America to set up housekeeping on the family farm. This time, successful matchmaking triumphed.

Jane and Boss Alex had ten children with two dying young. They were:

Alexander MçPherson, Jr.

Born: October 21,1827, LeRoy, New York

Died: February 14, 1896, LeRoy, New York

Sarah MçPherson

Born: April 16, 1829, LeRoy, New York

Died: March 18,1905, Bergen, New York

Eliza MçPherson

Born: April 4, 1831, LeRoy, New York

Died: March 29, 1874, LeRoy, New York

Jane MçPherson

Born: October 9, 1834, LeRoy, New York

Died: September 8, 1910, LeRoy, New York

Helen "Ella" MçPherson

Born: May 9, 1836, LeRoy, New York

Died: March 2, 1921, LeRoy, New York

Angus MçPherson

Born: July 29, 1838, LeRoy, New York

Died: June 25, 1841, LeRoy, New York

Donald Alexander MçPherson (my great-grandfather)

Born: May 28, 1840, LeRoy, New York

Died: February 8, 1887, Cross Village, Michigan

Angus MçPherson

> *Born: December 15, 1842, LeRoy, New York*
> *Died: September 14, 1845, LeRoy, New York*

John MçPherson

> *Born: September 28, 1845, LeRoy, New York*
> *Died: May 4, 1919, LeRoy, New York*

Catherine MçPherson

> *Born: October 6, 1848, LeRoy, New York*
> *Died: June 18, 1907, LeRoy, New York*

Jane could be very inflexible once she made up her mind about something. Two little cousins, both age eight, were in an upland field watching the men cutting a field of hay. Back in those days, fields were mowed by hand using scythes, which was very strenuous work. It was the custom to place a jug of water and a jug of liquor in the corners of the field so that the workers could refresh themselves as they made their way around the fields. The "laddies" secretly drank the liquor and one of them nearly died. When the lad had safely made a recovery, Jane told Boss Alex, "We will never again have a drop of liquor upon this place."

"Why Jane," he said, "How can I keep my men?"

"I will feed them," she answered. She did, and the men stayed. From that day on, her command was honored and the MçPherson homestead went dry long before Prohibition.[70]

Great-Great-Grandmother's obituary reveals how well her family and friends thought of her. It reads:

Though retiring in disposition had wonderful strength of character always genteel and fond of pleasantry, interested in her friends to a marked degree and zealous in all matters connected with her church of which she is one of the oldest members. She has been blessed with excellent health and her mind and memory were active to the last. During her sickness she would converse of things that occurred when she was a child in Scotland, and yet her mind was equally capable of taking interest in passing events.[71]

My Great-Grandfather Donald, 1880s.

---

70   McPherson, *McPherson of Genesee County*, 237.
71   McPherson, *McPherson of Genesee County*, 50.

THE THIRD GENERATION

Great-Grandfather Donald Alexander McPherson

Born: May 28, 1840, LeRoy, New York

Died: February 8, 1887 Cross Village, Michigan

Great-Grandmother Sarah Farnham McPherson

Born: June 6, 1848, West Bergen, New York

Died: August 13, 1925, LeRoy, New York

My great-grandfather was the seventh child of Alexander and Jane McPherson. I don't know anything about his childhood and no one is alive to interview who knew him. I know that he did volunteer to serve in the Civil War. On his war service record, I discovered that he was five feet six and a half inches. He had blue eyes, blond hair and a sandy complexion, and he was a farmer by occupation. On the eleventh of October 1861, he volunteered for three years of service at the age of twenty-one. He enlisted in LeRoy with the New York 100th Infantry Regiment Company B, and was mustered in as a corporal.[72]

The regiment left the state on March 10, 1862, and on March 13, he wrote a letter to his brother, John. It is a fascinating letter that gives insight into the morale and tourist attitude of Donald and his comrades as they made their way from Camp Morgan in New York to join the Army of the Potomac in Virginia. They arrived in Jersey City by taking the ferry and then took the Camden and Amboy Railroad to Philadelphia. While in Philadelphia, they were treated to a "good super" at a large saloon called The Soldier's Home. After finally arriving in Washington, D.C., he wrote about seeing the Capitol building and White House and blowing kisses to the "wenches" they saw as the regiment passed through the city. From his tent on Meridian Hill, he could see for miles and miles the encampments on every hill that surrounded his camp, as well as, the Washington, D.C. skyline and the Potomac River, some 20 miles in the distance. Each regiment had a brass band so music could be heard in all directions.

While making their camp on Meridian Hill, Donald witnessed a training exercise in the camp next to him. My great-grandfather writes, "Yesterday PM they had cavalry charges in the next camp to us [and] flying artillery. The horses would go with all their might on the

---

72   *Regimental Descriptive Book of Company B of the 100th New York Regiment*, National Archives.

cannons. It is worth something to see such sights as we can see here." Finally on March 14, they received their marching orders to cross the Potomac on their way to their first battle.[73]

Donald served in Naglee's Brigade with the Army of the Potomac, and participated in the Siege of Yorktown, Lee's Mill, and Williamsburg.[74] On May 19, 1862, he was treated for a condition called debilitas for exposure and chronic dysentery. He probably lost a lot of fluids and blood from constant diarrhea. Dysentery was a common affliction among soldiers in those days because of poor sanitation and contaminated water. In 1862, the only treatment was oral hydration and bed rest, resulting in many deaths. Donald was probably extremely anemic and not recovering very fast.[75] He was released with a medical discharge just nine months later on July 22, 1862 in Washington, D.C.[76]

Donald's spirit of volunteerism and patriotism was passed onto his daughter, Catherine (Chapter 23), who volunteered and served with the British and American Nursing Corp during World War I, as well as his grandsons Neil (my father, Chapter 28), and his youngest brother Bill (Chapter 29), who joined the Army during World War II.

After Donald's return to the farm, he met my soon-to-be great-grandmother, Sarah Farnham, of Stone Church, New York. They were married on October 23, 1867.

In the early 1880s, my great-grandparents moved to northern Michigan, where my great-grandfather took a job in a Lake Michigan town called Cross Village, which was known for its thriving lumbering business. His luck did not change for the better, however. He suffered from tuberculosis, which he believed he contracted during the Civil War, and died of heart disease in Cross Village, Michigan on February 8, 1887, at forty-seven years of age. My great-grandmother became a widow at age thirty-eight, with young children and no means of support. His remains were taken back to Western New York, where he was buried in Stone Church, the location of Sarah's family burial plot. With his passing, the whole family relocated back to Western New York and lived with Great-Grandma's family until they could get on their feet. On February 1, 1894, Sarah bought a house on 33 Summit Street in LeRoy for $1,050.[77] On May 7, 1888, Great-Grandma hired P. J. Lockwood, a Washington, D.C. attorney, to represent her petition for a widow's claim for pension, since a doctor told Sarah that the tuberculosis was most likely contracted during his time as a soldier in the Union Army. She wrote heartbreaking letters to the Pension Bureau trying to get a pension for Donald's military service. By 1890, she still had not received any benefits. For years the family never knew if she ever received any help from the government, until I found a form in the National Archives that shows she was paid $30.00 a month, which stopped at the time of her death.[78]

---

73 My cousin, David Frost, found this letter in his family archives that was written from Donald, my great grandfather, to his younger brother John, David's grandfather, on March 13, 1862 while Donald was serving in the 100th Regiment, New York State Volunteers.

74 "100th Regiment's Battles and Casualities: Civil War, New York" (New York State Military Museum and Veterans Research Center, March 19, 2006), http://dmna.state.ny.us/historic/reghist/civil/infantry/100thInf/100thInfTable.html.

75 Based on a conversation with my cousin, James MacPherson, CEO of America's Blood Center, and former registered nurse.

76 "Certificate of Disability for Discharge for Donald A. McPherson," Army of the United States, National Archives.

77 "Deeds Book 180," Track LV, (Batavia, New York: Genesee County Clerk), 158.

78 "Widow's Claim for Pension," Act of 14 July, 1862, National Archives.

There is one person alive who knew Sarah. My cousin Pauline remembers her as a tiny woman with squinty eyes who always wore her hair in a tight bun. Pauline said she was always smiling and was a pleasant person to be around, with tireless energy. Sarah had a really rough life. Besides having a husband with severe medical problems, two of her children died in early adulthood. Her oldest daughter Imogene was only thirty years old and married when she died in Niagara Falls, New York in 1898 of heart failure, and her son Alexander died at age twenty-two from malarial fever in 1897.[79] Alexander left LeRoy at age twenty and moved to Deckerville, Arkansas, where he was worked for a lumber firm. Their bodies were transported back to Stone Church for burial next to their father.[80]

On August 13, 1925, my great-grandmother died at age seventy-eight. She was a strong role model for her children, especially Catherine. A brief prayer service was held at the McPherson home on Summit Street, after which she was taken to the Stone Church Cemetery where she was buried next to her husband and two children.[81]

Great Grandmother Sarah, 1890s.

79   City of Niagara Falls, Genealogy Record, Local Registration Number 1340.
80   McPherson, *McPherson of Genesee County*, 98.
81   "Funeral of Mrs. Sarah F. McPherson," *LeRoy Gazette*, August 15, 1925.

CHAPTER 23

The Fourth Generation

The children of Donald and Sarah MacPherson are:

Imogene MacPherson

> *Born: July 16, 1868, LeRoy, New York*
> *Died: May 9, 1898, Niagara Falls, New York*

Catherine (Kitty) Margaret MacPherson

> *Born: September 24, 1872, LeRoy, New York*
> *Died: December 22, 1967, Batavia, New York*

Alexander MacPherson

> *Born: December 22, 1874, LeRoy, New York*
> *Died: September 17, 1897, Deckerville, Arkansas*

Mary Fay MacPherson

> *Born: May 30, 1879, Covington, New York*
> *Died: February 6, 1949, LeRoy, New York*

Donald Alan MacPherson (my grandfather)

> *Born: August 5, 1884, Cross Village, Michigan*
> *Died: August 13, 1957, LeRoy, New York*

The fourth generation is composed of my grandfather, three great-aunts, and a great-uncle. This generation moved to different parts of the country and became the first of our MacPherson branch to be educated beyond high school. My Great-Aunt Kitty became a symbol of a twentieth century woman when she earned a degree in nursing, served in World War I, traveled the world, remained unmarried, and then lived a life of independence. All were born in the nineteenth century but embraced the twentieth. Sadly, there is very little information on Imogene, Alexander, and Mary Fay. The information I do have on them is from death certificates and obituaries.

In comparison to the contemporaneous first generation of Sicilians who lived in LeRoy, the MacPhersons had long since assimilated into American culture, but never lost the links to their Highland heritage. It was this generation that visited Scotland and reconnected with their Highland heritage, and started the first genealogical study of our family.

CHAPTER 24

Great-Aunt Catherine (Kitty) Margaret MacPherson

Born: September 24, 1872, LeRoy, New York
Died: December 22, 1967, Batavia, New York

Great-Aunt Kitty was the second child of my great-grandparents, Donald and Sarah McPherson. She was very short, barely five feet tall, with a slight build. My great-aunt was very stylish into middle age and cut a very striking figure. She favored chic, black velvet dresses, with her favorite jewelry, white pearls, and big fancy hats with feathers. She was a fascinating person by all accounts, and the most remarkable member of our branch of the MacPherson family. She lived what seemed a very fulfilling and exciting life. There are very few photographs of her that have made it through the ages, since she hated having her picture taken and avoided all cameras. My earliest recollection of her stem from when I was around seven and she was in her mid-eighties and still living in the MacPherson house at 33 Summit Street in LeRoy. I remember this little old lady sitting in her chair with red rouge applied in perfect circles on her cheeks. It made her look like one of my sister's dolls or a movie star from the 1920s. Whenever we made a visit, she made us treats like her delicious sugar and molasses cookies. Kitty was a very kind woman who adored all of her nephews as well as her grandniece and grandnephews, and we felt the same about her. Since Kitty never married or had a family of her own, we filled that gap in her life.

My cousin, Jim MacPherson, recalled that when he was very young, she read to him from the children's classics, and then as she got older, the tables turned and he read to her. I have a book that belonged to my father that Kitty gave him when he was young. The book has incredible pen and ink illustrations by the famous late nineteenth century illustrator, Howard Pyle. As a child, I copied them over and over. Of all of the relatives I had on both sides of the family, Kitty was the one who cared most about learning for the sake of learning, and tried to pass on her love of discovery to us. She studied art and read the classics. My Sicilian relatives, on the other hand, knew that education was the most important avenue out of poverty and the best way to gain respectability, but at the same time believed that one should have a professional skill at the end of formal instruction in order to find a place in the workforce. Instead, Kitty read for the pure joy of learning and self-cultivation.

Jim also vividly remembers his visits to see our great-aunt: "My memories are [of] her reading by the hour, plus she had great picture books with animals, places [and] drawings. Also of her sitting at the head of her huge (at least I thought it was) dining room table where she opened her correspondence with a sharp gold opener, and wrote letters to friends, and ate her dinners alone. Records of the talking books would play in the background on some of my visits." On one of my own visits to see her, I remember seeing that gold envelope opener and the piles of letters sitting next to it. I had never seen anything like it before, and when I later saw an actress use one to open letters in a movie, I thought that Great-Aunt Kitty was indeed a very sophisticated and elegant woman.

Nothing is known about her early life with any certainty, but one can connect the dots and make educated guesses about the events that shaped it. One of the most stunning discoveries I made in researching this book happened in May of 2010. I was looking in the LeRoy Historical Society archives for information on the Barone and MacPherson families, when I came across a sepia-toned photograph of a young woman. "Kitty McPherson" was written on it. The woman had the signature round McPherson face and what appeared to be wavy blond hair and blue eyes. I did a double take and wondered, 'Was this my great-aunt?' I checked Donald McPherson's genealogy book, *The McPhersons of Genesee Country*, which I found on a shelf in the archives, and discovered that there were several Catherine McPhersons born in the nineteenth century and had "Kitty" or "Kittie" as a nickname, but they all lived in the early or mid part of the century. With help from the Historical Society Director and Archivist, we dated the photo to the 1890s. The woman in the photo was wearing a uniform worn by women who attended Ingham University (1837–1892) in LeRoy, the first exclusive women's institution of higher learning in this country, teaching classes in art and literature. According to the Ingham files, a Kitty McPherson attended school in 1888. In the pension records at the National Archives, Kitty and her family had moved back to LeRoy by 1888. Since Kitty was born in 1872, she would have been sixteen, which is within the age group of women who attended Ingham University. As I kept looking at the photograph, the woman I saw had an uncanny resemblance to my daughter, Caitlin, and my cousin, Jim MacPherson, said that she also looked like his daughter, Julia. The picture was a revelation to my daughter, since the only relatives she remembers are her Sicilian relatives, and the person in this photo with blond hair, blue eyes, a little nose and a round face, looked nothing like them. When I showed her the picture of Kitty she exclaimed, "Finally, someone who looks like me. Now I can see where I came from."

BREAKING STEREOTYPES

Great-Aunt Kitty was fifteen years old when her father died. She watched him suffer for years with tuberculosis, so this family tragedy could have been the catalyst that inspired her to become a nurse. Toward the end of her father's life, he must have been hospitalized and Kitty would have seen the work of the nurses first hand taking care of him. Since her father had volunteered to serve in the Union Army during the Civil War, his service may have given her the idea to join the Red Cross Nursing Corps just before World War I. In both wars, the spirit of patriotism was at a fever pitch in America, and men rushed to join the fight. The Red Cross Nursing Corps was more than a nursing school; it also prepared nurses for battlefield duty.[1] Being well read and educated might have given her a broader worldview of life and inspired her to help humanity in a noble cause.

---

1   "A Brief History of the American Red Cross," *American Red Cross*, accessed November 30, 2010, http://www.redcross.org/about-us/history.

Kitty was a product of the area in which she lived, so she might also have been influenced by Clara Barton to become a nurse. Since Kitty was well read, she probably knew who Clara Barton was since she lived only thirty miles away in Dansville, New York. Barton started the Red Cross in 1881.[2] She was a heroine of the Civil War and could have been an inspiration to my great-aunt to pursue a similar career.

There was no formal training to become a nurse until some time after the Civil War. By the late 1880s, most big hospitals had their own programs. Usually a woman was given training in exchange for working at the hospital. After so many hours of coursework and rotating through various types of patient care, graduates were given a formal cap and made a nurse.[3] Therefore, one can assume that Great-Aunt Kitty's training was mostly on-the-job training. In 1896, at the age of twenty-four, she graduated from the Buffalo General School of Nursing and began her unconventional life. In her own words, she was "was something of an adventuress, a true pioneer and most of all, a determined soul who meant business in a new profession that was going places." She felt like "an emancipated woman."[4]

By 1900, she was night supervisor at Buffalo General Hospital (General Hospital as it was known in 1900) and in 1908, at the age of thirty-six, she was Superintendent of Nursing at the German Hospital in Buffalo, New York. Such confidence, ambition, and determination may well have developed from her understanding of her place in the culture established in the area by the McPhersons. In departing from the standard expectations for a woman, perhaps Kitty was exhibiting that independent "Highlander" spirit that defied conventional norms, because mainstream though they were in the U.S., the McPhersons always took pride in the reputed fierceness and independence of their Highland culture.

In 1914, my great-aunt joined what was called Queen Alexandra's Royal Nursing Corps and spent eighteen months overseas serving with the British Expeditionary Forces in Belgium during World War I. While in Europe, she was so impressed by the bravery and devotion to the wounded of the Catholic priests and nuns, that in the 1920s she converted to Catholicism, which I imagine did not sit well with the rest of the devout Protestant McPherson family. This action gives one an indication of how independent my great-aunt was in living life on her own terms and staying true to her convictions. I could not see this happening with any of my Sicilian relatives, since the guilt would have been too intense to take, and the family reaction would have totally isolated anyone who left the church. In Kitty's case, her decision to convert to Catholicism did not hurt her standing with the family, since she remained a revered figure throughout her life. The McPhersons just didn't talk about her conversion very much.

While in England, she had an opportunity to travel to Scotland and found out that the spelling of McPherson in use by the family for generations was inaccurate. As I mentioned in the previous chapter, in Scotland, the Gaelic spelling of our last name is "Mçpherson." She discovered that the correct English spelling is "Mac," so in the 1920s, Kitty, her sister Mary

---

2   "A Brief History of the American Red Cross," *American Red Cross*, accessed November 30, 2010, http://www.redcross.org/about-us/history.

3   Lois Mastin Diehl, "A History of the Buffalo General Hospital Training-School for Nurses," *Journal of Nursing* 1, no. 11 (August 1901), 790–795.

4   From a newspaper clipping that is an undated fragment found in a relative's archive. The article was written by Anna Scibetta and was published in the *Buffalo Evening News* around 1946. At this time the article cannot be located.

Fay, and brother Donald, legally had their last name changed to reflect the correct spelling. The Scottish spelling of Macpherson, however, is with a lowercase "p," so they didn't get it entirely right. When I was growing up and saw the McPherson orchard sign across from Black Alex's homestead on the Oatka Trail Road, I thought it was an Irish family. My father corrected me by saying, "We are all Scots, but we spell it the right way thanks to Aunt Kitty."

There was a rumor in the family that while serving in the Queen Alexandra's Royal Nursing Corps, Kitty had an affair with the English poet, Rupert Brooke (August 3, 1887 - April 23, 1915). He wrote the "War Sonnets," and was considered one of the great poet-soldiers of his time. Brooke saw his only action in the defense of Antwerp where the British forces were overrun and experienced a marching retreat through the war-torn landscape until reaching safety at Bruges. It was on this retreat that he was moderately wounded in October 1914, and if she did in fact meet him, it was probably because he was one of her patients in the hospital base in Belgium. After his convalescence, Brooke returned to England, and there he contracted influenza, which turned out to be the first in a series of wartime illnesses.[5] Brooke had a reputation as womanizer. He was reputed to have had many affairs with women of all ages. If they did have an affair, there was a wide age difference between them, with Brooke having reached the age of twenty-seven while she was forty-two.

The MacPhersons accepted the liaison as truth and passed on the story to younger generations, supported by Kitty's owning a book of poems by Brooke, published in 1915, in which she had pasted a picture of Brooke from a New York Times article dated April 22, 1917. The article was about letters Brooke wrote during the war. Perhaps this is a bit of indirect documentation of the reputed affair. It is also possible that Kitty might have just met him or fallen in love with his poetry, since they had war experiences in common.

At the end of her service to Britain, Kitty received a letter of commendation and a distinguished service cross from King Charles V. My great aunt was so proud of it that she had the medal framed and hung directly over her favorite chair.

It is interesting to note that Kitty's military service to England is a reversal of the Highlander's exclusion from mainstream British culture, and a path to assimilation taken by many Highland Scots, who joined the British Army as a way to participate in the mainstream. Yet for Kitty, this service was done from her place in the dominant, American culture to which she belonged, and she worked in England not as an outsider, but as a member of a mainstream group that did not experience the exclusion that her ancestors had witnessed and sought to escape. Americanization had smoothed her path to acceptance by the culture her ancestors had left because it stereotyped and excluded them.[6]

When the United States entered World War I on April 15, 1918, Kitty volunteered to serve again, this time in the U. S. Army Nurse Corps. According to her war record, she received $15.00 a month. In order to join, my great aunt had to lie about her age; she was forty-five! This was not the usual age for someone to join the army and go to war. Since she had already served for eighteen months with the British, she knew what to expect and figured she was equal to the rigors that awaited her.

---

5   "Rupert Brooke," *About.com*, accessed November 17, 2009, http://europeanhistory.about.com/od/rupertbrooke/%20a/biorupbooke.htm.

6   Based on a conversation with Dr. Charles Burroughs, Case Western Reserve University, Cleveland, Ohio.

On the day I found the photograph of my great-aunt at the LeRoy Historical Society, I also found a fascinating interview with her that told of her wartime experiences and was published in the LeRoy Gazette, dated July 16, 1919 while she was on furlough. I also found her official war record signed by Lt. Col. Caldwell, Surgeon General of the U.S. Army. Together they give an accurate account of her wartime experiences.

After Kitty took her oath, she was assigned to Red Cross Base Hospital 23, which was organized in January 1917 by the General Hospital in Buffalo, New York,[7] but needed immunization shots and "cantonment work"—that is, further training—and was sent to the Base Hospital at Camp Meade to the Nurses Mobilization Station in Maryland. From there, by way of New York City, she was shipped to Europe with the Atlantic Division American Expeditionary Force sailing on the English ship, Carmania. This was a dangerous voyage, since it was during the height of the submarine warfare in the Atlantic. The division landed in Liverpool and was received by a musical band and a cheering crowd that escorted them to the train station. From there, they traveled through the beautiful midland country and on to Southampton where they crossed the English Channel to LeHarvre and then to Blois in central France. Fortunately, they arrived just before the Battle of Chateau Thierry. After this victorious battle, the casualties were so great that the nurses had to move their suitcases outside and give up their beds to make room for the wounded, but this was still not enough as the yard too was filled with soldiers on litters.

A short time later, Kitty and nine other nurses were assigned to Base Camp 26, which was twenty-nine miles from Blois. This large hospital base was in great need of nurses. My great-aunt remarked that the food at this base was excellent. This hospital was large and well equipped with the latest medical technology and even contained x-ray equipment. Kitty remarked in the newspaper article that "After long hours on duty it was very depressing to hear long motor trains passing all night to the front, and then see the boys marching by with their heavy packs, a few dropping out from illness and weariness, but most of them cheering the Red Cross nurses and singing 'I don't want to get well.' The nurses cheering and calling after them good luck."[8]

The First World War had very concentrated action, and on the Western front this meant static trench warfare where the front lines hardly moved forward or backward.[9] The American hospital bases were located miles behind the fighting, so it is not surprising that none of the American nurses died as a result enemy action. The war was described by Ellen N. La Motte, a former nurse in World War I, in her book, The Backwash of War, "as months of boredom, punctuated by moments of intense fright." At a field hospital, ambulances kept rolling in with the "dirty, dying men, and the guns off there in the distance! Very monotonous, and the same, day after day, till one gets so tired and bored." All the while, the war dragged on in the distance. "The weariness of it—the sameness of it! The same ambulances, and dirty men, and groans or silence. The same operating rooms, the same beds always full,

---

7   Joseph Ford, *The Medical Department of the United States Army in the World War*, vol. 2 (Washington, D.C.: United States Printing Office, 1927), 649.
8   "Another LeRoy Woman Returns from War Work," *LeRoy Gazette*, July 16, 1919.
9   Joshua S. Goldstein, "The Women of World War I," in *War and Gender: How Gender Shapes the War System and Vice Versa* (Cambridge: Cambridge University Press, 2001), http://www.warandgender.com/wgwomwwi.htm.

in the wards. This is war."[10] When Kitty had the opportunity to transfer to another hospital base, she probably jumped at the chance just for a change of scenery.

While at Base Camp 26, however, the pneumonia and influenza epidemic hit, causing 2,200 casualties. The camp had only a capacity for 1,500 patients, so consequently many were on litters on the floor. "Army nurses played a critical role in fighting the worldwide influenza epidemic of 1918."[11] Influenza spread quickly where people lived in crowded Army posts, port towns, and urban areas. "More than 200 nurses lost their lives because they contracted influenza while nursing their patients on the wards."[12] The nursing staff where Kitty was stationed was also depleted by the epidemic, but remarkably no deaths were recorded at the whole base.

My great-aunt reported that not only was the workload heavy, but the responsibility of the nurse was very great. On night duty, a nurse would have as many as twelve wards to look after; and complicating everything even further, the corpsmen, though willing, were often inefficient, not understanding the necessity of precaution against contagion.[13] Even though the corpsmen were willing to help, they often made a difficult situation worse, adding to the stress of tending to the wounded and flu patients. Since American Army nurses during World War I were not commissioned officers but appointed into the Army Nurse Corps, sometimes the lack of status created difficult situations where the corpsmen refused to accept the nurse's authority.[14] In the LeRoy Gazette newspaper article, Kitty referred to the corpsmen as "inefficient."[15] I think that was what she very diplomatically meant. Despite the hardships Kitty encountered as a wartime nurse, she did have fond memories of France and talked about furloughs in Paris, Blois, Tours, and southern and eastern France. She liked to talk about the "glorious sky, so bright and blue by day and wonderful stars at night, the beautiful canals bordered by trees of mistletoe and fields covered with poppies and other wild flowers, the beautiful vineyards and chateau covered with climbing

Great-Aunt Kitty in Scotland, 1918, discovering her roots. It looks like she moved the rocks.

---

10   Ellen N. La Motte, "'This Is How It Was': An American Nurse in France During World War I," in *The Backwash of War* (New York: The Knickerbocker Press, 1916), http://historymatters.gmu.edu/d/5326.

11   "The Army Nurse Corps." *Women in the Army*. n.d. Web. 17 June 2010.<http://www.army.mil/women/history>

12   "The Army Nurse Corps," *Women in the Army.*

13   "Another LeRoy Woman Returns from War Work," *LeRoy Gazette*, July 16, 1919.

14   "The Army Nurse Corps," *Women in the U. S. Army.* n.d. Web. 17 June 2010.

15   "Another LeRoy Woman Returns from War Work," *LeRoy Gazette*, July 16, 1919.

vines with roses."[16] The teenage girl who lost her father at the age of fifteen had gone a long way. Maybe the traveling Kitty did when she was young when her family moved to Michigan from New York gave her the realization that there was a great big world to be explored, and gave her a thirst for adventure. With the publication of the article in the LeRoy Gazette, the larger-than-life persona of my great-aunt started to take shape within the family, and they started to treat her like royalty.

After the war, Kitty was assigned to Walter Reed Army Hospital, and while there she contracted influenza in February 1920. She was hospitalized for a month with anemia, so this must had been a very serious case. She might have been worn down from her experiences in France and needed a month of bed rest to recover. Kitty was relieved from active service on April 9, 1920, and returned home to LeRoy to resume civilian life.[17]

The Conversion of Great-Aunt Catherine, *2011.*
Egg tempera on panel.

My tribute to Kitty, *The Conversion of Great-Aunt Catherine*, is based on the photograph I found at the LeRoy Historical Society when she was in her twenties. I was struck by her beauty, especially the intensity of her eyes. In my interpretation, I saw that the photograph depicted a strong, young woman with much determination and self-confidence. She was gazing to the left out of the field of vision of the viewer, as if dreaming about the future. When her father died, Kitty had to deal with adversity early in life. They may have made her even more able to deal with the hardships, drudgery, and suffering she experienced as a wartime nurse. Instead of being content and accepting the limited opportunities that women had at this time in American society, she chose to live an independent life on her own, without a husband or a family. For the setting of her painting, I chose a Scottish landscape complete with a loch from the Highlands with a dramatic sky opening above Great-Aunt Kitty's head, which represents her proud Highland heritage. The lower part of her body is emerging out of the darkness, contrasting dramatically with bright sunlight revealing her youthful face. The dramatic effect of the light acts as a spotlight shining down on her, and represents the moment of her conversion to Catholicism in which she saw the "light." I merged an equally dramatic sky from a painting by Crespi, titled *St. Gregory Delivers Another Soul to Heaven*, symbolizing the souls of soldiers who lost their lives on the field of battle during her years as an Army nurse during World War I. The other point of view is from a totally Catholic view of the world; now that she had

---

16   "Another LeRoy Woman Returns from War Work," *LeRoy Gazette*, July 16, 1919.
17   "War Record of Catherine M. MacPherson, Army Nurse Corps, April 15, 1918–April 9, 1920," War Records (LeRoy, New York: LeRoy Historical Society Archives, n.d.).

converted to Catholicism, her soul also had a chance to be delivered to heaven one day. The dove and hands at the top of the painting represent, in Catholic iconography, the Holy Spirit and God the Father, and were borrowed from a Verrochio painting, appropriately titled *The Baptism of Christ*.

CONFLICTING IMAGES OF WOMEN AS NURSES

In retrospect, women like my great-aunt stepped out of their roles preordained by society that kept women as homemakers and second-class citizens. They blazed the trail for women to be considered in a wholly different light. Women had been nurses in previous wars, but they were never part of the military. This war was different. The military provided this avenue for them to break free of societal gender barriers. They were responsible for hundreds of patients and they saw the grim realities of war. Women were patriotic and were encouraged to be tough, and they broke the stereotype of a woman as a delicate mother or housewife.

On the other hand, they were also expected by the military to be maternal figures to the wounded. So that none of the soldiers would make inappropriate advances to them, nurses' uniforms were designed to make them look like nuns. The uniforms were created to hide their womanly features and to project the nurse as the ultimate mother figure. In addition to their duties of treating the wounded, the nurses were charged with keeping up the morale of the soldiers by providing a maternal presence. They were expected to provide emotional strength and comfort as a replacement for the soldier's own mother in times of great stress. One only has to look at the famous Red Cross wartime poster, entitled *The Greatest Mother in the World*, which has an uncanny resemblance to an enthroned Renaissance Madonna. The "Greatest Mother" is dressed in long, billowy robes that hide her curves, and a cap that has the Red Cross insignia on the front. The nurse's cap resembled a nun's habit that made her look very matronly, therefore, marking them as sexually unavailable. She is holding a wounded soldier that is the size of a baby strapped to a stretcher, making the nurse a larger-than-life "mother" figure and protector.[18]

Even though both world wars shook up gender relations, after the wars were over the attitudes towards women's roles at home and at work remained remarkably consistent over the next fifty years.[19] I believe, however, that women like my Great-Aunt Kitty were the ones that opened a door and gave the world a glimpse of what women could do if given a chance. They gave strength to the women's movement and lived unconventional lifestyles before it became acceptable. They lived life on their own terms despite the obstacles society placed in their way to keep them in the home. After the war, she was viewed by our family as a respected professional, not as a homemaker or as a spinster. She was very independent and lived alone away from her family in a large city (Buffalo, New York). My great-aunt had an active social life and seemed to feel fulfilled even though she never married. She lived an independent life of work and travel, reflective of the opportunity for women provided by the emergence of women's rights activists in America in the twentieth century. To our family, she was a symbol of strength and determination.

---

18   "The Greatest Mother in the World." *Maine Historical Society*. Maine Memory Network, 2000–2011. Web. 30 December 2011.

19   Joshua S. Goldstein, *War and Gender: How Gender Shapes the War System and Vice Versa* (Cambridge: Cambridge University Press, 2001), 175.

POSTWAR LIFE

After her discharge in 1920, Kitty found employment as a private nurse and confidant to a wealthy family in Buffalo, New York. She lived with the family and took trips around the world with them. On our visits to my great-aunt's house, I remember the lantern slides and books of exotic places that she visited, but I don't remember her stories attached to these images since I was young and more interested in Roy Rodgers and the Lone Ranger. As a private nurse working for a wealthy family, she was able to travel to fascinating places and satisfy her venturesome spirit, an opportunity that she probably would never have been able to do left with her own resources. Eventually she left this job and worked for many years at Buffalo General Hospital as a supervising nurse until her retirement in 1938.

Great-Aunt Kitty, because of her career as a professional coupled with her postwar experiences traveling around the world, was more adventurous and independent than anyone I encountered in either my MacPherson or my Sicilian family. She was cultured, sophisticated, dignified, and well read. Consequently, Kitty achieved the status of a celebrity in the MacPherson family, and whenever she had Christmas off from Buffalo General and attended the Holiday festivities in LeRoy, everyone treated her like an aristocrat. My great-aunt was a larger-than-life figure, who was on the one hand a revered relative who loved us, and on the other hand, a very mysterious person whom we never fully knew. In my opinion, her decision to become a nurse liberated her beyond the accepted societal gender roles of most women in the late nineteenth to the mid twentieth century, and consequently, she was able to live an unconventional lifestyle that seemed to suit her.

Several years after Kitty retired, she returned to LeRoy and lived in the MacPherson family home on 33 Summit Street with her sister, Mary Fay. After Mary died in 1949, Kitty took in a series of blind boarders for companionship, to make some extra money, and to teach them how to live on their own. I have a dim memory of one of them. My cousin Jim MacPherson remembered visiting her several times when one of her houseguests was listening to records of talking books. Kitty had to stop taking in boarders when her own health and vision started to fade in the late 1950s when she was in her late eighties!

Great-Aunt Kitty was particularly fond of my mother since they were both Catholic, and when my parents were married, she gave Lena (Chapter 19) a beautiful string of pearls that became mom's favorite piece of jewelry. In fact, it was the best piece of jewelry she ever owned.

Great-Aunt Kitty with her ever-present string of pearls, Christmas 1961.

Kitty was one of the few MacPherson family members that she actually liked. In fact, when my mother died, my sister chose the pearl necklace for her to wear at her wake.

In the mid 1950s, when we had moved to Church Street, we lived within walking distance of Great-Aunt Kitty's house. I remember vividly one frigid winter day in particular when we visited her. It was so cold and windy that I remember getting a brain freeze on the walk over to her house. When we got there she met us at the door and invited us into the house. It was wonderfully warm, and I remember how friendly my mother and Great-Aunt Kitty were to each other. It was certainly a more pleasant vibe than the one I got when we visited Grandma MacPherson. My great-aunt was a pack rat and her house was cluttered with piles of books, newspapers and magazines. As her blindness set in and Kitty couldn't read her books any more, she bought her first television, but she had to sit inches from the TV set to make out the images.

After we moved to Lake Street and Mom rejoined Sicilian culture, we didn't make the trip across town to visit Kitty at her house. We did see her occasionally at a Christmas gathering at Grandma MacPherson's house, which was always a treat.

As Kitty reached her nineties, she got strange and senile. On one occasion she walked up and down the streets of her neighborhood, yelling at her neighbors for imagined transgressions. When my great-aunt realized what she had done, her erratic behavior embarrassed herself so much that she institutionalized herself in a nursing home in Batavia. Life in the nursing home was so unbearable that after a short time she left it and returned home and tried to live on her own again. By this time she was almost blind and realized that living alone was not an option anymore, so in 1964 she went back to the nursing home for good.

Dementia set in fairly quickly after that, and before long she didn't recognize anyone. Grandma MacPherson (her sister-in-law) visited her often. Grandma told us that even though the Kitty we knew was gone, she would sit in the dark and recite books and poems she had memorized, much to the amazement and delight of the staff and other residents at the home. Maybe some of her recitations were of works by Rupert Brooke?

When Mom heard about how bad Kitty was, she made arrangements for us to be driven to the nursing home to see her. When we went into her small dark room, it looked more like a cell than a living space. The room had only a bed and a chair. We were shocked to see our beloved great-aunt curled up in the fetal position with her face to the wall. She was totally out of her mind and didn't know who we were.

Mom talked to her as if she was lucid just in case she could understand us. My sister and I told her what we were doing in school, and after what seemed like hours we finally left. That is the last and most unfortunate memory I have of Great-Aunt Kitty.

On the way home Mom cried. She was stunned and couldn't get the image out of her head of her curled up on the bed. We never went back to see Kitty.

On December 22, 1967, Great-Aunt Kitty passed away at the age of ninety-five. Since Kitty was Catholic, the funeral took place at St. Peter's Church, just down the street from us. It was a short and demoralizing service. I wanted to ask Monsignor Healy to let me be one of the altar boys for the service even though my family weren't members of the church, but my mother thought it was a bad idea. He might have made an exception in my case since he liked my Aunt Franny (Chapter 20) so much.

Only a handful of relatives attended her funeral, one of them being my Sicilian grandmother, Calogera Barone (Chapter 3). Great-Aunt Kitty and Calogera to my knowledge never met, even though they lived in the same town. Yet, when Kitty died, Calogera was one of the few people who attended the funeral. She wanted to go with those of us who had known Kitty, because our great-aunt had been so supportive to us, and Grandma thought she belonged at that funeral to show respect—a typical Sicilian custom. We also suspected that not many of the MacPhersons would be in attendance because it was in a Catholic church, so it was imperative that we attend.

Kitty's casket was draped with the American flag, and at the cemetery there were Highland bagpipes playing and a twenty one-gun salute was offered in her honor. It was a dignified end for such an adventurous woman who was a loyal patriot and a proud, distinguished descendant of a Highland clan. Kitty was buried in Stone Church Cemetery, West Bergen, New York, in the family plot next to her parents, her brother, and her sisters.

CHAPTER 25

Grandfather Donald Alan MacPherson

Born: August 6, 1884, Cross Village, Michigan
Died: August 5, 1957, LeRoy, New York

Donald Alan MacPherson, my grandfather, was the fifth and youngest child of my great-grandparents, Donald Alexander MacPherson and Sarah MacPherson, and he was the only one of the family to be born in Michigan. When he was only three and a half years old, his father (Chapter 22) died. Grandpa was not a large man, remaining trim his whole life. He was about five feet eight inches tall with blue eyes and sandy hair. He was a very tolerant man and was not given to the bias and racism that infected most of the non-Italian community in LeRoy.

His older brother, Alexander, died at age twenty-three while working for a logging firm in Arkansas, so Donald was the sole surviving male who made it to old age. Whenever family members and friends talk about him, they remember him as a great father and a very friendly man. By all accounts, everyone liked him, and he was known for always having a joke to tell.

Donald MacPherson, *2011. Oil on canvas.*

Women especially found him irresistible. The painting I chose to commemorate his life portrays him when he was still a bachelor and a man about town. This is the charming person with whom my grandmother fell in love and married.

Donald left school at the end of eighth grade. Among the family documents, there is one that certifies that he passed the required entrance examination on June 20, 1897 for the Niagara Falls City Schools. In 1897, his two sisters, Imogene and Kitty, lived there. For unknown reasons, he moved to Niagara Falls and probably lived with his oldest sister, Imogene, who was married at the time. Imogene died on May 9, 1898 of heart failure, so it may be that he moved to Niagara Falls to help Kitty, who was a nurse working at Buffalo General Hospital, take care of his oldest sister. They were a close family, so it is not beyond the realm of possibilities.

Grandpa and others at the Saratoga Sanitarium, late 1940s. Left to right: Maggie, Don, Louise (Maggie's sister) and Warren Ganyiard (Lousie's husband).

In 1904, at the age of twenty-six, Don moved to St. Louis, Missouri and made a living as a printer, and at one time was a salesman for a large manufacturing company. My Uncle Bill told me he was a very good billiards player and played in tournaments throughout the Midwest. My grandpa returned to Le Roy, New York around 1917 when he met my Grandma, Marguerite (Maggie) Lewis. My cousin Pauline told me that on his return to the area, he had heard that some nice looking new girls just moved into town and he wanted to meet them. The girls were Marguerite and her older sister, Louise, and her younger sister, Dorothy. Obviously he hit it off with Marguerite, who recalled many years later that he was very charming. They were married in February of 1919. Marguerite was barely twenty and he was thirty-five. When an aunt found their marriage certificate, family members were amused and surprised that she was five months pregnant with their first child, Donald.

Like his sister Kitty, Don was also proud of his Highland heritage. In the 1920s, he assisted his sister to get our surname legally changed from McPherson to reflect the correct English spelling of our Scottish name, MacPherson. During the last few years of his life, he started to research and compile a handwritten genealogical record of our family. His grandson Jim remembers him sitting at the dining room table with his sleeves rolled up and lots of papers and several books in front of him doing his research.

Don was brought up as a Presbyterian, but after marrying my grandmother, he became a member of the Methodist Church of LeRoy. According to the obituary he wrote shortly before his death, he was a Mason and a Shriner. The Masons are a fraternal organization dedicated to forging social networks, mending social divisions, and supporting philanthropic causes. According to the bylaws, membership is open to all people of all religions and races.[1]

---

1   Bruce Marshall, "What Does It Mean to Be a Mason?," Prospect Lodge, 2011, http://www.prospect-lodge.org/mason-m.htm.

Grandpa served as a Doorkeeper, or the Outer Guard. The Doorkeeper's responsibilities required him to stand guard on the outside of the lodge with a drawn sword to keep non-members from entering the building. The Shriners are an arm of the Masons and are dedicated to helping children and families in need, and are bound by shared values and the desire to have fun.[2] I can see why my grandfather was attracted to both of these fraternal organizations, since he was an easygoing man with few prejudices. In addition, the first organized lodge was thought to be located in Scotland, so I am sure this had extra attraction for him. These organizations also helped him network when he sold insurance.

Like his father, Don was sick most of his life and battled what his doctors thought was tuberculosis, but was more likely emphysema. He was adamant in telling people that he did not have tuberculosis but just ulcers on his lungs, since people tended to shy away from people who had TB, an infectious disease. Regardless of his illness, his doctor recommended that he be sent to a TB camp in Colorado for several years when he was about fourteen or fifteen. It broke his heart to be away from his family for so long, instead spending his time among old sick people. Due to his poor health, Grandpa worked sporadically, making a living selling insurance for Metropolitan Life. He suffered from emphysema his whole life, so as a consequence, as he got older he hardly worked at all.

Grandpa MacPherson making his daily rounds in the early 1950s.

Shortly after World War II, Grandpa went to the Saratoga Sanitarium. When his doctor saw Donald, he exclaimed, "Why did they send me a dead man?" His stay at the sanitarium helped him immensely—he recovered sufficiently, and after two years of treatments, he returned home and lived several years of relatively good health. His doctor prescribed that he take extensive walks every day, but this good health was not to last, since he chain-smoked cigarettes. Every morning at breakfast he coughed up the previous day's phlegm while he rolled exactly 40 cigarettes. Then he would dress up in a suit and head for downtown, where he played billiards and visited friends, relatives, and acquaintances.

On these long walks, he would visit his recently widowed sister-in-law, Louise, who had three young daughters. He became a father figure to his three nieces. Pauline especially looked up to him. She remembered that "Uncle Don" always had a joke to tell that made everyone laugh, and he always remembered their birthdays. They never forgot his benevolent support.

My memories of Grandpa are few, but the ones I have say something about his personality and why everyone liked him. I remember one early summer evening in 1956 we went to visit my grandparents. We were all sitting in the sun porch, including my father's brother,

---

2   "Shriners Believe in Brotherhood," Shriners International, accessed August 16, 2012, http://www.shrinersinternational.org/Shriners/Values/Brotherhood.aspx.

Bill. On one end of the porch sat Grandma and me. At the other end, Grandpa held court with my mother, my father, Uncle Bill, and my sister, Mary Kay. They were all laughing and making a fuss over my sister. Grandpa's outgoing personality overshadowed Grandma's more introspective and serious nature, so everyone gravitated to him (after all, he was a salesman).

Mary was sitting on Grandpa's lap and Uncle Bill was sitting in a chair across from them, Mary enjoying all of their attention. Since the MacPhersons only had boys, both Uncle Bill and Grandpa paid much more attention to Mary Kay than they did to me. Grandpa always wanted a daughter, and my sister was going to fill that role. I was really bent out of shape. I was used to being the center of attention when we visited my Sicilian grandmother, since she only had girls, and boys hold a special place within Sicilian culture. Grandma MacPherson and I felt left out. Since Grandma MacPherson had only boys, she didn't relate well to my sister, and over the years, Mary Kay never really warmed up to her. To a child, Grandma was not very approachable, and she could be characterized as being stern and cold. All of the fuss that Mary was receiving was beyond Maggie's realm of experiences. Maggie was not brought up to wear fancy dresses, and she thought that there was already enough fuss being made over Mary Kay and she didn't want to add to the spectacle. We sat by ourselves looking at all of the commotion on the other side of the porch, feeling left out. I was Grandma's favorite, but it sure seemed like it was a lot more fun to be on the other side of the porch. Grandma tried to make me feel better by assuring me that it was all right that we had each other but I killed that tender moment by telling her that I didn't care, I wanted to be with Grandpa. Several times I tried to get their attention, but Mary's charm always kept them captivated. My sister remembers that every time we visited our grandparent's house, she would run and jump into his lap. There was a special bond between them, something she was never able to establish with Grandma. Since Mary looks very Sicilian with olive skin and dark eyes, Maggie must have seen my sister as a clone of my mother, and that was maybe one of the reasons they never bonded.

The last time I saw Grandpa was just before he died in 1957. He had been sick and bed-ridden for some time, and when we visited him he was always upstairs. On this particular day, we were sitting in the living room and Grandma went upstairs to tell him we were there to visit him. I remember hearing his old spring bed and the floorboards creaking as he made his way slowly down the stairs. He was a shell of himself. He didn't talk very much and didn't pay much attention to my sister, and after a short time he went back upstairs to bed. In addition to emphysema, he was in chronic heart failure. He died on August 5, 1957. Grandma found him dead in bed from an apparent heart attack, the same cause of death and health conditions that led to the demise of his father. It was also discovered that he was also suffering from prostate cancer, but that was not the cause of death. He was a very sick man and he had suffered for years.

In the end, Donald was not a great provider for his family, but he left a legacy of having touched people's lives and making a difference through his kindness and concern for others.

Grandmother Marguerite (Maggie) Lewis MacPherson

Born: January 7, 1899, Perry, New York
Died: January 14, 1975, Batavia, New York

Marguerite, or Maggie, as many called her, was of English and German descent. She was the youngest daughter of Martha (1876–1946) and Charles Lewis (1867–1940). Like Grandpa, Maggie's education was also truncated, so she never made it beyond the eighth grade. Grandma, or Grandma Phersey, as the grandchildren called her, was tall reaching five feet ten inches with dark hair and hazel eyes. Throughout her life, Maggie maintained a very svelte figure and moved with grace and elegance. Physically, she was in stark contrast to my Sicilian grandmother, who was very short and rotund. Maggie was a very intimidating figure who was a classic matriarch with an incredibly strong, dominant personality. At times she could be quiet, cold, distant, and hard to talk to, but she could also be generous and kind. She was a real paradox.

Young Maggie, 2012. Oil on canvas.

My grandparents had three children, all boys: Donald, Neil, and Alexander, who were meek and intimidated around her. She was as strong as they were weak. Uncle Donald, the eldest son, converted to Catholicism after marrying, and finally told Maggie fifteen years later. When he summoned the courage to tell his mother, she responded by telling him that she had known for ten years. Because of her tall stature and serious exterior, she was an imposing figure to be reckoned with.

Maggie was a staunch Methodist and was a member of the Order of the Eastern Star, a religious organization for women that was a satellite branch of the Masons.[3] She was as devout a Methodist as my Sicilian grandma was a Roman Catholic. Because of her father's aversion to Sicilians and her Protestant detestation of Catholics, she never got along well with my mother. My mother's presence in the family caused great tension between them. Maggie had another daughter-in-law who was Catholic and was of Irish and German ancestry, and she got along great with her. MacPherson family members have agreed that my

---

3   About the Order of the Eastern Star. Grand General Chapter Order of the Eastern Star. 2012. Web August 16, 2012, http://www.easternstar.org/about_oes.html.

mother's ethnicity was the major factor for their rocky relationship. However, she loved all of her grandchildren and I never thought that she either singled me out or treated me different from her other grandchildren. On the other hand, my mother had a cordial relationship with Grandpa. They got along wonderfully, since Don acted as a buffer between Lena and other MacPherson family members. Lena recalled that she felt very comfortable around him, and when he died in 1957, she dreaded going to visit the MacPhersons.

Maggie grew up in an environment of intolerance, so I'm sure she was aware the of the Ku Klux Klan activities directed toward the Italians in LeRoy. Her dislike of Sicilians can also be attributed to the values she obtained from her father and reinforced by the social structure of the town, but surprisingly, her sister Louise did not acquire the same narrow-mindedness. The egg tempera painting *Clash of Cultures* is my take on this dark side of my grandmother. The painting is based on a photograph taken after my parents were married in 1946, on the supposedly happy day they received their marriage nuptials. The setting is 36 Lake Street, the home of my Sicilian relatives. Maggie, wearing a sash that identifies her as a member of the Order of the Eastern Star, looks less than thrilled at having a Sicilian daughter-in-law in the family. Swiss guards are standing on the doorstep occupying their traditional role as protectors of the Pope. The woman in the doorway is my Sicilian grandmother, Carrie, and it looks like she is guarding the door from the Protestant hordes. Carrie's body language is telling. She is hesitant about interacting with Maggie, so she is standing in the refuge of her house. Since many Protestants in 1946 thought that the Pope was the Antichrist, I created a Methodist's worst nightmare by putting St. Peter to the right of Carrie in the sun porch, holding the keys of the church, and Pope Pius XII, the Pope at the time of the wedding, seen in the upstairs bedroom window preaching a fiery sermon. In the sky opening above the house,

Clash of Cultures, *2010. Egg tempera on panel.*

heaven appears where angels are watching in anticipation of what will happen next. Maggie opens the first salvo of this religious war by stepping on a Swiss guard that got too close.

Christmas celebrations at the MacPhersons, especially in the late 1950s, were great affairs. There were always special guests, like Great-Aunt Kitty (Chapter 24) and of course cousins whom we didn't see very often. Uncle Bill would make an appearance and then the roughhousing would commence. Grandma MacPherson had very good taste and bought great presents. She always got an expensive toy and the requisite sweaters and pants, but we couldn't wait to see what special gift she bought us.

There was always drinking whenever the MacPherson brothers got together. Grandma never drank, but her sons were heavy drinkers. Bill and Neil, like most war veterans, drank to forget their demons. If the Sicilians drank at all, it was a little wine with a meal to help with digestion or to celebrate a wedding or holiday with a glass of Asti.

Christmas was divided between both families with a visit to the MacPhersons in the afternoon and then to the Sicilian celebration on Lake Street at night. In all fairness, by the time we got to Lake Street, most of the festivities were over, and many times we opened our presents as aunts and uncles were leaving. In those days, my sister and I never wanted to leave Maggie's house because we had so much more fun with everyone, but by 1962 after my parents' marital problems hit biblical proportions, going there for Christmas became awkward for all of us. Lena refused to attend the holiday gatherings so Grandma tried to make us feel comfortable, but without the presence of our mother, Mary Kay and I still felt out of place.

A distinct cultural difference that contrasted the two families was centered on food and its enjoyment. Holiday meals at the MacPherson's was an eating experience based roughly on the melded cuisines of the British Isles brought to America. Food was plentiful, but meat, potatoes, and plain vegetables was the standard. Grandma MacPherson's specialty was pot roast with whipped potatoes and gravy. Since that is what her boys liked, that is what she cooked every Christmas. The backyard was filled with currant bushes, red raspberries, black raspberries, and a small orchard that had pear and cherry trees. A fond memory I have of Grandma's house was the currant and red raspberry jelly she would make and the freezer full of frozen treats from her backyard, in stark contrast to the traditional specialties my Sicilian family made for each holiday that I detailed in Chapter 3.

As a child, I wasn't too aware of these cultural differences since my mother did not cook Italian food. Instead, she cooked the meals that my father preferred like creamed beef, pig hocks, and real minced meat pie. Actually, Mom made a pie from the minced meat that Grandma made for Dad one time and was so disgusted with the look and smell of the rotting meat that she told Dad in the future to have his mother make it for him. Yuck. The contrasts of the menu between the

Maggie and her boys, Christmas 1962. Left to to right: Bill, Neil, Maggie, and Donald.

two families were striking. There was no doubt that when I started eating Italian food I became a less picky eater.

It was because of Maggie that the family was able to live a comfortable life. Grandma had no choice but to be the rock of the family, since Grandpa never made much money and was in hospitals for years on end. For example, according to the 1940 census, Grandma worked full time and made $900, while Grandpa worked part of the year and made $600. This was a productive year for him, since in the years during and after World War II, his health deteriorated to the point where he stopped working. She was the cement that held the family together and made a living as a telephone operator and later as a supervisor for the Rochester Telephone Company at the same office Aunt Helen (Chapter 18) worked. A few years ago, I ran into a distant cousin who also worked for Grandma, and she told me that Maggie was the best boss she ever had. Maggie cared about the people who worked for her and was never overbearing, but very considerate.

LeRoy was one of the last towns to eliminate operator-assisted calls, and when my grandmother lost her job in the mid 1960s, she became a dispatcher for the town and village. Maggie had to retire early and lived on a very meager pension. Eventually, she found a part time job as a dispatcher for the village police. Between Aunt Franny working in the drug store on Main Street monitoring my every move and Grandma Phersey working in the village hall, my every move was scrutinized, so I had no room for any adventures.

When all of us moved in with my Sicilian grandmother—including my father, who was a Jehovah's Witness by then—we saw the MacPhersons less and less. Since my mother would not get in the car with my father because she thought he would take us to Kingdom Hall, we never visited Maggie, who lived just across town. It was Maggie who made the effort to keep in touch with us. In those days, when gas was $.29 a gallon, families went on Sunday drives in the countryside, usually ending up at a mom and pop drive-in restaurant (before McDonald's invaded the area) to eat supper. Maggie had a driver's license and owned a 1962 white Ford Fairlane with red and white interior. At least twice a year, she would call us up and we would spend Sunday afternoon cruising around going to no place in particular. My sister and I would be in the back seat, and Grandma would put on our favorite radio station for us to listen to while the adults talked in the front seat. The Sunday drives stopped after we got older and my mother got fed up with Grandma always taking Neil's side on every issue.

As my sister and I drifted away from the MacPhersons, we lost track with relatives on that side of the family, so a devastating event that happened to Maggie barely caught our attention. She had always been a good friend with a neighbor named George, who lived a few houses from her. One could walk to George's house by walking across lots through Grandma's backyard. His wife had been an invalid for a long time, and there were many rumors about Maggie and George. His wife died, and that Christmas Eve he proposed to Maggie and gave her an engagement ring. My cousin Jim MacPherson was there with his parents and witnessed their wedding announcement. According to Jim, Grandma was transformed into a bubbly young girl when she made the announcement. It was a very exciting moment and everyone was happy for Grandma. Family members never saw her that happy again.

On this particular Christmas night, there was a major snowstorm that made driving home treacherous, but everyone made it home without incident. The next morning, Jim's parents, Uncle Don and Aunt Marcie, received a phone call from Grandma that shocked them. Grandma told them that she found George stone cold dead under the snow about halfway between the houses. He left her house at some point that night, and apparently had a fatal heart attack walking in the blizzard on his way home. Since he lived right next door, the heart attack was just one of those things, and not a result of getting lost in the snowstorm.

Grandma was heart broken. Jim remarked, "They were a cute couple, and even I could see the joy in her heart." Grandpa had been such a burden for so many years and George was giving her so much pleasure. She seemed to lose interest in living and went downhill after that. Maggie was never that happy again. In just a few short years, she was diagnosed with Parkinson's disease.

Even though I didn't see Grandma all that often, she still thought about me and cared about my welfare. In June of 1969, not long after the death of her fiancé, she intervened in my life at a crucial moment when I needed her most. I had been working in an Italian grocery store for three years that was owned by one of my distant cousins, Agostino Rubino. After all of those years, I was still making minimum wage, which in 1969 was $1.25 an hour. I wanted to quit and get a job with one of the large grocery chains in town, since if I had started there I would have been making much more than minimum wage. My mother wouldn't hear of it, since it would have been an insult to Augie, and she clung to the immigrant outlook not to make waves and to be grateful for any job you had. I had just graduated from high school and was waiting to go to college in the fall, and was wondering how I was going to afford the tuition and art supplies. I wasn't the most gifted student in the world, so I wasn't going to receive any scholarships.

One day when I was working in Rubinos, out of the blue Grandma MacPherson came into the store to see me and wanted to know if I had a better paying job lined up for the summer. When I told her that I was stuck working for Augie, she asked me, "How would you like to work with Uncle Bill at Texaco?" I had lost contact with Uncle Bill after the breakup of my parents and it had been some years since we had spoken. He worked for a Texaco company gas station near the LeRoy exit on the New York State Thruway (Interstate 90) where the starting salary was $3.25 an hour—an incredible amount of money for 1969, especially for a summer job for a kid just out of high school.

I wasn't sure that Uncle Bill would be enthusiastic about pulling strings to get me a job and working with me, since he was hurt that he didn't have any contact with my sister and me. I also didn't know anything about car repairs, but Grandma assured me that I did not need to be a mechanic and that I would pick up things along the way. I told her of course I would be interested. She was happy to hear this and told me not to worry about Uncle Bill, because if he had any objections she would make him get me a job. When I told my mother she was pleasantly surprised, and to this day I don't know why it was alright to leave Rubinos for Texaco but not for Star Markets. Grandma called me up a few days later and said that I was to report to the Texaco station, and that Uncle Bill would be there to show me the ropes. The job was a godsend and I don't know what I would have done if she had not intervened. She still cared about me and was concerned about my future. I look back to the visits I made to see her and I remember how warmly she treated me. She was very interested in what I was doing, and I really appreciated her intervention at a crucial moment in my life that turned out to be very pivotal to my future academic success. It ranked right up there with my Sicilian grandma lighting candles to the Blessed Mother whenever I had a big exam. Maggie even liked to look at my artwork.

Grandma met my wife one time, shortly after we were married in 1973. Since we were married in the Adirondacks and the drive was about seven hours in those days, she did not attend the wedding. I'm sure Grandma also felt that she wasn't wanted and would have felt out of place. She greeted Linda warmly, and we spent a nice afternoon with her. I regret to say I don't remember seeing her ever again; she died about a year and a half later in January 1975.

When my sister married in 1974, between the wedding ceremony and the reception, she brought her new husband to meet Grandma. Maggie did not attend the wedding since her Parkinson's disease was starting to surface, and being the proud person she was, she didn't want to make her presence into a spectacle. They sat on opposite ends of the living room with Mary in her wedding dress. After few moments of silence, Grandma asked Mary, "Are you sure you made the right decision?" Mary was so mad and felt really uncomfortable about the callous statement Grandma made in front of her husband of a few hours. Mary still couldn't make a connection with her.

The end was not pretty; it seldom is. With the onset of Parkinson's disease, she was wracked by tremors, muscular rigidity, and weakness of movement. The disease devastated Grandma both mentally and physically. This very proud women who always dressed well despite her financial position and carried herself nobly was reduced to a trembling, unco-ordinated old lady. She became very depressed in the months before her death. The disease also robbed her of her cherished independence because she couldn't drive or walk very far. In the words of my cousin Jim MacPherson, who became a registered nurse and is CEO of America's Blood Center, whenever he visited her, he could tell that it was clear to him that she often just sat or napped on the couch, often in the dark. She didn't read or watch much TV, and probably just napped the days away. My father Neil visited her every day, and that is probably what kept her going.

Jim remembers that at Christmas at his parents' house, she was quiet and sad. Just after New Year's, Uncle Neil thought that she had pneumonia and took her to the hospital. Maggie wasn't in the hospital very long before she died. She was ready. By this time, Grandma was living in a bizarre world where she imagined that she was a little girl living in her childhood home and wondering who all of the doctors and nurses were. On January 14, 1975, she died.

Grandma left a mixed legacy. She could be very magnanimous or very terse. To some she was a proud and courageous woman, but to others she was a moody and distant person who was hard to understand and get close to. When people remember her, they remember the disparity in her personality and how complex she really was.

CHAPTER 26

The Fifth Generation

The children of Donald and Marguerite MacPherson are:

Donald Charles MacPherson

> *Born: June 17, 1919, LeRoy, New York*
>
> *Died: April 22, 1976, Henrietta, New York*

Neil Lewis "Mickey" MacPherson

> *Born: June 27, 1921, LeRoy, New York*
>
> *Died: July 17, 1995, Chester, South Carolina*

Alexander William "Bill" MacPherson

> *Born: August 21, 1924, LeRoy, New York*
>
> *Died: July 22, 1995, Winter Haven, Florida*

The fifth generation of three brothers typifies what it meant to be American, since they did not have any societal restrictions and worries about assimilation. They followed whatever path life took them on. Donald was the most successful, Neil, my father, was lost his whole life, and Bill was the wild one. All of them took pride in their Scottish heritage and heartily accepted the Sicilians in LeRoy, having friends from this ethnic group. Donald was very good friends with my Aunt Connie during high school and after graduation. Neil's favorite hangout before and after World War II was Great-Uncle Tony Argana's bar in the Eagle Hotel, and my great-aunt and great-uncle had an affectionate relationship with him. Uncle Bill thought his friend and co-worker Ross Martina was one the nicest men he had ever known, and had a warm relationship with his Sicilian daughter-in-law. The brothers seemed to accept the more tolerant views of their father about the Sicilians in LeRoy, rather than their mother's close-minded attitude.

Left to right: Donald, Alexander, Neil, ca. 1926.

CHAPTER 27

Uncle Donald Charles MacPherson

Born: June 17, 1919, LeRoy, New York
Died: April 22, 1976, Rochester, New York

Donald was the oldest son of my grandparents, Donald and Maggie. He was five feet nine inches tall and had brown eyes and auburn hair, with a patch of red in the back. In his 1937 high school yearbook, under his senior picture is written, "With a patch of red, here comes MacPherson." He was the most successful of all of his brothers, providing a comfortable middle class lifestyle for his family. My uncle was a great role model to his sons and was a highly moral person, but above all he was a very serious man.

Uncle Donald was born with a clubfoot, and although he had surgery to correct it, he still walked with a slight limp that, as he got older, became more pronounced, especially when he was tired or walked a lot. Uncle Donald was a friendly man, but I didn't see this side of him very much. I only saw him at Grandma MacPherson's house, where he seemed to me to embody a very odd combination of melancholy and agitation. Grandma seemed to bring this out in all her sons. When he did laugh, his face lit up, which surprised me. Since he was the oldest, both of his brothers deferred to him and showed him the utmost respect.

Family photographs from the 1920s and 1930s, when Donald and his brothers were young chil-

Uncle Donald, August 1942.

dren, reveal that they led lives very typical of other middle class American children. These photos show them playing football, riding scooters, roller skates, and tricycles—a stark contrast to my mother and her siblings living in abject poverty on the farm. The MacPherson boys were hellraisers as adults, so they must have been a handful for Maggie as children.

In high school, Donald was a serious student and was well liked. He was a Boy Scout, and one of his most memorable experiences was taking a train trip to Washington, D.C. with his troop in 1934. After graduating from LeRoy High School in 1937, Uncle Donald went to

Syracuse University, where he majored in engineering. His dream was short lived because it was still the Depression and he had to leave after one year for financial reasons. His father (Chapter 24) was essentially disabled and his mother did not make much money as a phone operator, so Uncle Donald came back to LeRoy to help support them. He got a job working as a soda jerk at the local bus stop and later a factory job working at Lapp Insulator, one of the local industries. The 1940 census reveals that while working for Lapp Insulator, my uncle made $476 a year.[1]

Around this time, he met his future wife, Marcella "Marcie" Roos, on a blind date. His best friend and fellow LeRoyan, Jim "Brownie" Brown, was dating Marcella's sister Margaret and introduced them. Aunt Marcie recalled that Uncle Donald was very romantic, and in a matter of minutes they were necking after my uncle picked her up at her home. Their youngest son Jim MacPherson related to me the content of some of their correspondence:

I have 30 letters exchanged between them during their courtship. These were written in between weekly dates. Many are very touching and show the exuberance and splendor of young love. In one, my father apologizes for not having the money to take my mother to plays and concerts like Brownie took Margaret. My mother responds saying fancy stuff isn't important. 'Didn't we have a great time ice skating together?' In the next letter my father says he will keep his ice skates in his car. These letters have become among my greatest treasures.[2]

Aunt Marcella "Marcie" Ann MacPherson

Born: October 24, 1918, Rochester, New York
Died: September 14, 2004, Rochester, New York

Aunt Marcie was of German and Irish descent and was the youngest of three girls. Her father liked the name Marcella, and Ann was a family name on her mother's side. Marcie's father was born in the U.S., but his parents emigrated from Germany in the late 1800s. Her great-grandmother's family (Fitzsimmons) was pure Irish. The Fitzsimmons had immigrated to the U.S. in the early 1800s to work on the railroad. Some of the Irish came to the US after the potato famine in the 1840s, although the Fitzsimmons were here long before, as indicated by a one hundred year old certificate they had of their ancestors being at the founding of Rochester in 1825.

Aunt Marcie was very outgoing and dominated a room with her large personality that was in direct contrast to my uncle's quiet demeanor. She was boisterous, lively, and affectionate. My aunt was about five feet four inches in height and had dirty blonde hair (that she dyed red in later years) and blue eyes. When my aunt was young, she had a striking resemblance to another redhead, the actress Lucille Ball. Her fingernails were always perfectly polished in bright red. My aunt wore very strong perfume, and whenever she hugged me and

---

1 1940 census, S. D. Number 39, E. D. Number 19–39, Sheet Number 4 B. Enumerated by Sarah Fitzgerald April 5, 1940.
2 Jim MacPherson, "Family History," March 15, 2012.

pulled me into her bosom, the aroma was so strong that I would lose my breath. She was a very warm person and would make such a fuss when she saw a family member, in stark contrast to Uncle Donald, who was much more reserved with his greetings. As a child, I always gravitated to her. Her son Jim characterized her in a conversation I had with him:

My mother, she had one rule: she'd love you as long as you loved her. She had a huge heart but heaven help you if you betrayed that love. That was the Irish in her; quick to love; quick to drop you when you became more trouble than you were worth. I remember when your sister [Mary] came to visit my mother maybe 20 years ago and I happened to be up in Rochester. My mother couldn't have been happier to see her and just gushed and gushed over her. It was like the absence had never been there. You can never get enough unconditional love in your life. It's what I've missed most since mom passed.

Aunt Marcie, late 1930s.

Marcie started out in public school, but a combination of having a bad experience and being very boy-crazy convinced her parents to enroll her in Nazareth High School, an all-girls Catholic parochial school in Rochester, New York. At one time, she dated Bob Wegman of the regional supermarket chain, but didn't like him. In fact, she hated Wegmans and never shopped there; however, later in life she couldn't believe that she dumped him. After graduating from high school, she attended St. Joseph's commercial school and learned secretarial skills. Her first job was a secretary at a doctor's office, but she quit after the doctor kept hitting on her.[3]

MARRIED LIFE

My aunt and uncle fell deeply in love, and they were married on October 30, 1940. Marcie was five months pregnant at the time with their first child, a boy named Don Jr., who was born on March 4, 1941. Because of their circumstances and their religious affiliations, Uncle Don being a Methodist and Aunt Marcie a staunch Catholic and pregnant, the ceremony was held in the sacristy at Holy Redeemer Church in Rochester, New York. Marcie was embarrassed and referred to her wedding as a shameful affair.[4] Grandma MacPherson, who was also five months pregnant when she married Grandpa, must have identified with Marcie, since Maggie took to her daughter-in-law and they became very close.

---

3   I am extremely grateful to my cousins, Don, who is an attorney, and Jim MacPherson, CEO of America's Blood Center, for the extensive biographical and personal family information they shared with me about the events that shaped their parent's lives.

4   Jim MacPherson, "Family History," March 15, 2012.

Since Marcie's mother was a notoriously bad cook, Maggie taught her how to cook all of the food that her husband preferred. Marcie commented years later that Maggie was the best mother-in-law a girl could have, which was in stark contrast with the acrimonious relationship my mother had with her. The newlyweds moved in with Great-Aunt Mary Fay, Grandpa Don, and Grandma Maggie in the MacPherson homestead at 33 Summit Street, where they lived until 1946 when they moved to Rochester.

My uncle received an automatic deferment from military service because of his residual clubfoot, which ended up being up being the break he needed in life. In 1942, he was hired by Photostat, a wet processing-copier company, as an engineer because of the shortage of trained engineers due to World War II, despite having only one year of college training. He was considered a (junior) peer among the other engineers at Photostat. He was thrilled. Most of these guys were too old to be eligible for military service, so Donald worked in an ideal situation where these wise and experienced professionals mentored him. He was in seventh heaven.

In the early days of World War II, gasoline was expensive and later rationed, so even driving to work became extremely difficult. For convenience, Brownie and Uncle Donald stayed in Rochester with their in-laws and drove back to LeRoy to be with their wives only on the weekends. On one of these trips, they had a very serious car accident. They were apparently drunk and they turned over the car on one of the back roads around Mumford, and both had lifelong scars on their faces from going through the windshield. They were too drunk otherwise to be hurt. After Brownie joined the army, Uncle Donald stayed with a friend from work because he was tired of taking a lot of grief for being a Methodist from his Catholic in-laws. Eventually he converted to Catholicism, but it took many years before he gave in. It was a bit strange that Aunt Marcie lived full-time with her in-laws in LeRoy while Uncle Donald lived in Rochester with his in-laws for most of the week during the war.

While his brothers were in the Army, Uncle Donald was able to work toward becoming a very successful professional that completely overshadowed their achievements. A combination of determination and lofty career goals was the key to his success, and were the characteristics that made him different from other family members. By the end of the war in 1945, Donald had a head start on the men who served in the military, and was working toward becoming an engineer without having to deal with the consequences of war service that many veterans had to overcome when they returned.

The living arrangements after the youngest brother Bill returned from the Army in December 1945 became even more crowded in the small house on Summit Street. In 1946, Aunt Marcie's mother asked her husband to intercede for her to convince his sister, Ceil (Cecilia), to let them move in with her in her big empty house on Clifford Ave. in Rochester, which was in the middle of a German neighborhood. Great-Aunt Ceil agreed to the arrangement, so Donald and his family moved out of the cramped quarters in LeRoy and into the relatively spacious house in Rochester. They stayed with Ceil for 25 years. Now Uncle Donald had a relatively short commute.

My aunt and uncle had an active social life. My cousin Jim remembers that Marcie loved to entertain, and there seemed to be constant parties and BBQs at their house. The neighbors also had lots of parties. Shortly after my parents were married, they too became part of this social circle and went to the movies with Don and Marcie every weekend. Marcie and

Lena were very close for a few years and then their friendship cooled. Marcie was hurt and never really knew why my mother distanced herself from her, and in fact, neither do any of us. Donald and Marcie were also very religious and were heavily involved in the church events at Holy Redeemer Church right across the street.

Uncle Donald was providing a great life for his family. His daughter, Jean Marie, was born the following year, and now their family was perfect and complete, having a boy and a girl. My cousin Jim relayed to me a tragic event that forever changed my aunt and uncle's relationship, but ultimately strengthened their bond. One evening in 1947 they had a big party at their house. Jean Marie was only a few months old. Aunt Marcie asked my uncle to change her diaper. Uncle Donald put her down on the bed and went out to get something to clean her up. When he came back she was gone, or so he thought. He figured Aunt Marcie had picked her up.

Actually, she rolled off the bed and ended up squished between the bed and the wall. Poor little Jean Marie couldn't cry because she was suffocating. By the time they discovered her, she was not breathing and they didn't know what to do. My aunt ran down the street to a local doctor, but he said his wife was sick and he couldn't come, and that they should call an ambulance. Jim asked his mother about the circumstances of her death and wondered whether she held it against his father. She said not for a second. His grief was so inconsolable that she just needed to love him more to help him recover. Jim also remarked that talking about Jean Marie as he grew up was taboo. There was one small picture of her, but nothing else in the house to remind them of her. I think this was the reason I always thought Uncle Donald was always sad and melancholy, even though I didn't know about this tragedy. It was quite a burden for him to carry around. To me, there was always a sadness that haunted him.

Although very involved with the Catholic Church, Uncle Donald had not converted. He was so impressed with how the priests and nuns of Holy Redeemer Church comforted his wife after Jean Marie's death that he decided to become Catholic. When he told his mother-in-law, she sniffed, "It's about time." That response did not set well with my uncle. Since he was a proud and complex man, he waited ten years until she died before he actually converted.

Jim was born after the death of Jean Marie as a replacement for her. He was spoiled and had a happy childhood. Don, on the other hand, was the oldest son and always seemed to be at odds with both his parents, especially his mother. I remember times at Grandma's house he would argue with them and push them to breaking point, and then Aunt Marcie would tell her husband to take care of it. Uncle Donald would always say, "Stop making your mother so upset!" Sometimes my cousin would push the right but-

Jean Marie, 1947.

tons that would make my uncle hit the ceiling, and that really scared us but he seemed unfazed. My sister and I couldn't believe he would push his father so far. I think that is why we kept our distance from Uncle Donald, who was, in hindsight, a very nice man to us. A vivid memory Jim has of one their fights was Don running around the dining room table and Aunt Marcie chasing him with a rolling pin. She got in a couple of direct hits on his arms. It is a comical image reminiscent of a slapstick comedy routine.

If the kids made my aunt upset, then she took it out on her husband and made his life miserable. In 1967, at the height of the Vietnam War, Jim told his father that he was applying for conscientious objector status with the draft board, and was joining the Quakers. His father hesitated for quite a while and said, "I support your decision, but this will really upset your mother." (It did.) He only wanted peace and quiet, and when the kids upset her, she took it out on him. Aunt Marcie admitted as much the night he died, saying, "He put up with a lot of shit from me."

In 1956, Aunt Marcie also started working at Photostat. Marcie's reason for going back to work was that her money could be used to splurge on the family. They were the only family in their neighborhood to have a color TV, and neighbors would drop in on Sunday evenings to watch Bonanza, the only regular series in color, and sometimes color specials. This was also the start of vacations to a resort in the Adirondacks. At first it was just a week, but my aunt and uncle loved it so much that eventually they booked their stay to last three to four weeks. By the 1950s, Uncle Donald was providing his family with a comfortable upper-middle class lifestyle. From my perspective they seemed rich. Uncle Donald bought new cars and took his family on vacation to places like Canada and the Blue Ridge Mountains.

Beside the affluent lifestyle they lived, my aunt and uncle were very good role models for my cousins. Marcie was a liberal and very active in Democratic politics. Uncle Donald was very tolerant of the Sicilians in LeRoy and got along well with my mother. As I described in the chapter on my Aunt Connie (Chapter 17), Donald was very good friends with her, even though their friendship made Marcie very jealous. By deeds, my aunt and uncle taught their two sons to accept people who were different than they were, and passed on their value system to their sons. When Don, their oldest son, was stationed at Keesler Air Force Base in Biloxi, Mississippi in the early 1960s, he witnessed an ugly racial altercation. Don noticed that all along the beaches on the Gulf coast he never saw any African Americans. On one day while at the beach, a group of black men and women set their chairs and towels near to him. It wasn't long after they got settled that a group of who he described as "Hitler Youth" descended on them and started harassing them and also started assaulting them. Before things got out of hand, the police showed up and escorted all parties off the beach. The episode left a bad taste in my cousin's mouth, because he could not stand the stench of racism.

One of the lasting memories I have of Aunt Marcie is of the stories she told. On a visit to her house in the 1980s, she recalled a Sunday afternoon drive they took with another couple. They were driving out in the countryside on a very hot summer day. Uncle Donald was driving and they came upon a roadhouse. As was the tradition among the MacPherson men, they didn't pass a bar without stopping, particularly one they had never been in. The men told the women that they would be just a minute and that the women should wait in the car. As the minutes passed by and the women were getting hotter and hotter waiting in the car, my aunt exclaimed that they are in there having more than just one beer. The women became very agitated and went into the bar to drag out their husbands and resume their Sunday drive. They found the men were having a good time and that just infuriated them even more. Marcie yelled at her husband, "Why did you ditch us?" Her husband looked up at her and said, "Well now that you're here do you want a drink?" Marcie said it was hot and all, and a drink sure sounded good, so they relented. My aunt said it was such a good place that they stayed the whole afternoon, and that "we had beers out our ears." I had never heard of that expression before and it tickled me. She had a unique way of telling a story.

In 1966, with Great-Aunt Kitty in the nursing home, her house on Summit Street was left vacant. Donald's youngest brother Bill had just gotten married, and he approached Grandma about moving his family into the empty house. She gave them permission even though the house was going to be left to both Grandma and Uncle Donald. Great-Aunt Kitty's passing in 1967 precipitated a fiasco between the two families. Donald was inclined to let them stay, but Marcie was so upset that they moved in without asking for their consent, and hard feelings existed for years. Despite the fact the Uncle Bill and his family lived in the house with the threat of eviction hanging over their heads, he built an in-ground swimming pool. That was the last straw for Marcie. Once the will was probated, my aunt and uncle forced Bill to either pay half of the appraised value in cash or move out. They could not raise the cash so they moved out. Aunt Marcie even forced Uncle Bill to take out the pool. It became the talk of the town when Bill had the pool dug out of his back yard and then had it transported on a large truck through LeRoy to the backyard of his new house. A ten-year feud ensued, with Marcie even having strained relations with her mother-in-law Maggie, whom she adored. After a decade of acrimonious feelings, the two brothers, their families, and Grandma got together to reconcile their differences with a pool party at Uncle Bill's house.

Some of Marcie's vindictiveness might have stemmed from how much she resented Maggie favoring her other sons, Neil and Bill, when Donald was, in my aunt's estimation, the only success of the three. Both my father and Uncle Bill were blue-collar workers and did not have the disposable income of their older brother. While my father clearly was the least successful of the three brothers, Uncle Bill did struggle at times, but after his marriage, his family lived a comfortable middle class lifestyle. Grandma never acknowledged that success to Donald, and it irked Marcie for years. Uncle Donald understood and loved his brothers, and they looked up to their big brother, but Marcie would not accept that Maggie was very proud of him but couldn't show it. Maggie did not want to make her less successful sons feel inferior. Aunt Marcie was very kind to others, but was mean to her in-laws. I guess when sibling rivalry became an issue, jealousy and irrationality became obstacles too strong to overcome.

In 1970, Don and Marcie decided to leave the house they had been sharing with Aunt Ceil since 1946 and build their own house in the suburbs. They offered to buy a house with an apartment for her but she didn't want to leave her home. The surrounding neighborhoods had started to deteriorate when the 1964 race riots erupted just blocks from their house. Jim told me about a close call Uncle Donald had on the morning after the first night of rioting. Uncle Donald unknowingly drove through the area at about 6:00 a.m. on his way to work. He was shocked at the broken windows and damaged cars. Just as he was about to turn around and go a different way, a roving gang of young black men and women with bats and sticks surrounded his car. He was terrified and fearful he'd have to run them over to escape, but almost as quickly, another group of African Americans told the younger ones to back off. My uncle got to work and was mightily shaken. For five nights they could not enter or leave the neighborhood between 7:00 p.m. and 6:00 a.m. All of the neighbors would sit in front of their houses and watch National Guard troops stop and search every car that was out and about. According to my cousin, in the years after the riots, as the Jews and Ukrainians who lived in nearby neighborhoods left for the suburbs, poor blacks moved into these sections and there were increasing incidents of theft and assaults.

Six years after the riots and feeling increasingly unsafe, they were ready to leave. By this time, Photostat, now called Itek, moved their center of operations from downtown Rochester to the nearby suburb of Henrietta. So to be close to work, this is where Don and Marcie built a modest red house. Henrietta was not the most affluent suburb in the Rochester area, but it was filled other middle class families like them looking for a better life.

Now my aunt and uncle were able to have amenities that were difficult to add to the small lot they had in the inner city. Now they could accumulate whatever they wanted and build their dream house to suit their tastes. The MacPhersons loved swimming, so Uncle Donald put in a pool when he built his house in Henrietta. To relieve stress, he would take a few laps everyday regardless of the weather. He would start swimming in the spring as soon as he would open the pool and kept going into the late fall.

As Uncle Donald reached his fifties, my cousin Jim told me an incredible story about him. One day, Jim got a call from his mother to say his father was hyper and acting very strange. He was experiencing an anxiety attack. Jim went over to their house and Uncle Donald was very agitated. Jim called a friend who was a family physician and asked if he could see his father immediately. Fortunately, he said yes. Jim drove his father to the clinic where he spent about an hour. When Uncle Donald came out of the visit, he clearly was much more relaxed but still slightly worried. The doctor told him to cut back or eliminate his alcohol consumption, which was considerable. The doctor also suggested that my uncle join AA as a substitute for any psychiatric visits.

On the way home, Uncle Donald told Jim a remarkable and revealing story that explained this emotional turmoil. Sometime in 1946 or '47, a man named Joseph Wilson called each of the engineers at Photostat to ask if they would join Haloid Corporation. Haloid had been around for over thirty years, but they had stumbled upon a way to make massive copies using a "dry," rather than wet, chemical process. Each was promised a piece of the company if they joined Haloid. As Jim remembers it, most if not all the other engineers left Photostat, except his father. He stayed out of loyalty. Photostat had made him an engineer even without any degree or experience. Haloid became Xerox, and each of those engineers leaving Photostat became multi-millionaires. Many years later, my uncle felt that he had failed his family; he could have been a millionaire.

The episode scared him, so he quit drinking and joined AA. But after a few months, he felt everyone else at AA was so worse off, he quit and started drinking again. He felt much more stressed out not drinking, so he drank moderately as way to help him cope with stress.

When my sister was married in 1974, my aunt and uncle were the only MacPhersons invited to the wedding, since my mother had alienated all of the others. After the ceremony, they came across the street to visit my mother who was gracious and friendly to them. I had not seen them for almost ten years. Marcie was the same old wonderful person I remembered, but Uncle Donald was friendlier and seemed more at peace. It was a very pleasant reunion.

A few years later, on the evening of April 22, 1976, Uncle Donald did not feel well. He was cold and was sweating profusely, and was as pale as a ghost, but kept saying he was fine. Marcie called for an ambulance, but he lost consciousness and fell on his bed. He died before he reached the hospital. Uncle Donald was a sick man and he didn't even know it. He had extensive colon cancer but he had no pain. He went to the doctor for checkups but they didn't catch it. The reason for his chills and sweats was that his bowels had a rip in them, and he had nasty infection that spread from his peritoneum to his blood. Marcie said he never complained of pain but was taking large amounts of Tums in the days before he died. In many ways, it was a blessing that he went so quickly, because if he had survived he would have been mostly in pain and very sick for the last few months of his life.

Aunt Marcie continued to work and retired in the early 1980s when she took an early retirement when it was offered, since by this time, Itek was barely hanging on. It took ten years for Aunt Marcie to get over the death of her husband. During that time, she went into a deep depression and never left the house. Helen, her sister, became a constant companion. Helen died after a brief illness when my aunt was still in her sixties, and after that Marcie became addicted to the senior center and made a number of bus trips there. She was constantly going somewhere and hardly ever home. But by her early eighties, she had developed severe emphysema, heart failure, and diabetes, and felt betrayed by God, so she dropped him. As Jim relayed to me, "She became pretty housebound, and the last year was a tough one. My mother lived one year longer than she wanted to. I remember her saying just a month or two before the end that she cursed God for taking away her body but leaving her mind intact. She had stopped saying her nightly rosary and other prayers because she was mad and figured she'd done enough. "If I haven't said enough prayers already to get into heaven, then there is no heaven and no God," she said.

In the last year of her life, Marcie fell and broke her knee. When she went to the hospital, she learned that she had terminal cancer, which was too much for her to process. She was sent to a nursing home where she became unresponsive after a few days. Jim described to me his visit with his mother:

She was thrilled to see me, but as I went to fix her pillow, she grabbed my head and squeezed as hard as she could and said, 'Jimmy, please kill me. I need to die.' The look on her face was agonizing. I told her there was nothing I could do. It was really in her hands and God's. Her eyes filled with tears, and she nodded a bit as she let go of me. Within a few hours she went back into a sleep from which she never recovered. Two days later I got a call at work that she had extensive pneumonia. I saw God's hand.

My aunt had always hoped that she would die from what she called "old man's disease" because she had watched many of her family members die peacefully from pneumonia. Days later, the family was informed by the medical staff at the nursing home that she had pneumonia, and on September 14, 2004, she passed away. Marcie lived a very good life, and at the end did not suffer very much. Just like my Sicilian grandmother, she got her wish and died peacefully in her sleep.

CHAPTER 28

Neil Lewis "Mickey" MacPherson

Born: June 27, 1921, LeRoy, New York
Died: July 17, 1995, Chester, South Carolina

My father was the second child of Donald and Marguerite MacPherson. He was handsome and looked like a typical Scotsman, having blond hair and blue eyes with a big round face. In his prime, he stood at five feet eleven inches and was very muscular and incredibly strong. By middle age, he weighed 245 pounds. Despite his large size and physical strength, we knew him as a quiet, gentle man around his family.

He was also a very humane and compassionate individual who had a soft spot for animals, especially dogs. When I was three years old, he brought home a cocker spaniel puppy for me that I named Putsy. A few years, later when we moved to our no pets-apartment on Church Street, he had to find a home for Putsy. Dad found a couple who lived on his bakery route, and he was able to check on Putsy weekly. I was devastated when we had to give him up, but Dad gave me regular reports through the years until Putsy died. Later, when we lived in our apartment on Church Street, he became aware of a blue merle collie that had an abusive owner. The poor dog was mostly blind and spent its days locked in a shed. My father was determined to save the animal and relentlessly pestered the owner. He finally did coerce the owner into giving him the dog (my uncle told me that my father threatened the man with bodily harm if he didn't give up the abused animal). The dog's name was Rex, and he was a mess. On the day we went to pick him up, my mother, who was not an animal lover, tried unsuccessfully to talk some sense into Dad. What was he going to do with the dog once we got him, since we couldn't have pets in our apartment? My father was resolute in saving the poor animal and thought that he could talk Uncle Joe Burkart into taking him since Joe was also a dog lover.

When we picked up Rex, Mary and I fell in love with him. He was beautiful, but every time someone closed the car door, he started shaking and shivering. Dad told us that he was afraid of his previous owner and thought he was going to be abused. Mary and I were horrified that anyone would do that to a dog, so we tried to calm him down. The dog was a tough sell to Uncle Joe, but after several hours of pleading, he finally took it. Sadly, even though my father saved Rex, the dog was in really bad shape and may have been beyond help. He was old, blind, arthritic, and was scared of everything. Mercifully, after a few weeks, Uncle Joe had the dog put down. Years later, Uncle Joe would bring up the subject of Rex and ridicule my father for adopting such a pathetic creature, but I was proud of him and understood his motives. I know Neil's intentions were very admirable, but he had no real plan on how to take care of the animal once he saved it. As in many circumstances throughout his life, he had made an impulsive decision without assuming any of the responsibility. My sister and

I share our father's love of animals and have rescued our share of homeless dogs and cats, giving them good homes. Later in life, after my parents separated, Dad took care of Grandma MacPherson's Brittany spaniel when her Parkinson's disease prevented her from taking care of her beloved pet, and Dad's constant companion in his lonely, later years was a French poodle named Poncho.

As much as my father related to animals, he had a harder time with his relationships with people. He had an inclination to be sarcastic and judgmental towards others. As a parent, he was not a great father and did not seem to care much about how we did in school, nor did he ever attend any of our plays or little league games. As a child, many times I wouldn't see him for weeks on end, since he would go to work at dawn and then come home after I would be in bed. It wasn't all work. He required my mother to do the parenting.

Neil had a strange childhood that affected him his whole life. When my grandparents, Donald and Marguerite, were first married, they lived with his family, my great-grandmother, and Great-Aunt Mary in the MacPherson home on 33 Summit Street in LeRoy. The house was very small and they soon had a son, Donald and then Neil. The house had no bathroom inside (just an outhouse) for the four adults and two children who lived there. When Neil's younger brother Bill was born in 1924, at the age of three, Neil was forced to move out and live with his Grandma and Grandpa Lewis, his mother's parents, at 24 Platt Ave., a few blocks away. No one was sure why my father was chosen to be designated mover instead of his oldest brother Donald. The move was one of a series of emotional jolts that my father received in his life that may be what made him introverted and distant. He never talked about it and avoided the subject whenever my mother brought it up. Uncle Donald always thought that his brother developed an "odd" attitude toward life after being pushed out of his own

Neil's high school graduation photo, 1939.

home. In one sense, the move was actually good for my father, since his maternal grandparents' house was much larger and had modern amenities like a bathroom with running water. In later years, when my father was lost emotionally and destitute, I remember Maggie, his mother, doting over him giving him money and trying to save him from a life of misery.

This decision affected the relationship between Maggie and Neil for the rest of their lives. It seemed to me that their was a distance between them in their relationship, even though they loved one another. Maggie always seemed to be trying to make up for sending my father away and was always reaching out to my father, but he responded with very short answers and seemed irritated with her or was just indifferent. I don't think he ever forgave her for choosing him as the one to leave home. It was a very sad situation for both of them.

Neil was an average student in high school but had an aptitude for math. He enjoyed participating on the gym team that gave gymnastic exhibitions during the school year. After Neil graduated from high school in 1939, he got a job as a foreman at Veitel Hosiery. This is where he met my mother Lena (Chapter 19) and started up a relationship with her that was interrupted by World War II.

My father was very proud of his Scottish heritage. In the Highlands, the Mçphersons were known as a fighting clan and were involved in some of the most stirring events of Highland history. The Mçphersons were usually among the first to show up for a battle and were known as vicious fighters. When it was time for men to step up during World War II, my father volunteered and joined the Army, just like his ancestors had done for generations back in the Highlands. On September 15, 1942, my father volunteered for military service and was inducted the next day in Rochester, New York. He volunteered so that he could choose the Army branch (infantry, artillery or armor) he wanted to serve in. Since he knew he was going to be called up at anytime, he thought this was the way to avoid serving in the infantry. By serving in the artillery, he expected to be behind the battle lines blasting an unseen enemy and in relative safety. It didn't work out that way.

He trained at Fort Bliss, in west Texas near El Paso, where he became a member of the Fifth Army and was assigned to the 532nd Anti Aircraft Artillery-Automatic Weapons Group, becoming proficient in the use of the Browning Automatic Rifle (BAR). The BAR was a heavy (about fifteen and a half pounds), early assault rifle and had a spiked bipod that supported the end of the barrow, allowing for greater effectiveness and accuracy, especially when firing in bursts. After using it for a while, like many other riflemen, he took off the bipod to make it lighter to carry during missions. The performance of this rifle was very much like a light machine gun, and its benefit was that it was much more portable than one. The person using a BAR was a very important man in the unit, and formed the nucleus of the team providing cover during assaults and thwarting counter-attacks. The firepower of this weapon was quite ample if handled by a man who really knew how to use it: "The BAR was unanimously acknowledged to be the backbone of the Infantry squad. Related experiences of junior officers and NCOs indicated that the Germans also held this view. In all Infantry engagements the enemy constantly gave priority attention to the BAR in the squad. The BAR was credited with the disruption of many enemy counter-attacks."[1]

In February 1943, after five months of training, he was sent to Tunisia in North Africa, where he was promoted to the rank of corporal. He saw extensive action in the African and Italian theaters of operations, especially the Tunisian, the Naples – Foggia and the Rome – and Arno Campaigns, where he and his comrades supported the Anti Aircraft Artillery (AAA) units by supplying infantry cover against German and Italian forces. After the Germans retreated from Africa, the 532nd landed in Palermo, Sicily and then Naples where my father found himself in sunny Italy, which became a cruel joke since Italy would experience one of the wettest and coldest winters on record. After occupying Naples, Rome became the next target. The only obstacle in their way was the Gustav Line that ran through one of the

---

1 G3 Section, Headquarters 15 Army Group Italy, A Military Encyclopedia, Based on Operations in the Italian Campaigns. 1943–1945 (Italy: Printing & Stationary Services CMF, 1946), 179.

most rugged and mountainous areas in Italy. This is where the monastery of Monte Cassino is located and the site of one of the bloodiest battles of World War II, and is sometimes referred to as the Italian Stalingrad.[2] My father was one of the unfortunate soldiers who fought in this battle, which war historians agree was one of the most unnecessary undertakings in the history of the war.

Strategically, the Germans had the advantage with the monastery situated high on a massif, which made an assault virtually impossible because of the rugged terrain. From this impenetrable perch, they could hold off a far superior force by fortifying this rocky massif with artillery and mortars. Those unfortunate enough trying a head-on attack on the monastery would be caught in a murderous maze of pillboxes, wire, and minefields. This suicidal mission was further complicated by the fact that Italy was experiencing one of the wettest winters on record so any movement had to be through knee deep mud.[3] By the time the battle began, assailing Cassino was a dubious strategy. In fact, history shows that General Mark Clark's insistence on taking this objective was generated more by personal glory than by any strategic advantage. Major General Fred L. Walker commented in his diary, "The great losses of fine young men during the attempts to cross the Rapido River to no purpose and in violation of good infantry tactics are very depressing. All chargeable to the stupidity of the higher command."[4] My father grew to hate General Clark with a passion because of the unnecessary carnage he inflicted on his men.

Neil is in the center, flanked by two of his army buddies. Italy, 1944.

Finally, after many delays because of the weather, the battle began at 6:00 p.m. on January 20, 1944. Sometime between January 20 and January 21, my father's artillery position received a direct hit from Nebelwerfer fire during the attempted crossing of the Rapido River. Amazingly, he was only slightly wounded, while his best friend who was in the foxhole with him was decapitated and mangled beyond recognition. After two hours of shelling by intense mortar and artillery fire, my father carried one man and led another to safety. He volunteered to return to the scene and look for more wounded, but his officers refused him. The casualties of this

2   John Ellis, *Cassino, the Hollow Victory: The Battle for Rome, January–June 1944* (London: Aurum Press, 2003), xii.

3   Matthew Parker, *Monte Cassino: The Hardest-Fought Battle of World War II* (New York: Anchor Books, 2004), 39.

4   John Ellis, Cassino, *the Hollow Victory: The Battle for Rome, January–June 1944* (London: Aurum Press, 2003), 110.

battle were so staggering, with most of my father's unit either killed or wounded. The aid stations were crowded with wounded soldiers, so he went back to his post at the front. My father did not report his wounds until the next day when he was hospitalized and most of the shell fragments were removed.[5]

For his bravery he was awarded a Bronze Star for valor, an Infantry Combat Badge[6] for bravery during a battle, a Purple Heart for being wounded, and a promotion to sergeant all at the tender age of twenty-two. On April 22, 1944, Major General Geoffrey Keyes awarded him his bronze star in front of assembled troops.[7] He told me that he was offered a promotion to master sergeant but was adamant about wanting to stay a corporal. The survivors of Cassino had such a profound sense of comradeship that when my father had a chance to be promoted and have a safe desk job for the rest of the war, he declined. When he told me, I couldn't understand why he didn't take the promotion so that he could ride out the rest of the war in relative safety. He explained to me his pangs of guilt for surviving the battle were too strong that he didn't want to abandon his men for a desk job and have the death of more men on his conscience. He said the responsibilities of being a corporal were enough of a burden to carry for the rest of his life. A. B. Sally, a sergeant in the 88th Division, explained in John Ellis' scholarly, well-written book, *Cassino: A Hollow Victory*, the deep sense of comradeship and its inherent obligations:

> Why do I fight? ... I don't know, unless it's because I feel I must because I'm expected to. If I should fail to do what is asked of me, I would betray the trust of the men fighting with me. And if I betrayed this trust ... in my own eyes I believe I would be so despicable that no longer would I feel worthy of the comradeship of men ... It seems that there is an urge inside me that compels me to go with my buddies when they attack and to sweat it out with them in defense and ... to endure seemingly useless privations, all to what may be a useless end.[8]

As a compromise, my father accepted a promotion to buck sergeant, the lowest rank of sergeants that allowed him the chance of staying with his men.

After the battle, the focus of the war in the Italian Campaign changed due to the success of the Army Air Corps and AAA units. With the fading of the Luftwaffe, the AAA unit's role became less critical to the success of the Italian Campaign. The remnants of my father's AAA battalion and other coastal artillery units became the 2nd Battalion of IV Corps of the new infantry division, the 473rd. He spent the rest of the war fighting in the mountains and coastal region with the infantry, starting at Montecatini on January 1945, and finally ending in Genoa in April 1945.[9] By May of 1945, he had earned enough points on the Advanced Service Rating

---

5 "LeRoy Soldier Home on Point Discharge," *LeRoy Gazette*, June 26, 1945.

6 Even though my father was attached to an artillery battalion, he was awarded an infantry combat badge because he provided infantry support through his participation in the Automatic Weapons Group.

7 "LeRoy Soldier Home on Point Discharge," *LeRoy Gazette*, June 26, 1945.

8 John Ellis, *Cassino, the Hollow Victory: The Battle for Rome, January–June 1944* (London: Aurum Press, 2003), 473–474.

9 http://www.pjaudinetsr.com/473page1.html is web site dedicated to the 473rd Infantry Regiment in World War II. The 473rd was attached to the 92nd Infantry "Buffalo" Division.

Score[10] that he was given a furlough on May 1, 1945. He told his brother Bill that it was a good thing the war ended when it did, because he wasn't going to go back. At the time of his furlough, there was talk about him being sent to the Pacific.

Uncle Bill told me that when Neil received word that he had earned a furlough through the "Point System," he took his BAR, his K rations, dug a deep foxhole, and threatened anyone who tried to make him go out on another mission that he would shoot them. They left him alone and my father lived in the foxhole for a week until he left for home.

Upon arriving in the States, he went to visit his aunt and uncle, Dorothy and Bill Jenkins, who lived in Philadelphia, instead of returning to LeRoy. It was an odd choice since he didn't even know where his aunt and uncle lived, and just showed up unannounced. His parents Don and Maggie (Chapter 25) were concerned since he never informed them of his intentions to visit Philadelphia so they had no clue of his whereabouts and were concerned about his disappearance.

Dorothy found Neil to be in terrible shape and never saw anyone so distressed as her nephew. He would leave their house every day and walk around Philadelphia, and they didn't know if he would be coming back. His aimless wandering became his daily routine. The survivors of Cassino were referred to as the "walking dead," and he fit this description perfectly. After fighting in North Africa and enduring the carnage he saw in Italy, he returned home a damaged man. Neil became very quiet and withdrawn, and in the words of Uncle Bill, "I hardly recognized my brother."

Certain noises would derail my father's mind. One day while sitting at the kitchen table, a plane went overhead and Neil dove under the table. One time, my Uncle Bill, a veteran himself, and the only person my father talked to about his war experiences, told me of the time they were driving down a country road and a car passed them and backfired, producing a noise like a gunshot. My father, who was driving, opened up the car door and rolled out of it. My uncle got the car under control and found my father lying in a ditch shaking. These weren't memories, but an actual war experience where his mind actually put him back into battle, where the sights, smells, and sounds were all around him.

These flashbacks transported him back in time to relive his nightmares. A quote from Laura Hillenbrand's book, Unbroken: A Story of Survival Resilience and Redemption, tells the incredible story of Louie Zamperini's survival and redemption, and explains in vivid detail the reality of these flashbacks. Louie's story gave me insight into the hell that my father persevered throughout his post-war life. She wrote, "One day Louie was overcome by a strange, inexplicable feeling, and suddenly the war was all around him, not a memory but

---

10   Adjusted Service Rating Score (ARS) was based on the "Points System" where a soldier was awarded one point for each month in service; one point for each month in service overseas, five points for his medals and badges, five points for each combat star his unit earned (my father had three) and twelve points for the number of children he had. Since my father was not married and had no dependents, his score was based entirely on his time of service and exploits in the field. When a soldier obtained eighty-five points, he was sent home and discharged. Sadly, it was very difficult for servicemen to reach this point total since most were killed long before they could reach this minimum score. For a detailed explanation of the ARS Points system from "Stars and Stripes" magazine, check out the web site at: http://warren421.home.comcast.net/~warren421/score.html.

the actual experience—the glaring and grating and stench and howl and terror of it. In a moment he was jerked back out again, confused and frightened."[11]

These traumatic episodes experienced by my father after the war shaped the remainder of his life. The specter of Cassino was behind all of the life-altering decisions he made that ruined his life; decisions like his drunkenness, being an absentee father, and an unreliable husband. The only relief from these nightmares was the solace he found in drinking himself into oblivion every night. Hillenbrand quotes Louie about how drinking was the only way he could make it through from one day to the next. "Drinking gave him space of time to let it all go. Slowly, inexorably, he'd gone from drinking because he wanted it to drinking because he needed it. In the daytime he kept sober, but in the evenings, as the aspect of sleep and nightmares loomed, he was overcome by the need."[12]

Walking Dead, 2012. Oil on canvas.

Obviously, Neil was suffering from the extreme effects of post-traumatic stress disorder, or "battle fatigue," as it was called after the war. He was so bad it is amazing that he was able to function at all as a civilian. In his day, psychiatric treatment was not something people let anyone know about for fear of losing their job or possibly their family. Lena never understood what Neil went through and told me one time that other veterans went through the same thing my father did and they weren't like him. With or without family support, servicemen like my father dealt with their demons the best way they could, and many veterans from that generation became alcoholics. Finally on June 20, 1945, mercifully, he was discharged from the army.

The oil painting, *The Walking Dead*, depicts my father in his army dress-uniform at the end of the war and is a painting about the post-traumatic stress syndrome that haunted him.

---

11 Laura Hillenbrand, *Unbroken: A World War II Story of Survival, Resilience, and Redemption* (New York: Random House, 2010), 178.

12 Ibid., 184.

His wristwatch reads 6:00 p.m., the time the battle began on January 20, 1944. At first glance, his cool, quiet exterior makes him look like a man to be reckoned with, but as one looks at the images in the background, a more complicated interpretation emerges. On the top left, Monte Cassino looms as a specter in twilight surrounded by mist and smoke from a Nebelwerfer firing it's round of rockets, an image that will haunt him his whole life. The Scottish thistle in the lower left symbolizes the fearlessness of his Highland heritage that he was so proud of. To the middle right of the canvas, the image of death, which I appropriated from the Northern European artist Hans Baldung Grien, approaches my father with a deal. Death holds a human skull and a Nebelwerfer rocket (a screaming Mimi) that hit his position during the battle. When a Nebelwerfer rocket was launched, it made a terrifying sound that added a paralyzing psychological factor that soldiers heard as the round was hurling through the air toward them. Death is offering my father the path to become a war hero, but it comes with the price of having to live with the horrors of the aftermath. Under the surface of calm resolve, there is a boiling pot of demons in him that will never be exorcised.

When Neil eventually returned to LeRoy after the war, he resumed his relationship with Lena. When he announced their engagement to his family, no one knew he even had a girlfriend. The MacPherson men have a tradition of being close-mouthed and not discussing anything of substance with anybody. Neil also must have known how his mother felt about him marrying a Catholic and the added indignity of being involved with someone from an "undesirable" ethnic background.

Shortly after they were married, my father got a chauffeur's license and had a series of truck driving jobs. The one he had the longest was driving a bakery truck that made home deliveries. He never made much money and he drank most of the time he was employed. Many times he brought home so little money from his paycheck that Mom wondered how we were going to buy groceries that week. He was always in a bar after work and on weekends. When he wanted to spend time with my sister and I, he introduced us to the joy of bar life at his favorite watering hole, where we drank sodas and ate potato chips all afternoon. Our afternoons at the bar were all fun and games until the afternoon turned into evening, with Mom calling up the bar every fifteen minutes telling Dad to bring us home. By then we both had stomach aches from all of the potato chips and soda we ate and drank all afternoon, so we were ready to call it a day.

The bar was a place of refuge where other veterans, like my father, went to escape. There were no women, just men who had served their country. My father felt comfortable in the company of men who were suffering like him, who understood his pain and he theirs. Not much conversation took place. Nothing had to be said; just the sounds of the clinking of ice in glasses and beer bottles hitting the bar were enough. With the passing of each hour these men went into a catatonic state that brought them peace.

Neil loved music, and was an amateur musician who played many instruments. In high school he played the saxophone, and after the war, he joined The LeRoy Drum and Bugle corps with his brother and picked up the fife. The bar he liked to frequent had a dance floor and an old piano where he jammed with an old barfly named Jack. Jack would play piano and my father would join him with the brushes on the drums. This was my first encounter with live music and I loved it.

Uncle Bill told me a story of one of their late night escapades. They were at a roadhouse called the Chessar Cheese. There was a large, rampageous ex-Marine at the bar bragging about his exploits during the war. After a while my father had enough and said to the man, "Those who brag about what they did in the war didn't do anything." The man took a burn to his words being challenged and being embarrassed in front of his friends, and he asked my father if he wanted to step outside and settle it. Uncle Bill said that the fight only lasted a short time because Neil laid out the guy with a couple of punches. Other times, however, he wasn't as lucky and came home with cut lips and blood on his shirts. My father wasn't afraid of anything and had ice water in his veins.

One time when we were living in an apartment house on Church Street in LeRoy, a tenant in a downstairs apartment was making supper when a grease fire went out of control and started to spread throughout the kitchen. As we stormed out of the apartment house, my father was just coming home for supper. He ran into the house, grabbed a fire extinguisher that was in the hall, and ran into the burning apartment and started to put out the fire before the fire department arrived. Some years later, after we moved to Lake Street, he had a part-time job working as a bartender in a bar down the street from us. (Not the greatest of places to be for a recovering alcoholic.) He closed up one night, and as he was turning into our driveway he heard the fire alarm go off. He looked down the street and saw the upper story of the bar on fire where there were rooms to rent. He drove back to the bar, ran into the building and helped people get out and then he realized that all of the night's money was still in the cash register, so he ran back into the building, unlocked the door to the bar and grabbed the cash register and safely made out with it. The firemen were not pleased with his heroics, but the owner sure was. He even brought home two of the men who rented rooms at the bar since they had lost all of their possessions and were homeless. They had minor burns on their faces and arms and were black from the smoke. After Lena treated them, she was not pleased with my father's invitation for them to spend the night, since they were complete strangers; especially when she found out that one of the men started the fire by falling asleep while smoking in bed. Neil ended up finding them another place to stay that night until they were back on their feet. From these two incidents, I got a glimpse into what he must have been like during World War II turning him into a valiant man of courageous deeds. He was the bravest man I ever knew.

Just as drinking was an escape for veterans, religion saved many of them from a total life of misery. While on his bakery route one time, a life-altering revelation by my father brought a drastic change in all of our lives. As fate would have it, some of the customers on his route were Jehovah's Witnesses. One day their message hit a chord that brought him the peace he so fervently sought, that he became a changed man. Practically overnight he stopped drinking and smoking, devoting himself to Jehovah's work. He believed that divine intervention had interceded on his behalf and saved him. He got rid of everything that was at the root of his ruined his years. My father was a mess because of his horrific experiences, but the Word of God brought him peace and soothed his inner turmoil. One would think that Mom, Grandma MacPherson, and the rest of the family would have been relieved that he found something to believe in that straightened up his life. It is not uncommon among people with PTSD to make drastic changes in their lives after being saved.

Up to this point, my father was never a religious person, when he was a young man or after he was married. He went to church on Christmas under duress with Grandma MacPherson, only because my mother told him it was the right thing to do. Lena never put any pressure on him to become Catholic, but she thought it only showed respect to his family for him to attend services with his mother at least on the holiest of religious holidays. Neil was an Easter/Christmas Christian, so when he informed my mother of his epiphany, no one believed him at first. He became exactly like Charlton Heston playing the role of Moses in the movie, *The Ten Commandments*. In the movie, after Moses went to the mountain to receive the *Ten Commandments* from God, he came down to give them to his people and underwent a transformation. His hair was frosted white and he had a strange intensity about him after he had just seen God. My father had that same far-away look in his eyes, and an intensity none of us had ever seen before. He was a changed man for the second time in his life.

There is a mental health term called "homeostasis." My friend Bob Herson, who is a social worker, explained it to me. It relates to how family members do not relate well to an often constructive dramatic change to an individual. It is an almost universal quality that occurs in families when an individual makes a significant change in their behavior. Other family members often have great difficulty with the change and unconsciously attempt to revert the person back to his or her original state. Even people with the best of intentions have great difficulty when a person that is problematic makes a change. An example would be an alcoholic family member who gets sober and has to deal with other family members undermining his sobriety. Years later, my mother and I were sitting around the kitchen table talking and out of the blue she said, "You know, I liked your father better as a drunk." Sadly, we all agreed with her.

As I detailed in the chapter on my mother (Chapter 19), my father was failing his family because he had such tunnel vision about being saved and saving others that he couldn't see what he was doing to us. When our financial situation almost put us out on the streets, Mom told Dad that we were moving to live with my Sicilian grandmother. He had the same reaction I did. He didn't want to move to Lake Street, the den of Catholicism, and he surely did not want my mother to get a job. I heard them arguing that he was the man of the house, and he started quoting the Bible about how women are subservient to men and that he is the only breadwinner in the household. Lena went crazy. She challenged him to get a real job and straighten up; until then we would be moving to live on Lake Street.

For years, Lena had to do all of the heavy lifting to provide us with some semblance of a normal life, since my father was just about useless when it came to being a parent. His post-traumatic stress disorder made him unreliable and uncommunicative. To hear him preach to her about gender roles was too much for her to take, since she had been taken advantage of and unappreciated for years.

We moved to Grandma's around Thanksgiving in 1961. I don't know how we made ends meet before we moved to Grandma's, and I know we were late with the rent most of the time if we paid it at all, and later, Grandma refused to accept it from us. Dad came with us when we moved in with Grandma, but Lena did all she could to discourage him to move with us. With his newfound religion, he declared that he belonged with his family, so wherever we went he was coming with us. It was ugly from the start. My mother moved into a bedroom by herself at the far end of the house, and my sister and I had bedrooms between them like a buffer zone. It was very symbolic, since from that day on, both of them used us in a holy war they were waging against each other. Lena tried to scare my sister and I by saying that if Neil ever tried to kidnap us, to make as much noise as possible and she or Grandma would call her sister Helen's husband Joe and he would save us. Neil would try to sway us by telling us how much better his religion was than Catholicism. My sister Mary wasn't comfortable around him anyway, because when she found him passed out in a chair she thought he was dead; but my mother's psychological warfare put her over the top. She tried to avoid him at all costs. I remembered the good times with him and tried to talk with him like before, but it was impossible since every topic he turned around to religion. Life was very bleak for all of us.

The relationship of my parents became like the storyline of a Puccini opera: very melodramatic and over the top. My father was the stoic Scotsman while my mother was the emotional Mediterranean, and they played their stereotypical roles to the hilt. Lena wanted Neil out, so she turned up the heat on him. I saw her do everything she could to make Dad's life miserable so that he would either leave or hit her so she would have grounds for a separation. One Sunday afternoon, Dad was cooking his meal (since Mom stopped doing anything for him) and she started in on him about making a mess and eating our food, and then it escalated into she hated him and so did the kids. He turned the other cheek. When his back was turned in a fit of rage, she picked up the iron frying pan and was just about to hit him on the back of the head, when I yelled to Dad to look out. He turned around and caught the frying pan in his hand inches from his head. Mom started crying and went up to her room. Dad thanked me for saving him and asked me if I wanted to go to Bible study with him. I went to my room and listened to music. Lena was pushed into a corner and did not know what to do. From her point of view, she was protecting her children from a deranged lunatic. I was shocked by her actions, but at the same time I knew she would do anything to protect us from harm.

My mother's actions seem extreme in this day and age, but in the early 1960s they were a cliché of the time, when society and people's interactions were more physical than today. But even under the circumstances of the times, this incident affected my sister and me in an adverse way. Both of us wanted out of the house and to have a home life that was less confrontational, where the parents got along and even loved one another. At this time, I spent as much time as possible at Aunt Florence and Uncle Joe Burkart's (Chapter 15) house hoping to avoid all of this conflict. Sometimes Mary came with me, but most of the time she withdrew and either went to a friend's house or tried to become invisible.

Both of my parents believed that their religion was the true one and would not compromise one bit. It was inevitable that the situation would reach the boiling point. Everything came to a head one Sunday evening in 1965. By this time, my father was a minister and started turning up the pressure on my mother to take us to Bible study. He was told at one meeting that if he couldn't convert his own family he might not be one of the chosen ones to go to heaven when he died. He gave Mom an ultimatum that he was taking us even if she didn't like it, unless she converted. All week my mother was upset that she didn't know how she was going to save us from going with him. Grandma, Franny, Mary, and I were all getting nervous as the day approached. Mom called up her sister Helen crying and saying she was at her wit's end. Helen told her not to worry, and that if Neil decided to force us to go with him to call her and she would send her husband Joe D'Angelo (Chapter 18) over to keep it from happening. Joe was an ex-marine sergeant who was in the Battle of Guadalcanal and was tough as nails.

When Sunday evening rolled around, Neil came down from his room and told my sister and I to "get your coats, on you're coming with me." The last thing I wanted to do was go, so I stood my ground and told him absolutely not. Mary was petrified and said nothing. Lena intervened and said he wasn't taking us anywhere. Neil got mad and yelled at us to get dressed because we were going, like it or not. With that, Mom snuck over to Grandma's apartment and told her to call Joe. He came in a matter of minutes.

He walked in the side door to our apartment and asked my father what was going on. Neil replied that it wasn't any of his business, that it was a family matter and that he should leave. Uncle Joe was cool and calm, and stood up to my father and said, "Lena and the kids are part of my family too, and I'm not going to let you take them anywhere if they don't want to go." My father went ballistic, "You little shit! I can crush you with one hand!" (Which he might have been able to do, but I wouldn't have bet on it.) Uncle Joe stood his ground and replied, "Don't be so sure. I've taken care of bigger guys than you." Then Joe said, "Neil I've always liked you. Don't do this. Your kids are scared of you and your wife is hysterical. Think twice of what you are doing."

Many thoughts raced through my mind. On one level I was intrigued by the fact that there was going to be a fight in our apartment, but then the thought, 'if Neil won we would be going to Bible study' did not thrill me. What about broken furniture? And where should I go to keep out of the way, but still have a bird's eye view of the altercation?

Just then, Grandma had heard enough and came storming from her apartment yelling in broken English, "You acting like a bunch of roughnecks! Nobody fights in my house! If you don't stop I'll call the cops! They'll take care of you!"

Both brothers-in-law stopped dead in their tracks. Even after everything that had happened, my father still liked Grandma and she was still cordial to him when she saw him. Joe, after all, was Italian and respected Grandma as if she was his own mother. Both men backed off, and my father told us that we lucked out this time, but next week we would be going with him.

Several of my uncles thought that Uncle Joe D'Angelo was out of line for sticking his nose into our business, but my sister and I were glad that he was looking out for us. Their feeling was that the world wouldn't have come to an end if he took us to Bible study. Maybe Mom made the situation worse than it was with her hysterical outbursts, but the bottom line was that we didn't want to go any place with him, especially to any religious-related outing to have his religion shoved down our throats. We were devout Catholics.

After this episode, Neil changed his tactics. If he couldn't take us to Bible study, then he would bring Bible study to us. One week he brought home a young couple from his congregation to our apartment while Mom was at work. For an hour we sat around the kitchen table and had bible discussions. It was an hour of agony. When Mom came home, she of course hit the ceiling and another fight ensued. Mom sought legal council, where she was told that our father could not take us out of the apartment against her wishes to a Bible study group, but he did have the right to preach to us at home. So every Wednesday night in the hour before Mom came home from work in Rochester, we had Bible study. One Wednesday evening, Dad summoned Mary and I to the living room for our Bible study. By this time, I was fourteen and I had enough of his preaching, so I stood my ground and refused to participate. As we stood arguing in the living room, he grabbed me and tried to force me onto the couch so I shoved him, knocking him to the floor. I felt pretty smug about what I had just done, but the next thing I knew, Dad had picked me up and threw me across the room, where I landed on the couch. I bitterly participated and grew to resent his tactics. That evening I finally experienced the volatile side of my "gentle" father.

After this episode, Lena went to a lawyer for advice and to the parish priest for his blessing to get a legal separation. Our priest, Father Zupa, counseled my mother to not do anything hasty and to give it another year. I couldn't believe that he told her that. We had been putting up with everything for years, and he knew of our situation. This was not a snap decision on my mother's part. Because Mom wanted to have the support of the church, she waited the year and then started legal procedures for a separation but my father wouldn't go easy. Even though she had obtained a legal separation on the grounds of mental duress, my father refused to leave. On the day the papers were going to be served, we packed up our belongings and moved in with Aunt Helen and Uncle Joe D'Angelo across town for a month. After Dad left and moved to the town of Nunda to live in a trailer to be close to his congregation, we went back home. The atmosphere was much more bearable, but all of the stress from my mother's marriage exacted a toll on her, and after the breakup with my father, whatever sense humor Mom had left was gone.

In 1969, I turned eighteen during the height of the Vietnam War, and in accordance to the law, registered for the draft. I was hoping I would be accepted into a college to study art and get a student deferment. As long as I kept my grades up, I could get another one for up to four years and then I would, in all likelihood, get drafted and go to war like my father. On one of his court-appointed weekly visitations, my father told me that he didn't want me to go to college nor go to Vietnam. He told me that if I get drafted, that he would drive me to Canada because he did not want me to have to go through the hell he did. By this time he had become a complete pacifist.

In 1970, when the second draft lottery was held for those born in 1951, I received draft number 185, but, thankfully, the highest lottery number the Selective Service chose that year was 125. So the draft board classified me 1A, available for unlimited military service, and got my one year of eligibility out of the way. When I graduated in 1973, I was able to start the next phase of my life. Dad was very happy for me.

In 1973, after I completed my B.A. degree at SUNY Oswego, I moved to South Carolina and attended the University of South Carolina where I received an MFA degree. Neil followed me and occasionally came in and out of my life. I was the only member of our nuclear family who would have anything to do with him. I would let him visit me only under the condition that he would not preach to either my wife or me. My father only preached to us one time, so I stopped him in the middle of his sermon and told him to leave and never come back. He became very distraught and asked me for another chance. I could see that he was very upset at this prospect, so I gave him another one. Neil never did it again, but always after one of his visits, a member of the local Jehovah's Witness Kingdom Hall would pay us a visit and would leave us with a Watchtower magazine to contemplate. Every meeting with my father was very awkward and we never had much to say to one another. He always seemed sad and guilty, like a dog that has just gotten into trouble.

My father lived a self-imposed life of poverty, since that is how Jesus lived his life. Neil read the Bible constantly, and worked just enough to feed himself. He lived in a rundown sharecropper shack on a large tree farm around Great Falls, South Carolina, and made a living selling firewood. After a section of forest had been logged, he would go into the area and scavenge anything that he could and then sell it. One day his chain saw got stuck in a cut he was making, and in the process of getting it out, one of his pinky fingers got stuck between two large logs and was mashed. After he got it free, it started bleeding profusely. Instead of getting medical help, he went home and bandaged it up the best he could with a handkerchief and took off for a Jehovah's Witness Convention that was being held that week near his house. In hindsight, this was the same reaction he had to being wounded at Monte Cassino, when he delayed medical attention for his wounds. When he got to the convention and his friends saw that his finger was bleeding and dripping through his bandage, they sent him to the nurse's tent to get attention.

Neil in the hospital in South Carolina, February 1992. Left to right: Neil, me, Fanny Lee, and Uncle Bill.

As fate would have it, a nurse who was a widow with several children treated him. This is how Neil met his future wife, Fanny Lee Parnell, a very polite Southern woman in the truest sense of the word. She had her eye on him for a long time, and seized the opportunity to make her move and rushed to take care of my father. His finger was so mangled that she drove him to the emergency room to get proper medical attention. Neil had finally found the missing piece in his life. Here was a woman with a family in need, who thought he was a real catch, and most importantly, shared the same zealous religious beliefs. My father was awarded a second chance to make up for the mistakes he made with us, and he made the most of it. Her children loved him very much, and he became a very good father to them. In 1985, when

I got my teaching position at SUNY Geneseo and moved back to New York, I didn't feel guilty about leaving him since I knew he had everything he needed for the rest of his life.

As their relationship grew, Neil finally asked Lena for a divorce so that they could remarry. When Lena received the papers to sign, she hesitated for a long time, thinking it was one more opportunity to get revenge on him. As I reported in my mother's chapter, after a few days of soul searching, she signed the papers and put them in the mail.

In the intervening years, Neil developed emphysema just like his father and grandfather from all of the years of chain smoking, and eventually developed heart problems. In February 1992, Neil had a massive heart attack and Fanny Lee thought he was going to die, so she called me. I went down to see him. He still was my father. I met his step-children, and they all told me how lucky we were to have such a caring parent and were thankful that I wasn't jealous of their relationship with him. I did have passing thoughts of wishing that he was as attentive to me as he was to them when I was young and needed a role model. We all would have had a happier and easier life if he had been more like the father he became. If they only knew what it was like having him for a father for the past forty years. On the day I was leaving, I went to see him one last time. It was then that he apologized to me for being an absentee father and how proud he was of me. I told him that I understood why he was the man that he was, and that I was glad he finally found happiness with a family who loved him and understood him. It was the first time that we ever made an emotional connection, and this strong and a heavy weight was lifted off both of us.

Dad made it through this close call, but in 1995, his heart started to get weaker, and on July 17 of that year he died. I never saw him again because I didn't want the best memory I had of him to be tarnished in any way. For years I hated Neil for never being around when I needed him, and I felt that I had somehow not lived up to his expectations and that was why he never spent time with me. After his death, I realized what a tragic life he lived. From moving out of his home as a child, to his war experiences, to his postwar ordeals, and then finally purging his demons only to find his inner peace lead to more pain and suffering for him and his family. He was adrift in a world of his own and soldiered through life, and, somehow, he was able to time and time again resurrect his life from the ashes and ultimately find peace, something that my mother was never able to do.

CHAPTER 29

Uncle Alexander William "Bill" MacPherson

Born: August 21, 1924, LeRoy, New York
Died: July 22, 1995, Winter Haven, Florida

Uncle Bill was the youngest of the children of my grandparents, Maggie and Don MacPherson. Bill, like his father, was very interested in his Scottish heritage, and he owned a book on our family's genealogy that he shared with me. It was his interest in our Scottish family history that got me thinking years later about the possibility of expanding the direction of my current research from a strictly Sicilian study to becoming bicultural in nature. He would have loved the information I dug up on relatives long gone. When I made a trip to Scotland to give a paper at the Biennial International Conference hosted by the Society for Italian Studies at the University of St. Andrews in 2011, I frequented many of the local pubs in Edinburgh and St. Andrews. As I was sampling the Scotch, local beers, and ales, I thought about how much Uncle Bill would have loved to be on the trip with me. He loved all things Scottish, and he would have had a great time eating the meat pies served in the pubs and listening to people speak the old Scots language.[1]

Uncle Bill and his movie star good looks, 1943.

Bill was at times a secretive person, but he was generally very friendly. From an early age, I only knew him as "Uncle Bill" and was very surprised when I started working with him at a Texaco service station to hear other people refer to him as Alex (he was named after Black Alex). He was five feet nine inches tall, and, like my father, was very strong and muscular. As he aged, he had a very imposing physical presence weighing around 220 pounds in middle age. His forearms and hands were massive, with stubby looking fingers that had the strength

---

1   "What Is Scots?," *Scots Language Centre*, 2015, http://www.scotslanguage.com/What_is_Scots%3F_uid2/What_is_Scots_%3F. The term "Scots" refers to the Scottish dialects found throughout Scotland. There is a fascinating website called Scots Language Center that explains all aspects of the dialect. Robert Burns wrote most of his poems in Scots.

of vice grips. He lived a very exciting life, and most people would say he lived life on the wild side.

Like his father, Uncle Bill was very charming and popular with the ladies. He was a very handsome man with brown eyes, and thick, beautiful, black curly hair that always seemed to stay perfectly in place. Women were said to have loved it so much that they liked to run their fingers through it. In high school his nickname was "Ty" because his classmates thought that he looked like Tyrone Power, a movie star.

Of all the MacPherson boys, Bill was the least judgmental and really related well to kids. He loved all of his nephews and his niece, but when we were young, I think my sister Mary and I were his favorites. Uncle Bill always seemed to be happy to see us, and when he flashed his engaging smile, his eyes would get small as slits. In all of the family photographs I've seen of him, he always had that "MacPherson grin" that seemed mischievous as much as friendly. Uncle Donald could be aloof and my father could be sarcastic and judgmental, but Uncle Bill greeted people with a smile and accepted them for whom they were. Long after my sister and I were adults, he still referred to me as Tommy and my sister as Mary Kay, names we had long since outgrown.

When we drifted away from the MacPhersons, Uncle Bill was hurt as much as Grandma MacPherson was about losing contact with us. I was surprised to find out how disheartened he was, since I thought I was more of an annoyance to him. Looking back, I can see how he missed Mary so much, since she was well behaved and looked like a little princess whenever we visited him at Grandma MacPherson's house, while I, on the other hand, was always looking to wrestle with him. My favorite name for him was "Uncle Bull", and whenever I called him that, he would chase me around the room making bull noises. He would grab me and throw me up into the air and catch me. I was scared out of my mind, but I never stopped taunting him because I liked the attention he gave me. But it was Mary whom he took on long drives to get an ice cream cone in his 1955 white, black, and coral Ford Sunliner convertible. Mary was neat and I was always too dirty from playing outside to sit on the white leather seats, so Mary was always his first choice. I was so envious. When I did get a chance to take a ride with him, Mary always sat in the passenger's seat up front and I was relegated to the back seat, with Uncle Bill occasionally turning around to make sure I was not touching anything with my dirty hands. Even though I washed them, he still thought they weren't clean enough.

Unlike his older brother Donald, Bill was indifferent about academics and never had any interest in pursuing a degree beyond high school. On March 12, 1943, Uncle Bill vol-

Uncle Bill with his ambulance, England, 1943. Note that "LeRoy, New York" is on the hood.

unteered and joined the army. Bill told me that his father cried like a baby when he took him to the bus station, since he was the youngest and my father had already enlisted in the Army and was fighting in North Africa. After receiving his basic training at Camp Pickett in Charlottesville, Virginia, he was assigned to the 9th Army as an ambulance driver and was shipped to England, where they trained and waited for months for the impending invasion of France. He told me stories of endless training and waiting for something to do. He spent his free time romancing the women around his base, and his only criticism of them was that English women only wanted to make love in a standing position. Finally—or mercifully, for the English women—on June 6, 1944, D-Day, he found himself in France.

His grisly job on D-Day was to go from body to body on the beach to see who was dead and to save who was still alive. My uncle told his son, who was also named Bill, that the belief that medics and ambulance drivers did not carry firearms because of the supposed protection afforded to medical personnel on the field of battle was not true. My uncle said that he and his buddies carried weapons, since the Red Cross insignia on the side of his ambulance made a nice target for the Germans. Later in 1944, after hurting his knee, he was assigned to a clerical position in the headquarters of the European Theater of Operations in the Communications Zone. He attained the rank of private first class and earned a good conduct medal, a victory medal, and a European Campaign medal. According to his Separation Qualification Record, his role was "performing various clerical duties in a medical detachment orderly room." Basically he kept the file system, typed reports, signed leaves, and kept records. His favorite duty, however, was playing revelry with his cornet every morning to wake up the camp. He told me that he was lucky and never saw action as an infantryman, unlike his poor brother Neil, who was dodging bullets and shrapnel from North Africa to Italy.

The "bad boy" of the MacPherson clan at my parent's wedding, June 1946.

After the Germans surrendered on May 8, 1945, my uncle was transferred to Switzerland and spent time in Davos. He loved Switzerland and planned to go back one day, but never did. On December 24, 1945, he received an honorable discharge and started his life as a civilian. After he got home he said, "I went over on a goddamn boat, I came back on a goddamn boat, and I will never get on another goddamn boat." Like my father, Uncle Bill was a musician and enjoyed all of the big band music of the World War II era. Shortly after returning to the States, they joined the LeRoy Drum and Bugle Corps together.

Soon after his homecoming, Uncle Bill married a woman by the name of Jean. The marriage did not last long. Apparently she was still having an affair with an old boyfriend after she had become engaged to my uncle, and it carried over into the marriage. The marriage lasted only a matter of weeks and she dumped him. Of course he was devastated and embarrassed, so the subject of his first marriage was taboo. I didn't find out about it until I was about 18 and then my mother swore me to secrecy.

Bill was always a wild kid, but after the breakup of his marriage, he especially lived life on the edge. He had an active social life, frequenting bars and roadhouses, drinking and carousing throughout the area. The MacPherson boys were always interested in cars, but Uncle Bill was car crazy. My uncle became involved with racing cars at the Spencerport Racetrack near Rochester and Lancaster Speedway in the Buffalo area, as well as street racing on the backroads of LeRoy in his spare time with his friends. He always had to have the hottest and fastest cars.

Friday Night, *2012. Oil on canvas. Uncle Bill with his "Hot Rod Merc."*

Like the many fortunate service men that returned to civilian life, Uncle Bill got caught up in the car-crazy phenomenon in post-war America. Once hostilities had ceased, those lucky enough to make it back wanted to make up for lost time. Hot rods and the cult of the American car had started to take off in California just before World War II. Once back, ex-GIs couldn't get enough of cool cars, all-American hamburgers and fries, and the girls they had left. Owning modified cars was an important part of self-expression and allowed many to enjoy the social life they desired. Many GIs missed the adrenaline rush that war provided, and wanted to relive the feeling without the disastrous consequences.[2] Getting behind the wheel of a cool hot rod and racing around the streets and backroads of LeRoy must had been a lot like driving an ambulance through the war-torn countryside in France. For my uncle, driving fast cars and picking up women was at the top of the list of things to do and fulfilled his conscious and unconscious dreams.

Like many car enthusiasts, Bill had a preference for a certain type of car. In his case, it was Fords and Mercurys. His favorite car among all of the cars he owned was his red 1949 Mercury Monterey coupe, or as he affectionately called it, "My Hot Rod Merc." Car enthusiasts and motorheads alike referred to it as "the cigar" because of its oblong shape. My uncle

2   Auto Editors of Consumer Guide, "History of Hot Rods & Customs," *HowStuffWorks.com*, September 2007, http://auto.howstuffworks.com/hot-rod2.htm.

liked to tell the story of how he used to take a ride to the nearby town of Mt. Morris to pick up some "Eye-talian girls." Mt. Morris was a tough blue-collar village that was predominately Sicilian. Ironically, some of my Barone relatives lived there. On these forays into town, he flirted with and drove around with several of the dark haired, Mediterranean beauties, and in the process flaunted his coup to their infuriated boyfriends. His all-American charm and bad boy good looks were far too much for the women to resist. Finally, their Italian boyfriends tried to put a stop to these insults by waiting for him on the outskirts of town to teach him a lesson, but he always eluded them in his Merc. Once again, the skills he learned as an ambulance driver in the Army served him well in peacetime. He enjoyed the danger and the chase of these excursions into "hostile territory."

The oil painting *Friday Night* depicts Uncle Bill in his bachelor days, getting ready to go out for a night on the town in his beloved Merc. His mischievous grin and robust physique was his trademark. Main Street LeRoy is in the background, waiting to be plundered by Bill and his cronies.

After his ill-fated marriage, Bill drank heavily and took unnecessary chances street racing in his cars. The following episode illustrates his dangerous lifestyle. An old friend of his named Dick told me a story of Uncle Bill about his street racing days. He had bought Uncle Bill's 1955 Ford Sunliner, and one Saturday at four in the morning, Dick and his wife were driving west from Caledonia to LeRoy on U.S. Route 5, when they came upon Uncle Bill. Bill was driving a Ford Galaxy and before they knew it, they were racing side-by-side, heading west on Route 5 toward LeRoy, eight miles away. Dick said they had their foot to the floor all the way, until finally Uncle Bill took the lead on the outskirts of LeRoy. Apparently Bill was toying with Dick and was saving just a little bit of his horsepower for the home stretch. My uncle's friend said they were lucky no one was coming eastbound because neither one of them would have been able to stop in time.

My uncle's stepson, also named Bill, gave a similar account of one of his adventures. "One such story was related to me by Jerry Stella [a friend and racing buddy] about when Alex [the name his children preferred] was literally pushing Dale Hammer's 1963 Ford 426 Galaxy down Route 5 in Limerock with his 406 Galaxy 500 XL convertible at well over 120 miles per hour—I mean literally on his bumper, and this was witnessed by several [people]." When Uncle Bill first bought the car, he hated it because he was disappointed that it was so slow. He had his friend re-bore the carburetor and perform other modifications, making it one of the fastest cars in the county. At age forty-nine, he still had that reckless streak and thirst for an adrenaline rush.

Aunt Beverly MacPherson

Born: January 19, 1931, Batavia, New York

Uncle Bill was heading down the road to self-destruction when fate intervened. When Uncle Bill met Beverly Houseman, she turned his whole life around. They met at the Spencerport Racetrack, where they were both there with other dates. Several days later he showed up at Beverly's house, and six years later they were married.

She had two children from a previous marriage, and his new family became the center of his life. Before he met Bev, his life had little purpose; but now it had direction. Bev and Bill enjoyed the same zest for life. They were made for one another, so they belonged to social clubs and spent some nights out on the town. Bev didn't keep him from enjoying his social life; she just toned it down a notch. They were married on July 12, 1963.

My uncle's two-step children, Bill and Sue, became his whole life. They needed a father and Bill wanted children. One time he told me that he loved Bill and Sue as much as if they were his natural children. He backed up his words by adopting them, and they took his last name. His stepson Bill even changed his middle name because he did not want his birth father's first name as his middle name.

Uncle Bill worked in a series of jobs, from making women's stockings to working in a mine, but the one that suited him the best was working as a mechanic for Texaco, Inc., on a company station on the New York State Thruway (Interstate 90) from 1959 to 1973. Since he worked for a company station rather than a privately owned gas station, he received union wages, so he was well compensated. When Grandma MacPherson got Uncle Bill to pull strings for me to work with him after I graduated from high school, I got to know him all over again. My first day on the job we reconnected, and after a few days, it was like we had never lost contact. When Texaco closed down the company station and Bill lost his job, the company re-assigned the management but not Uncle Bill. My uncle never played the corporate game, and when he repeatedly turned down promotions to be assistant manager, he put himself into a no-win situation. He worked for them for fourteen years, which was not enough to receive any pension, so he was fired with nothing to show for all of his years of service. Luckily, Bev had a great job working for Sylvania Electronic Products, an electronic company that made televisions in the nearby city of Batavia. During her years of employment, she worked in just about all facets of production and management, so she had a good pension and they had financial security in retirement.

Uncle Bill was someone we all admired and held in the highest regard. In the summer of 1964, his nephew Jim had just gotten his driver's license and was in LeRoy with his family visiting the Browns, relatives on his mother's side. Jim's father, Uncle Donald, had just bought a new car, and Jim persuaded him into taking the car out for a spin. He took it out on the expressway and floored it, and suddenly there was a very loud knocking under the hood. Jim panicked, and not knowing quite what to do, he went to see Uncle Bill, since he knew everything about cars. After listening to the noise, he reassured Jim that he had not done anything wrong and likely it was just a faulty valve lifter. Jim was still upset and anxious—and rightly so, because I remember Uncle Donald frequently having a short fuse. Uncle Bill did his best to calm his nephew down. By the time he drove across town to confess to his father, Uncle Bill, in all probability, had called his brother to give him the scoop, because by the time Jim got to the Browns, Uncle Donald was very understanding when he heard the details. Uncle Bill had a soft streak in him that made him want to protect those that were vulnerable, especially young family members.

Shortly after this episode, the family feud that involved moving into Great Aunt Kitty's house without getting permission from his brother Donald, and the moving of the swimming pool across town that I detailed in the Chapter 26, regretfully deprived Jim of closer family contact with his uncle, just like my parent's divorce took away precious years from my relationship with him. Events like these have stuck with me, and give insight into the empathetic character of my uncle. He was a very compassionate man inside that manly exterior.

Bill was such a character that there are many stories about him and his escapades, only a small amount of which I have already told. He was a very interesting and funny man, but his tough and courageous attitude sometimes took over. His close friends called him "The Cat," because whenever he went to his favorite bar, he would sit very quietly just like a cat in the corner on his favorite bar stool, sipping his "BV"[3] and water, and sometimes he would doze off and take a "catnap." One afternoon he was sitting and drinking his BV and dozing, when two migrant workers, who had had too much to drink, started getting belligerent, so the bartender shut them off. An argument ensued, and when the migrant workers realized that the bartender was not going to change his mind, they pulled out their knives. All this commotion woke up my uncle, and when he saw the two knives, true to his name, he moved quick as a cat, grabbed the two men by the back of their shirts, picked them up in the air and banged their heads together until they dropped their knives. When he put them down, they took one look at my uncle lurking over them and made a hasty retreat. Like my father, Bill was a very strong man, so I have no doubt he was able to pull off this incredible feat of strength.

One summer when I was working with him at Texaco, I witnessed his strength and his temper firsthand when I pushed his sense of humor to its limits. That summer he started wearing a nautical hat much like the Skipper on Gilligan's Island, so I started calling him "Skippy." I teased him for a whole week, and one day as we were passing one another at his favorite watering hole I said to him, "Hello Skippy!" I was taller than him, so it must have looked very ludicrous when he turned and grabbed me by the shirt with one hand and lifted me up so that my feet were off the ground and slammed me against the wall and said, "You little shit, I'm tired of your smart assed mouth." After some time he let me down, but it took a whole week, with Aunt Beverly interceding for me, to convince him to talk to me again. I realized then that he was like a big bear: you could push him just so far, but after he got mad, watch out. As far as I'm concerned, I have no problem believing the story about him lifting up and shaking the two migrant workers.

Even though Bill could be contentious, he was also kindhearted and sympathetic. He was concerned about how I was growing up and felt my pain of not having a father around. At times, he would see that the absence of my father was affecting me, so he would reach out to me and try to explain why things were the way they were. We developed a special bond working at Texaco. After work, I would head to his favorite bar and we would talk the night away. During the years I worked with him, Bill was very instrumental in helping me understand my father. He told me stories of my father's horrific war experiences that gave me insight into the way he was. My uncle helped me see the bigger picture, and I was able, over time, to rid myself of the anger I had toward Neil. Since my father was nonexistent in my life, Uncle Bill fortuitously entered my life at just the right time and helped fill the void my father left. I was fortunate to have two men who helped me through the difficult times as a teenager. First Uncle Joe Burkart (Chapter 15), then later Uncle Bill, filled the roles of mentor and surrogate on my way to adulthood. Since I was living with my Sicilian Grandma, Aunt Franny, and my mother and sister, he was a strong male role model at a time when I was rebelling and angry at the world. I had the utmost respect for him. He taught me how to change my oil

---

3   Black Velvet whiskey.

and make simple car repairs, something he thought was important that every man should know how to do. I was so proud that he was my uncle, and those that worked with him also had great respect for the man they called Alex. My uncle made me feel proud that I wanted to be an artist and encouraged me to pursue my dreams. He even told me that he thought I got my talent from him. I was also able to feel pride in my identity as a MacPherson and a Scot.

My mother, however, was not happy with me hanging around Uncle Bill, and tried to forbid me to have anything to do with him. She thought that Bill was a bad influence on my father and didn't want me to end up like the MacPhersons. Being only eighteen and still living at home, it took a while for me understand that I could do as I wanted, and before long I was seeing Uncle Bill as often as I pleased.

There is one incident that happened about this time, that as I look back I want to kick myself over. My father had a large photo album of Army pictures that my sister and I used to look at all of the time. It had staged pictures of him coming out of bunkers with his rifle, pictures of him standing on his hands on the beaches in Italy, and even one with him getting his medals from a general. I treasured those pictures, especially after Neil left and I was trying to make sense of everything. My father's war service was the one part of his life that I could look to and be proud. My cousins had fathers who were more successful in life, but mine was noteworthy in his own way; he was a war hero. It was something that made him special. Lena was adamant about throwing everything of his out after their separation, but I wanted to save those photos. They were the only evidence I had that showed that Neil wasn't a total failure in life. I hid them, but she found my stash and threw everything out. I should have given the box full of treasures to Uncle Bill for safekeeping, but it never occurred to me. Years later, when I told him about this incident, after he got through swearing, he went through his photo albums and got all of the pictures he had of Neil in the Army and gave them to me.

Uncle Bill came in and out of my life after I left for graduate school in South Carolina in 1973, so I didn't see him much in the intervening years. On his trips down to Florida in the winter, he would stop off to see my father in Chester, South Carolina, who would drive Uncle Bill over to our house. On one such trip, Bill came to visit us and became quite fond of my son, who had a red pedal car that looked like a sports car. Jesse would pedal his car to the top of our steep driveway and speed down it, and at the last minute would do a powerslide that stopped inches from the front steps, resulting in a perfect parallel parking maneuver. Bill thought my son was a real MacPherson.

In 1974, when my sister Mary was married, she had a heated argument with Mom about

Left to right: Aunt Beverly, my son Jesse, and Uncle Bill in Florida, 1988.

whether or not to invite Uncle Bill and Aunt Beverly to the wedding. Since the breakup of our parents, we had virtually no contact with them, as I outlined in Chapter 26. Mary wanted to invite them, but Mom was adamant about not sending them an invitation. My sister considered sending them one anyway, but in the end, she knew that Mom would have embarrassed Bill and Bev in some way in front of everyone. Uncle Bill was heartbroken and assumed Mary didn't want him there. Years later, when my family and I visited them in Florida, he brought up the subject and I could see he was still visibly upset about it. Bev said, "He was always hurt that he couldn't go to her wedding. I told him he could not be kept out of the church, but he did not want to cause problems with Lena."

When I finally got the teaching position at SUNY Geneseo in 1985, I was ecstatic, since I could now visit with him on a regular basis. I wanted to surprise him with the news of my job, so I waited until I went to see him in LeRoy earlier in the summer just before the big move. After I told him that we would be relocating back to New York, much to my chagrin, I found out that Uncle Bill and Aunt Beverly were moving to live in Florida in a few weeks. By the time we moved to New York later in the summer, they were gone. We did take a vacation to visit him once in Florida, and my aunt and uncle treated us with the utmost hospitality. My two children still remember that visit.

Colon cancer has ravaged both sides of my family, and Uncle Bill was one of its victims. In July 1995, I received a phone call from him. It was very unusual for him to call, and it was great to hear his voice. He told me he wasn't doing very well, and after some more conversation he told me that he loved me. I was surprised by this admission since the MacPherson men were not known for expressing their inner feelings. I wanted to go see him, but he didn't want me to see him the way he looked. He wanted me to remember him the way he was. I didn't want our conversation to end, but we had said everything that needed to be said and we hung up. A short time later, I convinced my sister to call him at his house to talk, but he had taken a turn for the worse and was already in the hospital. Mary hadn't talked to him in at least twenty years. Bev gave my sister the hospital number, but asked her to call the room when she was there. Mary did, and Bev gave the phone to Bill not telling him who it was and his eyes just lit up. Aunt Bev didn't even have to tell him who it was. My uncle was always hurt that he wasn't invited to her wedding, but in the end they reconciled. He was so happy that he got a chance to talk to my sister before he died. It was sad that it took this to bring them back together, since deep down inside, I think Mary was still his favorite.

His stepson Bill went to see him in his last days. On the morning as he was leaving for the airport to return to New York, he visited his father one last time. Uncle Bill insisted on shaving everyday, except on this particular morning, he was too weak to lift up his arms. As Bill was leaving for the airport, my uncle asked him to give him a shave as a favor. Of course he agreed, and as he was leaving after he was done, Uncle Bill called to him and rubbed his face and said, "That is the best shave I ever had." This complement meant a lot to his son. It eased some of his sorrow and became one last fond memory of his father to cherish. Uncle Bill left this world with his dignity intact, and with his passing he left a void that none of us was ever able to fill, not even with all of the memories we had of him.

EPILOGUE

Tracing my family's history enabled me not only to learn more about my personal history, but also to think about its significance within a larger context of emigration, immigration, and the complex encounters of diverse cultures. This project also made me focus on how the differences in perceptions and receptions impacted and affected the fortunes of different members of my family on the Sicilian and the Scottish sides. My project has been specific because it is about my family, but it has universal implications because every family has stories comparable to those of my descendants.

While I was completing my research and writing, I happened to see the documentary, *The Journey of Man: The Story of the Human Species*, which was written and narrated by Dr. Spencer Wells and sponsored by the National Geographic Society. It made me realize that my family's immediate and documented history was only a small part of who I was, because behind the Scottish and Sicilian heritage, there was the larger story of where those ancestors came from, after the groups that eventually became my family left Africa. After watching *The Journey of Man*, I wondered about the bigger picture of my ancestors' immigration to LeRoy.

In the documentary, Dr. Wells spoke about the Genographic Project and invited viewers to participate by sending their DNA to be analyzed. The test reveals one's deep ancestry along a single line of a direct descendent, when humans first appeared in Africa around 150,000 years ago, as well as the migration routes they took within Africa and when they left the African subcontinent.

My sister and I decided to participate in the project. I had my DNA tested to discover my paternal heritage, and my sister sent her DNA to find out about our maternal side. The DNA results I received included information that mapped my ancestor's migration route out of the African continent, the haplogroup of my ancestors, and other information that explains my deep ancestry. A haplogroup is defined by a series of Y-chromosome markers (or mutations) that are shared by other men in the paternal lines and mitochondrial DNA that we all have, inherited from our mothers that can be traced back to the beginning of humans.

The results revealed genetic markers that defined my paternal line's ancestral history that began roughly 50,000 years ago, most likely in Ethiopia, with haplogroup M168. The descendants of M168 became the only lineage to survive outside of Africa, making him the common ancestor of all non-African men, and therefore received the name Eurasian Adam.

The next ancestor in my lineage is the man who carried M89, a marker found in 90-95 percent of all non-Africans. He was born in either northern Africa or the Middle East, roughly 45,000 years ago.

As the Eurasian clan spread through the Middle East and Central Asia, my next ancestor is a man born around 40,000 years ago in Iran or southern central Asia, and carries the genetic marker M9. M9 and his offspring were nomadic hunters who followed the animals they hunted over thousands of years into the Eurasian steppe, until their path was blocked by the mountain ranges of southern and central Asia, the Hindu Kush in central Afghanistan, and northern Pakistan.

M45 is the next genetic marker, and he arose out of the M9 clan about 35,000 years ago when they moved north of the Hindu Kush Mountains and into southern Siberia. The Ice

Ages usually were the main factor that prompted these nomadic people to migrate in this case into southern Siberia.

Around 30,000 years ago, an individual in this clan carried the M207 mutation. The group started moving toward Europe. The descendants ultimately split into two distinct groups, with my lineage moving toward Europe. As my ancestors continued to move west, a man was born who carried the marker M173. His descendants were among the first large wave to reach Europe.

The M343 marker appeared as my clan made its way west through northern Europe. This western wave of migration went unabated until the ice sheets started expanding again and forced my clan into present-day Spain. As the earth warmed and the ice receded, my ancestors retraced their steps and moved north and ended up in present-day Scotland. M343 is where my paternal genetic trail ends.

Not surprisingly, the story that my sister Mary found out about our maternal lineage took a totally different path out of Africa. This saga began around 150,000 years ago with a woman nicknamed "Mitochondrial Eve," haplogroup L0. She represents the root of the human family tree. She was not the only woman alive, but the only one whose descendants survived to modern times. This group originated and remained in East Africa, and eventually split into two groups, haplogroups L0 and L1. With the appearance of L2 individuals, they split from their L1 predecessors and moved into West Africa.

The next ancestor is an individual that appeared around 80,000 years ago and broke away from L2 and began haplogroup L3. These ancestors are important since they were the first modern humans to leave Africa and head north into the Middle East. My descendant's next signpost is haplogroup N. This ancient haplogroup spawned many lines that spread over the rest of the globe. After several thousand years in the Middle East, individuals formed a new group called haplogroup R and began to move out of the Middle East and explore the surrounding area. Finally, we arrive at my own clan when a group of individuals emerged around 40,000 years ago to constitute haplogroup T. Haplogroup T has a wide distribution ranging from India and Pakistan to northern and eastern Europe. This is where the genetic clues get murky and the DNA trail goes cold. My haplogroup ends currently in present-day Romania, not the typical Turkey to Greece to Sicily route. But this isn't the end of haplogroup T. Further research will eventually move my descent's migration route closer to the present day, but for now, all I can do is to ponder how my ancestors got to Sicily.

The results of the Genographic Project made me think about my ancestry in a much larger way. The question is, how does the genetic information stack up against the culture of these two families? The three generations of Sicilians and the seven generations on the Scottish side to live in America are just a tiny piece of the story of our migration from when my ancestors walked out of Africa and ended up in LeRoy. Obviously, culture is just a tiny part of the study when it is compared to my deep family history. 150,000 years ago, the way people lived was very different from what developed in Sicily and Scotland because cultural identity is always changing. How much of this identity is in our present perception of who we think we are? Very little is left after only one hundred years of my Sicilian relatives and even less of an influence for the MacPhersons after over two hundred years.

I realize now that only considering the cultural aspect, my family members look at themselves in such a narrow frame of reference that they pass on to each succeeding generation a mistaken notion of whom we are. Growing up in a bicultural family and being immersed in the culture of my grandparents, we had a very limited view of where we came from. The Barones stayed within the Mediterranean character and brought it to America, but in reality, the real story is beyond culture. Questions remain. Who are the people in these haplogroups? And what does all of this actually mean?

After thinking about the significance of the DNA study, I realized that my family's history is just a snapshot of human history. I understood that my families' cultures were deeper and more diverse than the LeRoyan/Scottish/Sicilian history, and that at different times and in different places my family had been very dissimilar from what they are today. As my family's ancestors moved through all of those various countries that our haplogroups journeyed, they became the cultures of each time and place, changing with each move into something dissimilar from what they had been and from what they are now. Thus, our cultural origins and identities are not fixed but are, and have been, mutable. Who we are today is not who we were or who we will be. Even now, my family's cultures are changing as this generation marries and adds new cultures to the mix. Recent research on Scotland reveals that Scots have much more diverse DNA than had been thought. Alistair Moffat and Dr. James Wilson in their book, *The Scots: A Genetic Journey*, have come to the conclusion that Scotland is a nation of immigrants and is actually one of the most genetically diverse countries in the world. They assert that since Scotland is the end of the European continent, people migrating west couldn't go any further so they stayed there. In their research, Moffat and Wilson have found West African, Arabian, Southeast Asian, and Siberian ancestry in Scotland. Amazingly, 1% of Scottish men have Berber ancestry.[1]

My Mediterranean descendants have comparable mixtures, and I have come to learn that who we really are are our DNA, not the cultural layers that are acquired and developed in time and place. Ultimately, who we really are is our source genetic heritage, and that is something that we all have in common. While we are many and diverse, we are all really one. In researching my family's DNA, I came to the conclusion that the separation that we see when we look around is profoundly artificial because the one true thing is the links we have to each other. In thinking about this in connection with the types of discrimination and stereotyping that my Sicilian relatives lived with, I realized that as long as we remain trapped in narrow definitions of whom we are instead of enjoying the rich cultural diversity that exists, such narrowing diminishes the value of our history. In short, by thinking about DNA and culture, I have internalized the realization that using culture and race or gender and religion so that one group can oppress another is equally destructive for the oppressor and the oppressed, as the act of discrimination reduces the humanity in those who seek to deny others their fair share, even as it destroys the lives of those who are oppressed.

My Sicilian family survived and prospered, and my Scottish family did so as well at a time in America when there was room for growth even for those who were discriminated against. My family's past history is an example of the fates and fortunes of those who set out from home to look for a better life. Both sides of my family found a better life in nineteenth and twentieth century America. The twenty-first century history of my family remains to be

---

1   Charlotte Higgins, "Scottish People's DNA Study Could 'Rewrite Nation's History'," *The Guardian*, (August 14, 2012), http://www.theguardian.com/uk/2012/aug/15/scotland-dna-study-project.

written, but I was recently told that my branch of it will continue in the grandchild that my son and daughter-in-law will soon have.

1. Scottish and Sicilian Recipes

Euphemia Walker's Shortbread

My brother-in law's grandmother, Euphemia Walker, was born in 1890 in Dundee, Scotland and died in 1980 in Pittsburgh, Pennsylvania. Her shortbread is the best I've ever had, and it is labor-intensive to make but the work is worth the effort.

Ingredients:

- ½ pound of high quality butter (high quality butter makes it easier to work with)
- 2 ¾ cups of white flour
- Scarce ½ cup of rice flour
- ½ cup of sugar

Directions:

Cream the butter then add all of the sugar and the flour (a little at a time).

Knead or use a stand mixer. A stand mixer works best since the dough will clump in 3-4 minutes.

The dough is ready when it suddenly clumps together.

Press it in an aluminum pan approximately 7 inches by 9 inches and roll it out with a small glass until it is smooth then take a fork and poke holes in it.

Bake at 350 degrees Fahrenheit for 45-65 minutes or until golden brown.

As soon as it comes out of the oven, cut the shortbread immediately and leave in the pan to cool.

Great-Aunt Mary Argana's Artichoke Fritatta

(Told to me by Anthony Cinquino)

Ingredients:

- One or two cans of artichokes hearts, drained and washed.

- Cut the hearts in half. If large, cut again

- Four to 6 eggs gently beaten

- 2 tbsp. of fresh ground Romano pecorino cheese (more or less to your liking)

- 1 tsp. fresh ground pepper

Directions:

Mix all ingredients together.

Heat a black iron frying pan with olive oil and a couple of crushed cloves of garlic in it.

The olive oil should cover the bottom of the frying pan—at least the height of one penny. (I guess this one of Aunt Mary's requirements!)

Heat up the garlic and oil to give it flavor then remove the garlic and get the oil hotter.

Here is the tricky part. When the pan is hot not smoking, add the egg mixture and artichoke mixture. Cover and cook for 1 to 2 minutes until the edges start cooking. Using a wooden spoon, gently push the eggs from the edge of the pan toward the middle, letting the uncooked egg mixture fill in behind spoon. Repeat 4 or 5 times. Cover and continue cooking for 1 to 2 minutes. Gently loosen the omelet from the bottom of the pan, place an inverted plate* over the pan and flip onto plate. Slide the omelet back into the pan for 1 to 2 minutes to cook the bottom. Eggs should be slightly loose; don't over cook. Slide omelet back onto the plate. Allow to cool and cut with a sharp knife. *Mangia!*

*I select a plate that covers the opening somewhat snugly because some of the egg will be liquid. This step takes some practice. Maybe do it over the sink until mastered.

Tony Argana's Christmas Sausage Recipe

Great-Uncle Tony was a very good cook/chef in his own right. As I mentioned in Chapter 3, he made an Italian sausage that was admired by all of his customers. It was a family tradition that he would make it for our Christmas Eve parties that everyone celebrated after Midnight Mass. If we were lucky enough, he would stop by our house a few days before Christmas Eve and drop off a few pounds. It was so lean that we would have to cook it with some olive oil just so it wouldn't burn in the skillet. It had such a unique combination of spices and meat that I have not tasted anything close to it. Commercially made sausage, when compared to it, is bland and too fatty.

Ingredients:

- 30 pounds of beef (chuck)
- 20 pounds of pork (boneless pork butt)
- 3-4 cups of Romano cheese
- 8-10 tbsp. of salt (optional)
- 1 ounce of red crushed pepper
- 8-10 tbsp. fennel seeds
- 2-3 cups of parsley
- 100 feet of casing (If you run out of casing make the remaining sausage into patties.)

Directions:

Sausage casings are salted and packed dry. To prepare them, rinse under running water. Hold casing under faucet and let water run through to separate. Soak casing in water for several days to remove the salt. Change the water each day.

Grind the meat in a meat grinder. After the second grinding, mix in the cheese and spices.

Grandma's "Family Secret" Carduni Fritti

(Fried Cardoons)

Every spring, Grandma and her brother-in-law, Tony Argana, would scour the country-side for this delicacy. *Cardunis* (burdocks) should be picked before Memorial Day, before the weather gets too hot and they become too tough and bitter.

Ingredients:

- 4 eggs
- 2 tbsp. grated cheese (Romano)
- ⅛ tsp. baking powder
- A couple of cloves of garlic minced
- Flour

Directions:

Trimmed stalks of *carduni* (young burdock) are cleaned (get all of the hair-like fibers off the stalk) and cook in boiling water until tender.

Mix eggs, cheese, garlic and baking powder with enough water, approximately ¼ cup to the consistency of pancake batter.

Coat the *carduni* with flour and dip 3-4 stalks of burdock into batter and fry in olive oil until golden brown on both sides.

Burdocks should be picked before Memorial Day. As the weather turns warmer, they get tougher and bitter and become inedible.

Grandma's Recipe for Sfingi

After a hard day of shoveling snow after a storm, as a reward, Grandma would make me a batch of this timeless classic Italian donut.

Ingredients:

- 3 eggs

- 1 cup of flour

- 1 cup of water

- About 1 tsp. of sugar

- 1 heaping tsp. Crisco (Grandma used lard)

- 1 tsp. baking powder

- ¼ tsp. vanilla

Directions:

Boil water and Crisco together. Pour water and Crisco and mix and let cool. When cool add 1 egg at a time and add baking powder, sugar and vanilla. Keep stirring until smooth.

Drop in hot grease with teaspoon. *Sfingi* are unusual since after they are placed in the hot grease, they turn over by themselves. Roll in powdered sugar.

Mangia!

Grandma's "Sacred Recipe" for St. Joseph Bread

Just about every Sicilian in LeRoy made St. Joseph bread from his feast day until Easter Sunday. It is a kind of bread that gets stale very quickly, so Grandma would make a few loaves and freeze them so that we could enjoy them during Lent. It is also great toasted for breakfast.

Ingredients:

- 3 ¼ cups warm water
- 2 pkgs. dry yeast
- 1 cup sugar
- ¾ tsp. salt
- ¼ cup plus 2 tbsp. shortening
- Stir in about 4 cups flour
- 1-3 tbsp. anise seeds (or more if you like it.)
- 3 tsp. baking powder
- 3 eggs beaten
- Poppy or sesame seeds

Directions:

Mix warm water, yeast, sugar, salt, shortening, eggs, flour, anise seeds and baking powder. Work dough and add more flour until right consistency (about 10-15 minutes). Usually it takes about 3 lbs. of flour altogether. Let raise 1 ½ hours or until double in bulk. Shape into loaves or celebratory shapes and let raise another hour or so on baking sheets.

Before putting in oven brush the top of the loaves with beaten eggs and sprinkle with sesame or poppy seeds. Bake at 350 degrees Fahrenheit for about 25 minutes on greased cookie sheet. Best when eaten hot out of the oven!

Aunt Mananna's Meatball Cookies

Aunt Mananna (Marianna Argana) made the best meatball cookies we ever had. She was the sister of Great-Uncle Tony Argana. We all looked forward to Christmas for a plate of these scrumptious treats.

Ingredients:

- 6 oz. cream cheese
- 1 cup Crisco
- 1 ½ cup sugar
- 3 eggs
- 1 cup milk
- 1 tsp. vanilla
- 5 cups flour
- ¾ cup baking cocoa
- 5 tsp. baking powder
- 2 tsp. cinnamon
- ½ tsp. nutmeg
- 2 cups chocolate chips
- 1 cup nuts (if desired)

Directions:

Mix all of the ingredients together and bake at 350 degrees Fahrenheit for 10-12 minutes.

You may have to add more flour. Frost with 10x sugar glaze.

2. MacPherson Family Tree

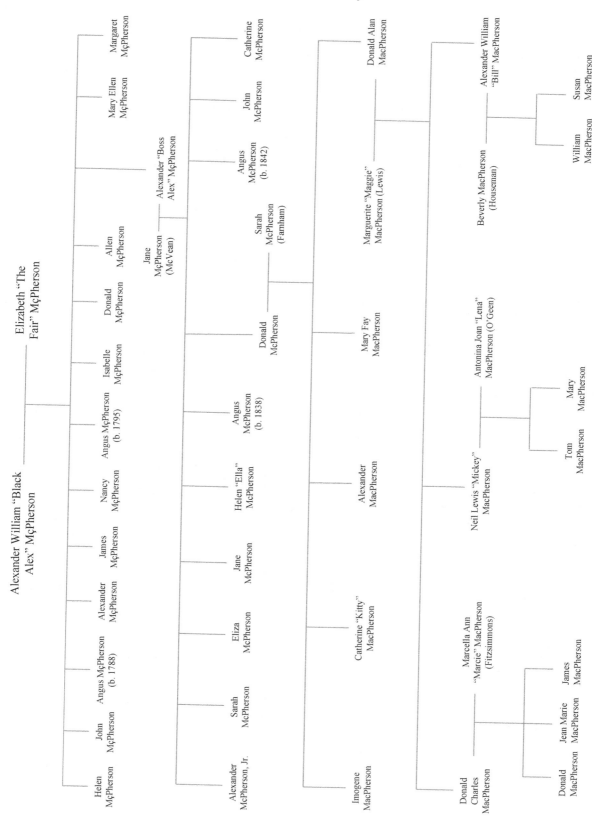

3. Barone Family Tree

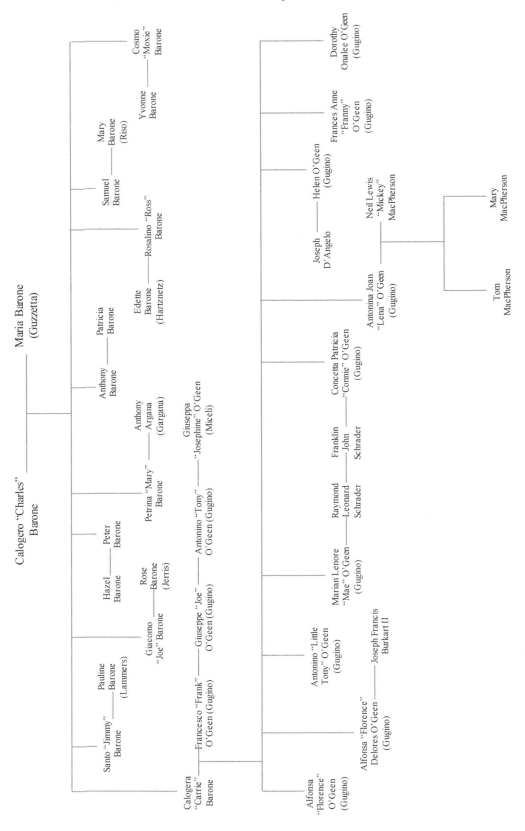

INDEX

Made in United States
North Haven, CT
19 June 2023

37937364R00148